REVENGE TRAGEDY AND CLASSICAL PHILOSOPHY ON THE EARLY MODERN STAGE

EDINBURGH CRITICAL STUDIES IN SHAKESPEARE AND PHILOSOPHY
Series Editor: Kevin Curran

Edinburgh Critical Studies in Shakespeare and Philosophy takes seriously the speculative and world-making properties of Shakespeare's art. Maintaining a broad view of 'philosophy' that accommodates first-order questions of metaphysics, ethics, politics and aesthetics, the series also expands our understanding of philosophy to include the unique kinds of theoretical work carried out by performance and poetry itself. These scholarly monographs will reinvigorate Shakespeare studies by opening new interdisciplinary conversations among scholars, artists and students.

Editorial Board Members
Ewan Fernie, Shakespeare Institute, University of Birmingham
James Kearney, University of California, Santa Barbara
Julia Reinhard Lupton, University of California, Irvine
Madhavi Menon, Ashoka University
Simon Palfrey, Oxford University
Tiffany Stern, Shakespeare Institute, University of Birmingham
Henry Turner, Rutgers University
Michael Witmore, The Folger Shakespeare Library
Paul Yachnin, McGill University

Published Titles
Rethinking Shakespeare's Political Philosophy: From Lear to Leviathan
Alex Schulman
Shakespeare in Hindsight: Counterfactual Thinking and Shakespearean Tragedy
Amir Khan
Second Death: Theatricalities of the Soul in Shakespeare's Drama
Donovan Sherman
Shakespeare's Fugitive Politics
Thomas P. Anderson
Is Shylock Jewish?: Citing Scripture and the Moral Agency of Shakespeare's Jews
Sara Coodin
Chaste Value: Economic Crisis, Female Chastity and the Production of Social Difference on Shakespeare's Stage
Katherine Gillen
Shakespearean Melancholy: Philosophy, Form and the Transformation of Comedy
J. F. Bernard
Shakespeare's Moral Compass
Neema Parvini
Shakespeare and the Fall of the Roman Republic: Selfhood, Stoicism and Civil War
Patrick Gray
Revenge Tragedy and Classical Philosophy on the Early Modern Stage
Christopher Crosbie

Forthcoming Titles
Making Publics in Shakespeare's Playhouse
Paul Yachnin
Derrida Reads Shakespeare
Chiara Alfano
The Play and the Thing: A Phenomenology of Shakespearean Theatre
Matthew Wagner
Conceiving Desire: Metaphor, Cognition and Eros in Lyly and Shakespeare
Gillian Knoll
Shakespeare and the Truth-Teller: Confronting the Cynic Ideal
David Hershinow

For further information please visit our website at edinburghuniversitypress.com/series/ecsst

REVENGE TRAGEDY AND CLASSICAL PHILOSOPHY ON THE EARLY MODERN STAGE

◆ ◆ ◆

CHRISTOPHER CROSBIE

EDINBURGH
University Press

Edinburgh University Press is one of the leading university presses in the UK. We publish academic books and journals in our selected subject areas across the humanities and social sciences, combining cutting-edge scholarship with high editorial and production values to produce academic works of lasting importance. For more information visit our website: edinburghuniversitypress.com

© Christopher Crosbie, 2019, 2020

First published in hardback by Edinburgh University Press 2019

Edinburgh University Press Ltd
The Tun – Holyrood Road
12(2f) Jackson's Entry
Edinburgh EH8 8PJ

Typeset in 12/15 Adobe Sabon by
IDSUK (DataConnection) Ltd, and

A CIP record for this book is available from the British Library

ISBN 978 1 4744 4026 4 (hardback)
ISBN 978 1 4744 4027 1 (paperback)
ISBN 978 1 4744 4028 8 (webready PDF)
ISBN 978 1 4744 4029 5 (epub)

The right of Christopher Crosbie to be identified as the author of this work has been asserted in accordance with the Copyright, Designs and Patents Act 1988, and the Copyright and Related Rights Regulations 2003 (SI No. 2498).

CONTENTS

Acknowledgements	vi
Series Editor's Preface	viii
Introduction: On Revenge Tragedy and the Shaping Influence of Classical Philosophy	1
1. *Oeconomia* and the Vegetative Soul: Thomas Kyd's Naturalisation of Revenge in *The Spanish Tragedy*	41
2. Fixing Moderation: *Titus Andronicus* and the Aristotelian Determination of Value	88
3. 'A fine pate full of fine dirt': Hamlet among the Atomists	132
4. 'Vein by vein': The Pneumatics of Retribution in John Marston's *Antonio's Revenge*	191
5. *Prohairesis* on the Inside: *The Duchess of Malfi* and Epictetian Volition	243
Epilogue: A Kind of Sensible Justice	295
Index	303

ACKNOWLEDGEMENTS

Writing is often an isolating process, but it also provides occasion for invigorating conversation and correspondence. The ideas on theatre and philosophy explored in this book have taken shape over many years, and the debt I owe to so many generous, insightful scholars is considerable. For their invaluable feedback and encouragement at various stages of this project, I wish to thank Douglas Bruster, Mary Thomas Crane, Andrew Cutrofello, Timothy Harrison, Heather Hirschfeld, James A. Knapp, Ryan McDermott, Curtis Perry, Willis Salomon, Donovan Sherman, Jennifer Waldron, John N. Wall and Brian Walsh. Thanks are also due to research assistants Elizabeth Beck, James Ensley, Ashley Grantham, Andrew S. Keener and Valerie Voight for their hard work on this and coterminous projects. I'm especially grateful to Emily C. Bartels, along with Ann Baynes Coiro and Ronald Levao, for their generous attention and good counsel that brought an expansive set of interests into shape in this project's earliest days. Peter Holland provided encouragement and guidance about the book's framework at a critical juncture, and I'm deeply grateful to Michael Witmore for many agreeable conversations about early modern natural philosophy and for helping me think through Renaissance atomism in new ways. Words fail when I consider my debt also to Russ McDonald, late too soon, a truly gracious mentor and friend, and quite literally the reason I study and teach Renaissance drama today.

My chapter on *Titus Andronicus* benefited immeasurably from the kind attention of Gail Kern Paster and the readers of *Shakespeare Quarterly*. I'm grateful to Arthur F. Kinney for his attention, early on, to my work on *The Spanish Tragedy* which appeared in *English Literary Renaissance* and, later, to the book as a whole. These earlier versions of Chapters 2 and 3 appeared as '*Oeconomia* and the Vegetative Soul: Rethinking Revenge in *The Spanish Tragedy*', *English Literary Renaissance* 38 (2008): 3–33 and 'Fixing Moderation: *Titus Andronicus* and the Aristotelian Determination of Value', *Shakespeare Quarterly* 58.2 (2007): 147–73. I thank both journals for permission to reprint portions of those articles here. I'm also extremely appreciative of the support, kind words and incisive feedback offered by Kevin Curran, Michelle Houston and the editorial board at EUP. This project was further supported by a Folger Shakespeare Library short-term fellowship, two Mellon Foundation fellowships through Rutgers University, and continued funding from North Carolina State University's College of Humanities and Social Sciences.

My work has benefited in ways too numerous to count by the continued support of my parents, extended family and friends. I'm forever grateful to Joan Graubit for her unfailing love, warmth and good cheer. Most importantly, I'd like to thank Kelly and Henry Crosbie for making the whole process, and everything in between, beautiful and worthwhile.

SERIES EDITOR'S PREFACE

Picture Macbeth alone on stage, staring intently into empty space. 'Is this a dagger which I see before me?' he asks, grasping decisively at the air. On one hand, this is a quintessentially theatrical question. At once an object and a vector, the dagger describes the possibility of knowledge ('Is this a dagger') in specifically visual and spatial terms ('which I see before me'). At the same time, Macbeth is posing a quintessentially *philosophical* question, one that assumes knowledge to be both conditional and experiential, and that probes the relationship between certainty and perception as well as intention and action. It is from this shared ground of art and inquiry, of theatre and theory, that this series advances its basic premise: *Shakespeare is philosophical.*

It seems like a simple enough claim. But what does it mean exactly, beyond the parameters of this specific moment in *Macbeth*? Does it mean that Shakespeare had something we could think of as his own philosophy? Does it mean that he was influenced by particular philosophical schools, texts and thinkers? Does it mean, conversely, that modern philosophers have been influenced by *him*, that Shakespeare's plays and poems have been, and continue to be, resources for philosophical thought and speculation?

The answer is yes all around. These are all useful ways of conceiving a philosophical Shakespeare and all point to lines of inquiry that this series welcomes. But Shakespeare is philosophical in a much more fundamental way as well. Shakespeare is philosophical because the plays and poems actively create new worlds of knowledge and new scenes of ethical encounter. They ask big questions, make bold arguments and develop new vocabularies in order to think what might otherwise be unthinkable. Through both their scenarios and their imagery, the plays and poems engage the qualities of consciousness, the consequences of human action, the phenomenology of motive and attention, the conditions of personhood and the relationship among different orders of reality and experience. This is writing and dramaturgy, moreover, that consistently experiments with a broad range of conceptual crossings, between love and subjectivity, nature and politics, and temporality and form.

Edinburgh Critical Studies in Shakespeare and Philosophy takes seriously these speculative and world-making dimensions of Shakespeare's work. The series proceeds from a core conviction that art's capacity to think – to formulate, not just reflect, ideas – is what makes it urgent and valuable. Art matters because unlike other human activities it establishes its own frame of reference, reminding us that all acts of creation – biological, political, intellectual and amorous – are grounded in imagination. This is a far cry from business-as-usual in Shakespeare studies. Because historicism remains the methodological gold standard of the field, far more energy has been invested in exploring what Shakespeare once meant than in thinking rigorously about what Shakespeare continues to make possible. In response, Edinburgh Critical Studies in Shakespeare and Philosophy pushes back against the critical orthodoxies of historicism and cultural studies to clear a space for scholarship that confronts aspects of literature that can neither be reduced to nor adequately explained by particular historical contexts.

Shakespeare's creations are not just inheritances of a past culture, frozen artefacts whose original settings must be expertly reconstructed in order to be understood. The plays and poems are also living art, vital thought-worlds that struggle, across time, with foundational questions of metaphysics, ethics, politics and aesthetics. With this orientation in mind, Edinburgh Critical Studies in Shakespeare and Philosophy offers a series of scholarly monographs that will reinvigorate Shakespeare studies by opening new interdisciplinary conversations among scholars, artists and students.

Kevin Curran

INTRODUCTION: ON REVENGE TRAGEDY AND THE SHAPING INFLUENCE OF CLASSICAL PHILOSOPHY

When Francis Bacon deemed revenge 'a kind of wild justice', he provided an apothegm that would prove irresistible to scholars studying retribution on the early modern stage.[1] The phrase has seemed perfectly apposite for a genre principally known for its spectacularly brutal violence. For what justice could be considered wilder than that administered by razing an entire court, then biting out one's own tongue, by grinding a mother's children into her pudding, or by offering a poisoned skull for one furtive, fatal, necrophilic kiss? Adopted as paradigmatic of the ethos and even aesthetics of theatrical retribution, Bacon's assessment has served to emphasise the barbarity and brutishness of the genre. Fredson Bowers' seminal *Elizabethan Revenge Tragedy* (1940), for instance, opens by figuring 'Blood revenge as [. . .] universal among primitive people' and 'the only possible action for the primitive individual', before concluding that 'Francis Bacon, with his usual acumen, recognized such a condition when he called revenge "a kind of wild justice".'[2] In a similar vein, Frederick Boas, in an influential reading of *The Spanish Tragedy*, accounts the final scene 'sheer savagery' as 'the wild justice of revenge turns to mere massacre, and a situation inspired by the true genius of tragedy collapses into a series of blood-curdling incidents'.[3] As a means of highlighting the genre's savagery, such appropriations of Bacon abound. Bacon's full statement, however, emphasises not savagery but disorder of a different sort as he deploys a *horticultural* trope to advance a judicial point: 'Revenge,' declares the essayist, 'is a kind of wild Justice, which the more Man's Nature runs to the more ought Law to weed it out.' If Bacon's famous dictum can be thought of as representative of early modern revenge tragedy, perhaps we might think of it as paradigmatic of the ways in which the plays' intense brutality exerts a profound gravitational pull on our critical hermeneutic, inviting us to see these plays principally in terms of sensationalism – in terms of primitive impulses, mere massacres and blood-curdling incidents – rather than as works marked by subtlety, nuance and the innovative engagement with some of the era's most foundational philosophical traditions.

To the extent revenge drama has registered as *philosophical* at all, critical attention has tended to concentrate on the morality and metaphysical implications of revenge itself, often with *Hamlet* privileged as a more extensive, sophisticated treatment than one finds among lesser plays. In this book, by contrast, I reveal how the revenge tragedies of Shakespeare and his contemporaries participate in the era's broader re-engagement with classical philosophy. This study examines how such popular, often sensational, plays could do intricate philosophical work, and it traces how theatrical appropriations of classical philosophy, in turn, could condition audience reception of revenge in subtle ways. Rather than investigate the influence of a single philosopher or branch of philosophy on the stage, however, I instead focus on ancient theories particularly invested in the relationship between immateriality and materiality in order to show how the revenge drama of the era could make retribution intelligible, perhaps sympathetic, by making it seem of a piece with the very fabric of the worlds the revengers inhabit. Revenge dramatists, I argue, adapt classical ideas about how the world operates on its most rudimentary levels in order to construct sophisticated ontological contexts for their plays. By articulating the aggrieved protagonists' final retribution in language evocative of these contexts, early modern dramatists, I conclude, help direct their audiences to understand vengeance as fundamentally appropriate, even organic, within the particular worlds their plays construct. Rethinking revenge tragedy as marshalling familiar classical doctrines to provoke certain kinds of audience response, this book thus reimagines the Renaissance stage – even at its most lurid – as a space especially suited for engaging and radically appropriating ancient philosophy.

For this wide-ranging inquiry into philosophy and early modern theatre, I take as my object of study five plays central to the revenge tragedy genre. The individual chapters that follow discover the influence of the Aristotelian vegetative soul on *The Spanish Tragedy*, the Aristotelian ethical mean on *Titus Andronicus*, Lucretian atomism on *Hamlet*, Galenic pneumatics on *Antonio's Revenge*, and Epictetian volition on *The Duchess of Malfi*. Through new reception histories for each philosophy, I examine how these diverse classical theories – each in its own manner concerned with the last waypoint between immateriality and materiality – shape revenge narratives on the stage. No early modern writer could see the vegetative soul, the ethical mean, the infinitesimally small atom, the ebb and flow of the most rarefied *pneuma*, or the hidden recesses of the Stoic will. Yet the writers studied here treat these concepts as ontological realities that structure the ways their characters think. Early modern dramatists persistently tether revenge into these ontological frameworks in order to render the final retributive act as fitting – even beyond overt appeals to audience sympathy – within their fictive worlds. In doing so, Shakespeare and his contemporaries not only provide more substantive ground for retribution than might be found in appeals to personal grievance alone. They also recuperate the immediacy such otherwise distanced philosophies or theoretical abstractions can hold for the suddenly marginalised or dispossessed.

By arguing that such a diverse range of philosophies shaped representations of revenge on the early modern stage, I do not seek to claim that the doctrines studied here hold an especial connection to revenge in themselves, that is, independent of the dramas in which they are employed. Nor is it my intent to suggest that the various strands isolated here – say, the Lucretian atom and the vegetative soul – are linked to, or are in conversation with, each other in substantive ways across these plays. Rather, my claims pertain to a genre, the multitudinous vibrant ideas that become obscured when we foreground too exclusively legal, political, or religious matters in our thinking about that genre, and the ways in which the era's received philosophies made available to dramatists a versatile toolkit for creating immersive playworlds, ones with internally coherent sets of ontological assumptions, which could then subtly frame retribution narratives for particular dramaturgical ends. Moreover, I'm especially concerned in this book with the appropriation of classical ideas still prevalent in early modern English culture for ends that are at once theatrically innovative and philosophically original. Revenge dramas have long been recognised as having distinctive 'moods' or 'atmospheres'. By discovering within these plays the subtle shaping presence of rich philosophical doctrines – each with a lineage and early modern commentary tradition of its own – I reveal how, theatrically, the very atmospheres of revenge tragedies work on the audience in more extensive, intellectually-rich, and *conditioning* ways than previously appreciated. At the same time, while I examine the theatrical effect of these shaping philosophies, I also reveal how, as much as revenge dramatists tap into pre-existing traditions, they also stretch those traditions to new, often politically or socially radical ends, in effect *doing* philosophy by testing out the implications of a given theoretical abstraction by placing it within the crucible of extreme circumstances. Preoccupied with their own set of theatrical concerns, the dramatists studied here draw on classical doctrines thematically apt for the unique needs of their individual plays, but, taken as a whole, they also exhibit a remarkable shared sensitivity to the potential of the era's philosophical heritage to help construct immersive worlds that, in their own right, act upon the audience. What binds these diverse classical philosophies together is the similar *function* they serve within their respective plays, as dramatists marshal and refashion in philosophically adept ways a broad spectrum of ontological claims endemic to their culture in order to create fully-realised worlds that, in turn, affect reception of the revenge narratives depicted.

Though organised around the issue of theatrical revenge, this book is concerned, then, with reciprocity of a different sort: the ways in which revenge drama *does* philosophy and the ways in which its revised philosophies condition audience apprehension of retribution. Preoccupied with reciprocity itself, even the finest criticism of the genre remains focused exclusively on matters of recompense as mediated through law, politics, or religion. But revenge tragedy – a genre especially attuned to the relationship between cause and effect, spirit and body, thought and action – proves particularly useful for reconsidering how the immaterial and insensibly material come to manifest themselves in lived experience. A unique medium for doing philosophy, revenge drama draws attention to the ligatures connecting foundational principles and how we order ourselves in society. In doing so, it exposes the considerable flexibility possible between theory and *praxis*, ontological assumption and social action. Integrating early modern drama with the era's complex, variegated intellectual histories, this book refigures how we understand one of the most popular subgenres of Renaissance drama and the ways in which classical philosophy, central to the construction of Renaissance culture itself, found expression and rearticulation in even the most sensational moments on the popular stage.

Establishing Revenge Tragedy as a Genre, Estranging Philosophy from Retribution

In his famous opinion regarding the definition of pornography, Justice Potter Stewart concedes the impossibility of defining 'the kinds of material I understand to be embraced within that shorthand description' and admits that 'perhaps I could never succeed in intelligibly doing so', before concluding this confession of hermeneutic frustration by adding, with a hint of defiance, 'But I know it when I see it.'[4] Critics of early modern revenge tragedy often find themselves sharing in Justice Stewart's epistemological and taxonomic dilemma, having to rely on a similarly intuitive approach toward definitions. When speaking of revenge tragedies, we seem to assume, more often than not, that plays such as *The Duchess of Malfi* are in, ones like *Macbeth* are out, whatever the relative merits of the justice served by the Bosolas and Macduffs populating the stage, seeking their retribution within unjust worlds. In recent years, scholars have increasingly drawn attention to the modern origins of our thinking about revenge tragedy as a genre,[5] yet even while registering the novelty and imprecision of this generic category have left the act of genre creation itself largely unexplored. My concern in the first part of this introduction is neither to fix in place a more precise definition of revenge tragedy nor to jettison altogether this appealing and perennially useful heuristic, but rather to show how the very instantiation of the genre in the early twentieth century contained from the beginning the seeds of such taxonomic confusions and, more importantly, established a mode of thinking about theatrical revenge that estranged retribution itself from the very notion of philosophical complexity. Although alert in varying degrees to the provisionality of this popular generic construct, criticism, that is, has yet to fully appreciate how the very process of genre creation has helped condition reception of retribution on the stage, foregrounding its more sensational aspects and, concomitantly, obscuring the remarkable range of classical philosophical traditions at work throughout plays associated with the genre.

Introduced by A. H. Thorndike in 1902 and amplified by Fredson Bowers in the first monograph on the subject in 1940, the concept of revenge tragedy as a definable genre would eventually become commonplace in the century's criticism, but even as Thorndike and Bowers laboured to codify the type, these foundational critics also betrayed in passing the imprecision endemic to the effort itself. Thorndike begins his expansive article by identifying 'revenge tragedy' simply as a tragedy 'whose leading motive is revenge and whose main action deals with the progress of this revenge'.[6] Citing *The Spanish Tragedy* as the progenitor of this tradition for the Renaissance stage, however, he proceeds to isolate from the play three characteristics that 'distinguish more specifically the revenge tragedy' as a genre. First, Thorndike asserts, 'the fundamental motive is revenge, and this revenge of a father for a son is superintended by a ghost'; second, there exists 'hesitation on the part of the revenger who requires much inciting and superabundant proof'; and, third, 'madness' functions as 'an essential motive throughout'.[7] Following the essential contours traced by Thorndike, Bowers likewise appends to the revenge motive a similar constellation of conventions. 'Revenge,' Bowers explains,

> constitutes the main action of the play in the sense that the audience is chiefly interested in the events which lead to the necessary revenge for murder, and then in the revenger's

actions in accordance with his vow. The revenge must be the cause of the catastrophe, and its start must not be delayed beyond the crisis. 'Revenge tragedy' customarily (but by no means necessarily) portrays the ghosts of the murdered urging revenge, a hesitation on the part of the avenger, a delay in proceeding to his vengeance, and his feigned or actual madness.[8]

Through the work of Thorndike and Bowers, revenge tragedy becomes identified, then, not only with the retributive act but also with ghosts, hesitations and madness – a series of traits to which later critics would append the prevalence of metadrama and that, in the aggregate, constitutes the revenge 'type'.[9] But as Bowers rather casually qualifies his claims ('customarily', 'by no means necessarily'), he signals, however subtly, the *aporia* at the heart of his and Thorndike's very project, for he detaches even as he invokes the very conventions meant to establish an identifiable type. Inadequate in itself to delineate a genre, revenge, it would seem, requires ancillary conventions that, at the same time, appear optional, dispensable. Difficult to pin down with precision, revenge tragedy depends upon something of a gestalt impression: we know the genre when we see it.

Although the conventions of revenge tragedy as outlined by Thorndike and Bowers have taken on a certain sense of cohesiveness in critical imagination, this *aporia* lies at the heart of their combined acts of genre creation, a fact that becomes more visible upon closer examination of how both critics treat Thomas Kyd's *The Spanish Tragedy*. Consider, for instance, Thorndike's depiction of Kyd's play as a revenge tragedy where 'the fundamental motive is revenge, and this revenge of a father for a son is superintended by a ghost'. As he labours to link the convention of a ghost to the *scelus*, or great crime, which animates the retribution narrative itself – all in order to delineate the distinguishing features of the genre – Thorndike subtly equivocates by figuring the revenging action as '*superintended* by a ghost'. For the ghost superintending Hieronimo's revenge in Kyd's play is not that of Horatio, the revenger's murdered son, but rather of Don Andrea, a figure who, having died in battle, holds at best a dubious claim to revenge and, more significantly, remains divorced from the murder of Horatio that sets Hieronimo's own revenging action into motion. If plays featuring either retribution or ghosts – and, indeed, even some, like *Macbeth*, which feature both yet keep them apart – fail to adequately signify a 'revenge tragedy', Thorndike's formulation requires a close relation between the two, something that the subtle disjunctures of Kyd's play trouble. A similar sense of unease regarding *The Spanish Tragedy*'s role as prototype for a genre can be witnessed in Bowers' more explicit engagement with its problematic nature. After declaring that Kyd's play 'is far from a perfect working-out of a revenge theme', for instance, Bowers notes how 'the actual vengeance of Hieronimo is not conceived until midway in the play' and then concedes that 'the ghost has no real connection with the play'.[10] Curiously, then, the fundamental characteristics of revenge tragedy imperfectly define *The Spanish Tragedy*, ostensibly the progenitor of the very genre itself.

The mixed reception of revenge tragedy as a genre during the years between Thorndike's introduction and Bowers' canonisation of the term further attests to the imprecision and provisionality inherent in the construct's defining qualities. In the immediate aftermath of Thorndike's article, scholars exhibit a notable tendency to perceive in the newly-established genre something at once instantly familiar and yet difficult to identify with precision. As early as 1904, Lewis Mott calls *Hamlet* 'a revenge play of the type discussed by Professor Thorndike two years ago and built, as he pointed out, upon a common and usual formula'.[11] In a similar fashion, in 1906, John W. Cunliffe, likewise citing Thorndike, stipulates revenge tragedy a matter 'familiar to students of Elizabethan drama', while Felix E. Schelling, writing in 1908, identifies Kyd's play as belonging to what is 'commonly known as the tragedy of revenge'.[12] Even as some adopted the freshly-minted genre as common, usual and familiar, however, others probed the parameters of Thorndike's formulation, at times rather trenchantly. Where F. W. Moorman adduces *Tancred and Gismunda* as 'another revenge tragedy' in 1906, E. E. Stoll declares *The Malcontent* a 'revenge tragedy', before aligning *Julius Caesar* in the following year with the 'Elizabethan murder and revenge play, the latter half of it, like *Hamlet*, containing a ghost to preside over the revenge'.[13] Amid these tentative attempts to test out the boundaries of the term, Rupert Brooke, the famous World War I poet, launches a particularly compelling, extended case against Thorndike's genre, something he deems 'a recently-invented genus', in *John Webster and the Elizabethan Drama* (1916). 'There is something in the idea, but not much; and it has been over worked', asserts Brooke, before expounding:

> To begin with, there are far fewer examples of this type than these critics believe. And it is not quite clear what is the thread of continuity they are thinking of. Is it the fact that revenge is the motive in each play? Or is it a special type of play, the criterion of which is its atmosphere, and which generally includes vengeance as a motive? If the second, they must include other plays in their list; if the first, drop some out [. . .] The whole category is a false one. It would be much more sensible to invent and trace the 'Trial-at-law' type, beginning with the *Eumenides*, going down through *The Merchant of Venice*, *The White Devil*, *Volpone*, *The Spanish Curate*, and a score more, till you ended with *Justice*.[14]

Brooke's counterfactual, a compelling argument in its own right, recalls the era's penchant for sub-categorisation, an impulse which produced, in addition to the more durable 'revenge tragedy', other categories, since discarded, such as the 'conqueror play', the 'romantic tragedy' and the 'homely circumstantial murder play'.[15] More importantly, as Brooke notes the novelty and arbitrariness of the genre, he exposes Thorndike's formulation as depending upon the constant shifting between two categories of criteria, neither of which, on its own, establishes a 'thread of continuity' capable of binding the genre together in itself. In the years immediately preceding Bowers' monograph Brooke rightly diagnoses the hermeneutic uncertainty which, in varying degrees, would plague studies of revenge tragedy throughout the century.

While Bowers' monumental study has since eclipsed Brooke's crucial question regarding the 'thread of continuity' binding revenge tragedies together, virtually every play associated with the genre nonetheless still receives at some point in the critical literature a telling disclaimer: namely, that it imprecisely fits the revenge tragedy mould. Thorndike and Bowers, as we have seen, signal the inadequacy of the revenge tragedy construct for describing Kyd's play, a concession which has since been echoed more explicitly elsewhere.[16] Perhaps most remarkably, however, a similar caveat attends even *The Revenger's Tragedy*. 'Paradoxically, *The Revenger's Tragedy* does not lie in the main tradition of Elizabethan revenge tragedy,' asserts Brian Gibbons in one of the starkest articulations of the notion, for example, as he depicts the play as 'breaking the pattern established two decades earlier in Kyd's *The Spanish Tragedy*'.[17] Indeed, critics have understood *The Revenger's Tragedy* as indebted as much to morality drama and Marstonian satire as to any revenge tradition,[18] and the play, moreover, has vexed those seeking conformity to a generic template by markedly omitting the ghost, a convention ostensibly common to the genre. *Titus Andronicus*, for all its horrors, also makes 'no mention of a ghost' and, if the sheer ferocity of the play's multiple acts of vengeance have kept it within the fold, it is not without the observation that, in terms of genre, certain 'formal parts have been discarded' along the way, including the masque or play-within-a-play.[19] In a similar fashion, *The Duchess of Malfi* may retain 'the dramatic framework of the revenge play but it contains fewer of the trappings of this type of drama', notably displacing the madness expected from the revenger onto one of the villains and, what's more, omitting the figure of the ghost, the latter a feature shared with *The Tragedy of Hoffman* as well.[20] Finally, as one recent study of revenge tragedy has it, '*The Atheist's Tragedy* and *The Revenge of Bussy D'Ambois*, might even be called "anti-revenge" plays, interesting less for the ways they instantiate the norms of their genre than for the ways they dissent from them.'[21] But if the case can be made – as it has been at different times, by different scholars – that *The Spanish Tragedy*, *Titus Andronicus*, *The Atheist's Tragedy*, *The Revenge of Bussy D'Ambois*, *The Duchess of Malfi*, *The Tragedy of Hoffman* and even *The Revenger's Tragedy* fit uneasily within the revenge tragedy construct, might it not be time to ask why this is so?

While most plays associated with the revenge tragedy type receive the disclaimer that they selectively incorporate the conventions of the genre, criticism on *Hamlet* remains conspicuously exempt from such genre anxiety, marking the play as singular in its conformity with this modern construct. But why does *Hamlet* fit seamlessly with the genre, even in its most minor characteristics, while other plays featuring revenge lack, in varying degrees, the genre's fundamental conventions? The exact correlation of the one and the procrustean position of the others suggests that Thorndike's model, remarkably enough, attempts to read revenge drama *through* the conventions common to *Hamlet*. Rather than simply situating *Hamlet* within the context of similar drama, that is, Thorndike *projects* Shakespeare's most famous play onto other texts, creating in one motion a coherent genre but one imperfectly suited to other plays. If *Hamlet* sits comfortably within the generic type, it does so because Shakespeare's play provides the very conventions for the genre itself: *Hamlet*, in short, *is* the type. Indeed, although Thorndike's title, 'The Relations of *Hamlet* to Contemporary Revenge Plays', signals his attempt to place *Hamlet* within the context of other early modern drama, it also registers his privileging of Shakespeare's work, his emphasis on *Hamlet* as the point of departure for his inquiry. For while Thorndike admirably seeks to situate Shakespeare within the context of his contemporaries, even striving to appear 'fair in this effort', he nonetheless contrasts 'the great man and the smaller men from the point of view of their contemporaries', noting that 'in the other revenge plays we have found attempts to deal with the same themes to which Shakespere gave *final* expression. The other men were in some degree struggling to express similar artistic moods and a similar range of thought and feeling'.[22] The predisposition to read *Hamlet* as superior, while in itself not surprising, clearly conditions the terms of the genre itself, as *Hamlet* becomes, first, the prototypical revenge tragedy and, finally, the exemplary one.

Using revenge to connect – and a sense of philosophical depth to contrast – *Hamlet* with other plays featuring retribution, this act of genre creation figures Shakespeare's play as emerging from a pre-existing construct it would then come to surpass. In its earliest iterations, this manoeuvre also served to frame other revenge drama as merely sensational, a critical disposition toward revenge plays that, even amid our own age's greater appreciation for their theatrical potency, has helped perpetuate neglect of their capacity for profound engagement with multiple, variegated philosophical traditions. When F. S. Boas argues that '*The Spanish Tragedy* [. . .] with revenge and madness as its main themes, anticipates in certain aspects Shakespere's mighty work,' he depicts Kyd's play principally as an inferior precursor to *Hamlet*, a claim Fredson Bowers makes more explicitly in his foundational study. 'Shakespeare,' Bowers avers, 'almost alone *unshackled* himself from the form, although in *Titus Andronicus* he experimented with it and in the final *Hamlet* achieved the *apotheosis* of the revenge play.'[23] That Bowers diminishes not only Kyd's play but also Shakespeare's own early treatment of revenge may not surprise, but that he does so while assuming *Hamlet* emerges from a readily identifiable form reveals how the very construction of the genre itself has served to distinguish Shakespeare's most famous play from other instances of theatrical revenge. Genre serves, that is, to highlight *Hamlet*'s sophistication, diminish the accomplishment of other plays, however intricately designed they might otherwise seem.[24] As *Hamlet* so adeptly transcends the parameters of the genre it was actually used to construct, other revenge plays concomitantly become understood as melodramatic, lurid bits of stage spectacle designed to appeal to popular tastes, frequently receiving thereby 'the casual and dismissive labels "decadent", "exploitative" and "gratuitous"'.[25] More contemporary criticism has rightly worked to correct this imbalance by drawing attention to revenge drama's intricate *dramaturgical* designs – the interweaving, for example, of intrigue, *pathos* and cultural anxieties in order to generate perennial audience interest – but assumptions about the play's limited *philosophical* horizons have notably still obtained, a vestige of this earlier critical legacy. Having secured *Hamlet*'s distinctiveness, the revenge tragedy genre helped align theatrical retribution with a sense of crude sensationalism, leaving little room – even now after greater critical acknowledgement of such plays' clever dramaturgical strategies – for appreciation of revenge drama's deep, and surprisingly broad, engagement with the philosophical.

If *Hamlet*, unique among revenge plays, has been credited with a broader range of philosophical interests while concomitantly seeming the quintessential revenge tragedy, the act of genre creation has also nonetheless subtly reinforced a sense of estrangement between philosophy and retribution even in this most lauded play. For while the protagonist philosophises, so the narrative conventionally goes, he does not revenge; when he revenges, he does so suddenly, on impulse, with comparatively little rumination.[26] This estrangement of philosophy from revenge in critical discourse has roots in Romantic assumptions of *Hamlet* as, in Augustus Schlegel's phrasing, a 'tragedy of thought', a play 'inspired by continual and never-satisfied meditation on human destiny and the dark perplexity of the events of this world'.[27] Explicitly setting Hamlet's philosophical disposition against his physical act of revenge, Schlegel concludes that 'The whole is intended to show that a calculating consideration, which exhausts all the relations and possible consequences of a deed, must cripple the power of acting.'[28] In Schlegel's reading, calculation debilitates; philosophy and revenge stand as irreconcilable opposites. Building on Schlegel's thesis, William Hazlitt likewise frames the play as a 'tragedy of thought', highlighting 'Hamlet's indecision to act', 'his over-readiness to reflect', and 'the abstruse reasoning in which he indulges'.[29] In the same vein, Samuel Coleridge perceives in the protagonist 'a great, an almost enormous, intellectual activity, and a proportionate aversion to real action'.[30] Writing during the ascendancy of revenge tragedy as a genre, A. C. Bradley dissents from how Schlegel and Coleridge configure the precise nature of this tension,[31] but he notably reaffirms that, throughout the play, the 'energy of resolve is dissipated in an endless brooding on the deed required'.[32] The perennial inclination to perceive a conflict between thought and action in *Hamlet* finds tacit but powerful support in revenge tragedy's codification of hesitation as central to an entire genre. As *Hamlet* shifts from 'tragedy of thought' to 'revenge tragedy', then, criticism retains the assumption – rooted in the Romantics, reaffirmed by a newly-minted genre – of a latent tension between philosophy and retribution.

With the sensationalism of retribution so thoroughly foregrounded in our critical hermeneutic, inquiry into the philosophical traditions operant within most revenge tragedies has tended to concentrate on the moral and metaphysical issues pertaining to revenge itself. The protagonists of revenge tragedies – violently defying corrupt rulers, contemplating suicide, potentially running afoul of divine law – have prompted from critics, that is, productive studies into the ethics of seeking personal justice, a mode of inquiry that has quite naturally extended to consider legal, political and religious matters. If other philosophical considerations have remained estranged from our understanding of retribution, sitting uneasily with the grotesque moments of revenge tragedy, these more familiar areas of critical study seem almost intrinsically consonant with the play's sensational aspects; seem, as it were, even to emerge from them. For how else are we to understand both the origins and ramifications of intense violence and extreme behaviour other than to think of their legal, political and religious implications? This easy coincidence, this almost symbiotic relationship, helps account for how critics could, with no apparent sense of contradiction, allude to 'the philosophic melodrama of the Kydian-Senecan revenge motive'.[33] Indeed, to the extent revenge tragedies as a whole have registered as philosophical at all, it is largely in this general sense of their Senecanism: their concomitant interest in grotesque moments of violence and the resultant, extensive ruminations centred on the psychology and social dimensions of responding to intense personal trauma. Focusing on the *agon* of protagonists isolated within unjust polities and a seemingly indifferent, perhaps hostile universe, revenge tragedy criticism has directed attention towards the emotive excesses, histrionics and sensational acts that, in turn, have served to delimit the kinds of philosophical traditions perceived as germane to such plays.

From the Intelligible to the Sensible: Revenge, Classical Philosophy and the Ontology of Embodied Acts

While revenge tragedy as a generic construct has principally directed attention to matters of law, politics and religion, we might nonetheless supplement and extend our use of this evocative term by considering how these plays marshal retribution and even its sensational moments to participate in a more expansive mode of philosophical inquiry. A useful, enduring heuristic, revenge tragedy, that is, deserves more precise interrogation of the philosophical substructures that give rise to what is often – imagistically and rather emotively – glossed as simply its 'moods' or 'atmospheres'. In his famous manifesto 'The Theater of Cruelty', Antonin Artaud argues persuasively for the theatre as a unique space that brings even the most abstract of theoretical ideas to audience attention precisely through shocking the senses and rendering philosophy, as it were, tangible. 'One does not separate the mind from the body nor the senses from the intelligence,' Artaud explains, 'especially in a domain [such as theatre] where the endlessly renewed fatigue of the organs requires intense and sudden shocks to revive our understanding'.[34] For Artaud, philosophy not only *can* co-exist with the sensational but more precisely *depends* upon it: revitalisation of the senses is prerequisite for revival of the mind. 'It is not, moreover, a question of bringing metaphysical ideas directly onto the stage,' Artaud continues by way of qualification, 'but of creating what you might call temptations, indraughts of air around these ideas,'[35] and as he expounds on how the theatre might help breathe life into philosophy, he posits a vision of the stage as a virtual extension of the audience member's own body, something that (in an almost organic fashion) channels one's attention. 'It is a question then of making the theater, in the proper sense of the word, a function,' explains Artaud, 'something as localized and as precise as the circulation of the blood in the arteries or the apparently chaotic development of dream images in the brain, and this is to be accomplished by a thorough involvement, a genuine enslavement of the attention.'[36] Theatre, functioning like part of the body, serves to captivate the mind and does so, moreover, in order to prompt philosophical rumination. 'It is through the skin,' Artaud concludes, 'that metaphysics must be made to re-enter our minds.'[37] But if, following Artaud's theory of theatrical dynamics and the presence of the philosophical within performance, cruelty and the sensational may serve as able means for exploring metaphysics, what sort of other philosophical work might revenge more specifically accomplish?

As much as retribution naturally lends itself to examining issues of law, politics and religion, revenge on the early modern stage, as it turns out, also proves especially well-suited for investigating matters of ontology across a diverse array of philosophical traditions. At every stage, revenge tragedies remain keenly alert to different states of *being*. More particularly, revenge dramatists, as we will see, frequently take up as central to their plays the differences between immaterial or imperceptible states of being and material or perceptible ones, the traversal across these varied states, and the ways in which the comprehending mind makes sense of such relations. Although played out in myriad ways throughout revenge drama, this interest in the relation between different modes of being can be perceived, in its broadest contours, in the very emergence of retribution itself. Unique among other theatrical devices, revenge persistently draws attention both to its own becoming, to the very process by which it enters into being as a distinct conceptual category, and, at the same time, to its own constitutive antecedents, the precise precipitating events without which this new thing could not exist as itself. To be sure, all theatrical acts are ones of instantiation and remain dependent on preceding events for coherence. But these features of revenge – its distinctiveness as a new and separate quantity, its dependence upon a specific localised antecedent that *must* be invoked as a condition of its own becoming, and its alertness thereby to the procedure of its own instantiation – set the retribution narrative apart in kind. In the interim between *scelus* and final retributive act, revenge proper notably does not yet exist, the reiterated desire for, and intricate planning of, vengeance only serving to underscore its absence and create anticipation for its arrival. Moreover, retribution's dependence on a constitutive antecedent at the moment of its instantiation invites consideration of distinctions between conceptual categories. Neither a permutation of the initial *scelus* itself nor an act capable of existence without explicit invocation of it, revenge thus exists as separate yet dependent. As an act that enters into being after a long period of delay while also invoking an even earlier moment central to its own constitution, revenge remains markedly invested in both the precise moment of instantiation and the relational aspects between conceptual categories.

The other conventions associated with the revenge tragedy genre also direct attention in their own ways toward the process of becoming and the relation of a quantity or quality to its antecedents, further creating, to adapt Artaud's evocative phrase, indraughts of air around ontological concerns. While madness, ghosts and metadrama share no essential links to revenge, these devices function in notably similar ways. Madness, of course, stands apart as singular, a state of mental being distinct enough to warrant its own designation, and dramatists devote considerable attention to its development over the course of their plays. If a stratagem, the madness functions not unlike metadrama, knowing and self-referential, but, even if real, contains the seeds of the rationality which preceded it and, indeed, principally becomes understood *as* madness by contrast to the previously well-ordered mind. For the 'process of reading madness' remains largely dependent on discerning how the 'cultural remnants' emerging from the afflicted 'have connections with [. . .] the characters' pre-mad history'.[38] In a similar fashion, the early modern ghost, 'by definition distinct from the living man', draws attention to its own instantiation not only by its sudden, shocking arrival to a community but also by recounting the narrative of its own separation from the body.[39] Distinct entities brought dramatically into being, ghosts inevitably recall their antecedents. They 'belong to the past, to a history that should have closed with their death, and yet they reappear to trouble the present.'[40] Various moments of metadrama, finally, inevitably recall the circumstances of their own formation both within the fiction of the plays themselves – where characters divide parts, learn lines, discuss final stagings – and also beyond. For metadrama by its nature 'uses reduplication to *internalise* the origin and causality of the scene'.[41] Although none of these conventions works in precisely the same mode as the retribution narrative itself, each foregrounds a process of entering into being that recalls that which came before, establishing prevailing conditions within the theatre amenable to exploring ontological matters of all kinds.

Through such conventions which emphasise the relationships between cause and effect, spirit and matter, absence and presence, and even idea and action, revenge drama consistently exposes the perceiving subject's central role in making sense of – in effect, creating – the links between the imperceptible and perceptible, immaterial and material. The challenge of bridging the divide between the observable material world and that which undergirds and gives rise to it falls primarily to the protagonist, but despite the audience's privileged position, we too frequently share in the endeavour. At its most basic level, the revenge narrative prompts a type of thinking backwards to the unseen. As the character seeking redress must discover the often elusive origins of the initial crime – must uncover, that is, its perpetrators, even its motive – revenge drama trades in probabilities rather than certainties. Just as the unrecoverable past must be discerned only by its subsequent effects, minds likewise cannot be known, can only be traced through embodied action. These issues of the relation between the perceptible and imperceptible, material and immaterial, find alternate, almost ironic, expression when revenge drama incorporates a ghost, a figure at once sensible yet ethereal, who concomitantly recalls divestment from the corporeal even while embodied (for the audience) on stage. The revenge dynamic which prompts in protagonists and audiences alike a mode of thinking backward to underlying causes – all as a means of making sense of present conditions – does so, that is, not simply in a social sense but also in a more broadly philosophical one. At every stage, revenge drama draws attention to the fluid boundary between the observable world and that which underlies it and informs its very construction, to how that boundary gets traversed, and to how the perceiver makes sense of such traversal. In doing so, revenge tragedies open for fresh scrutiny the relation between ontology and *praxis*, between the world's imperceptible, immaterial and most rudimentary processes and the shape or condition of embodied, lived experience.

Though we rarely speak in these terms when considering the revenge tragedy genre, we're already used to understanding these plays, in a distinctively religious register, as especially well-suited for drawing our minds backward to the imperceptible and immaterial, as the interrelation between the divine and mundane shapes virtually all critical discussion of retribution on the stage. Well-rehearsed in previous criticism and otherwise bracketed out here in order to bring other strains of intellectual history to the fore, the religious implications of retribution have long invited us to consider the nexus between ontology and embodied action. For in the injunction *vindicta mihi*, or vengeance is mine, we hear the reverberating voice of an invisible God who stands above the play's crimes waiting to mete out justice, an imperceptible force promising to make visible, indeed palpable, the reality of divine presence. Whether instantiated literally in the mechanism of a this-worldly scourge and minister or simply promised in the form of torment in the afterlife (or even still in Vindice's parodic reference to its apparent absence in *The Revenger's Tragedy*), the concept of physical intervention by an unseen deity permeates audience imagination, prompting a continual rumination, along religious lines, on the ways in which the imperceptible and immaterial will find expression in the perceptible, material world. Indeed, so ubiquitous is this promise of the invisible sword of God hanging above the heads of wrongdoers that the very notion informs the legal and political prohibitions against vengeance also so comprehensively covered in existing work on the genre. To such discourses I will briefly return in the book's epilogue, devoting this study instead to the myriad other ways the era's revenge narratives prompt consideration of both the sensible world and the abstract, intelligible concepts that give that world shape and meaning. Whether via vengeance itself, the many conventions commonly associated with the genre, or the era's myriad religious, political and legal discourses, revenge tragedy has, at every turn, directed attention backward from the observable world to the ontological realities undergirding it. What's remarkable is how dramatists make use of such linkages between ontological assumption and embodied action across an even more diverse set of philosophical discourses as well, finding ways to connect their plays' particular dramatic concerns with deeper substructures shaped by early modern iterations of classical philosophy.

Taking a cue from the energies of revenge drama itself, this book likewise began as a kind of thinking backward from the perceptible and material to the imperceptible and immaterial within prominent revenge tragedies. The works of Kyd, Shakespeare, Marston and Webster studied here provide a representative cross-section of the genre as received, and among the plays' other marked affinities is a coincident, shared dramaturgical strategy of marshalling recurrent tropes – ones attuned to the particular concerns of each given play – in order to signal the underlying ontological assumptions which fundamentally condition the atmosphere in which the revengers operate. Thomas Kyd imbues *The Spanish Tragedy*, for instance, with reduplicated tropes of the vegetative, most saliently in the figure of Hieronimo's garden, a stage property crucial to the *scelus* and the first casualty of a bereaved parent desiring revenge. From first to last, *Titus Andronicus* presents explicit physical trauma of various kinds to thematise the very notion of excess itself. In *Hamlet*, Shakespeare persistently recalls to attention the dirt and dust to which our bodies return. John Marston's *Antonio's Revenge* depicts a world where blood quite literally smokes, emanating fume and vapour throughout the play. And the characters populating the claustrophobic, repressive world of *The Duchess of Malfi* repeatedly allude to contained and desperate animals. What animates such a wide array of heterogeneous tropes? Why do they appear in even the most marginal moments, taking on, thereby, a sense of indispensability for these plays? What if these images, so clearly linked thematically to the central conflicts of their respective plays, extend beyond mere literary ornament to instead invoke philosophical traditions that, in turn, provide more fully-realised frameworks for their revengers than we've previously appreciated? What philosophies might give rise to such recurrent images, that is, and how might those philosophies, once perceived, revolutionise how we understand these plays? The early modern era was deeply syncretic and the commercial stage famously eclectic. While recuperating these neglected strands of intellectual history requires, by its nature, a tight focus, the powerful shaping forces of the philosophies uncovered here do not, of course, preclude the contributing influence of other traditions as well. Yet in each case, as we will see, the dramatists studied here drew on particular philosophical concepts not merely adventitiously for incidental effect but rather comprehensively as part of larger dramaturgical strategies. The project of this book has been to understand why and how this is so.

The following chapters reveal how playwrights such as Kyd, Shakespeare, Marston and Webster adapt a remarkably diverse range of classical philosophies that treat, at heart, ontological matters, and how, by doing so, the authors provide their narratives of retribution with philosophical substructures that if not justify at least make reasonable such violent resistance to tyranny. Uniquely suited to the particular dramatic concerns of their respective plays and unique, too, in their distinctive approaches to tracing embodied action to its various immaterial or insensible ontological grounds, the philosophies represented here nonetheless share a markedly similar purpose within these plays, permeating the action and creating distinctive atmospheres that help condition reception of the retribution presented onstage. Where revenge itself invariably prompts a thinking backward to antecedent causes and revenge tragedy as a genre has continually recalled the invisible workings of the divine in the material world, revenge on stage, as it turns out, also astutely reimagines a broad spectrum of ontological assumptions, drawn from classical philosophy, which undergirds early modern culture. Revenge dramatists, that is, frequently tap into their culture's intellectual history to marshal shared conceptions about how the world works on its most fundamental levels. While the specific doctrines these dramatists employ span a wide array of classical authors and theories, such philosophies function in allied ways across plays, as they serve to create the prevailing conditions – what previous generations of criticism gestured at through labels such as 'mood' and 'atmosphere'

– which frame, and therefore subtly shape reception of, retribution on the early modern stage.

I begin in the next chapter by examining Thomas Kyd's *The Spanish Tragedy*, the play most frequently identified as the progenitor of the revenge tragedy genre and one conventionally characterised as histrionic and sensationalistic. Indeed, even if contemporary critics have come to more fully appreciate the complex dramaturgical strategies by which Kyd's play attains its theatrical force, few today would credit the dramatist with either philosophical depth or the studied mastery of classical material. Yet *The Spanish Tragedy*, a play especially alert to the struggles of the underclass to secure a place amid a corrupt aristocracy, a place in which one's progeny and household may take root and flourish, makes a stunning turn to the era's Aristotelian faculty psychology as a means of presenting a fully-realised, immersive world for its revenge narrative. *The Spanish Tragedy*, I argue, creates a subtle *apologia* for the 'middling sort' by challenging the socially constructed predicates of aristocratic privilege. A scrivener's son, Kyd understood *oeconomia*, or household management, as both the means for material advancement among the 'middling sort' and a potential threat to aristocratic insularity. His translation of Torquato Tasso's *The Householder's Philosophy*, a work rarely studied by literary scholars, reveals an abiding interest in the political import of natural philosophy on class structure. More particularly, through his sophisticated revision of Aristotelian faculty psychology, Kyd appropriates early modern understandings of the vegetative soul – the imperceptible source of all reproduction, nutrition and growth inherent in all living things – to reveal middling ambition as a natural phenomenon. By presenting the latent desire for growth and development as the consequence of an innate psychology, Kyd's play transforms revenge into an understandable outgrowth of thwarted ambition, a type of reproduction by absence, when all lawful means of material advancement become foreclosed. Rather than simply irrational and brutish, or, conversely, highly calculative, revenge appears throughout Kyd's play as *instinctively* reproductive as well. Through such clever manipulations of the era's predominant Aristotelian theories of the impulse to reproduce and grow, Kyd links his revenge narrative, set amid sharp class antagonisms, to a philosophical substructure that, through the very ontological predicates permeating the play, help position Hieronimo and his household as both sympathetic and, what's more, very much of a piece with the natural world in which they operate.

Staying with Aristotle but turning to his ethical theory, my second chapter examines Shakespeare's *Titus Andronicus* to consider a different, though analogous, manner in which the ontology of imperceptible things – in this case, the theoretical abstraction of transcendent ethical value – gets worked out amid the very material realities of the play's extreme brutality. Here, I argue that Shakespeare structures his earliest revenge tragedy around the variable ways the theoretical concept of an ethical mean finds instantiation in embodied action, depending upon context. *Titus Andronicus*, I reveal, examines through its sensational horrors and multiple acts of vengeance how designations of moderation and excess may be constituted, unsettled and reconstituted in a polity destabilised by shifting ethical referents. By examining Shakespeare's engagement with the Aristotelian ethical mean – the theoretical point of moral equilibrium between two diametrically opposed, immoral extremes – this chapter explains how the construal of ethical value in Elizabethan England invited contest. *Titus Andronicus* exhibits a preoccupation with fixing moderation, both in the sense of locating but also repairing it as well, to imagine a world in which immoderation threatens to become the norm. By treating the contextual determination of moderation and the mean's ontological fixity as compatible, *Titus Andronicus* creates a flexible rigidity that positions Titus as both horrible and sympathetic in his revenge, as he negotiates the shifting terms of Rome's civic contract. The play's apparent dislocation of victim and villain derives from the theatrical possibilities inherent in the mean's fluidity, yet the ethical mean paradoxically provides a readable matrix of heroism and villainy. Resituated in a world grown uncontrollably immoderate, Titus acts in direct proportion to his surrounding context, his grotesque revenge functioning, remarkably, as a brutal but necessary type of moderation-in-extremity. Such an unexpected refiguration of moderation as signifying what would otherwise register as extreme reveals Shakespeare's *Titus*, in much the same way Kyd's *Spanish Tragedy* managed for Aristotelian faculty psychology, to be engaged in a radical reappropriation of classical thought as part of a dramaturgical strategy designed to create a playworld that itself shapes reception of the revenge enacted on stage. In doing so, Shakespeare, like Kyd before him, explores the remarkable plasticity possible between ontological theory – in this case, the ethical theory of transcendent value – and its embodiment in lived experience.

Where *The Spanish Tragedy* and *Titus*, directed by the unique needs of their narratives, make use of different classical theories treating the transition of ontological abstraction into embodied acts, *Hamlet*, a play preoccupied with the composition of bodies, minds and spirits, explores this nexus from the other direction: obsessively telling over matter's backward drift into increasingly attenuated states, fading, it might seem, even into non-existence. In my third chapter, I recontextualise *Hamlet* within a strain of early modern atomism, shorn of its atheist metaphysics and Epicurean ethics, which made available new ways of thinking about bodies and minds. Since atoms never fully dissolve, they afford the posthumous body a type of perennial identity: component particles remain integral, theoretically capable of later reconstitution. Moreover, atomism reads perception and memory as material phenomena, the effects of imperceptible motes impressing the mind. In this chapter, I reveal how both these strands of atomist thought – the body as particularised, perception and memory as material imprints – shape the course of Hamlet's revenge. Desirous to forget his own suffering yet enjoined to remember his father, Hamlet will both brood on his own bodily dissolution and intricately plot his vengeance. While these two processes have seemed inherently at odds, both reveal Hamlet's surprising *un*willingness to dissociate fully from the material world. In his ruminations, Hamlet repeatedly reveals a profound *attraction to* the ontological implications of having one's body composed of indestructible, imperturbable particles, promising, even amid the grave's obscuring dust, a kind of continued existence. In his revenge, Hamlet, who perceives time and collective memory in materialist terms – as capable of being 'set [. . .] right' when 'out of joint' and able to 'soil our addition' – will likewise seek to reshape the material contours that give rise to remembrance as he secures the legacies of his father and uncle. By attempting to reshape the court's communal memory, the most immediate register of historical time, Hamlet's revenge, I argue, operates as a type of material accretion to the past, palpably remoulding both murder and incestuous union as containing – and as principally defined by – the horror that redounds on the villainous. For as much as *Hamlet* directs attention to the afterlife and the fate of souls, then, the play also anchors its action into an ontology sympathetic to materialism (even in its most attenuated forms), heightening Hamlet's tragic condition by imbuing him with a keen sense of loss toward a material world whose promise, and even comforts, always remain imaginable but also, at least for him, ultimately elusive.

Hamlet prompts us to contemplate the fine line between the faintest particulates of matter and what lies beyond, its materialism, in this way, creating an ontological framework within which the desire to recover, or at least appreciate, the positive valences of the physical world makes as much sense as the impulse to connect with the undiscovered country of the immaterial one. Written at the same time as *Hamlet*, John Marston's *Antonio's Revenge*, a play keenly interested in the corporeal effects of emotional trauma, likewise takes up as central to its conditioning framework the point of contact, as it were, between materiality and immateriality, repeatedly turning as it does to the subtle pneumatic workings of the human body. For early modern thinkers, *pneuma* signified both spirit and matter, the word simultaneously pointing to both imperceptible soul and the perceptible smoke or fume emanating from the blood. Marston's play, I argue in my fourth chapter, adopts a specifically Galenic understanding of corporeal pneumatics, a theory that imagines indraughts of air merging with, and exerting influence over, blood distributed throughout the body. Where Hamlet perceives in matter's finest particles an enviable freedom from disturbance, Marston's protagonist dispenses with the fiction of imperturbability altogether and – indebted equally to Galenic anti-Stoicism as to Galenic physiology – instead understands the disordered *pneuma* present within the body as a site requiring healing, an interface between body and soul that bears the burden of trauma upon each. In order to reveal Stoic *apatheia* as fundamentally contrary to nature, Marston depicts the interior workings of the body as automatically and by necessity processing the effects of trauma. The Marstonian body markedly absorbs, refashions and transmits back outward – in a fluid physiological cycle – the distemper caused by sudden tragedy. Marston remarkably figures revenge, that is, as the necessary rectification of disordered *pneuma* within a process of instinctive self-healing. By translating this essential operation of physiology upon encountering distress – one that exists right at the boundary between immaterial soul and the faintest wisps of corporeal matter – into social relations, Marston tethers his play's revenging action into the very fabric of his playworld's ontological assumptions, surprisingly positioning vengeance, as he does, as a visceral reaction to trauma designed to satisfy the body's deepest need for constitutional equilibrium.

Where Marston situates his revengers within a framework particularly attuned to how the subtlest physiological processes affect the psyche, John Webster's *The Duchess of Malfi*, the focus of my last chapter, plumbs the deepest recesses of the human soul in a different register. Intrigued by the notion of an inviolable internal state always just beyond the reach of external, material forces, Webster takes as his prevailing concern less the physiological effects of trauma which so preoccupied Marston and more the social disruption a theory of untouchable volition could pose to a repressive political regime obsessed with dehumanising its citizenry. Beginning with the play's curious use of animal lore for depicting an oppressive court, I examine how Webster draws on the Epictetian doctrine of *prohairesis*, the rational capacity for choice that distinguishes humanity from the bestial, to shape the disparate courses of action taken by his characters. Within Epictetian philosophy, those who assent to false impressions, or *phantasiai*, enslave themselves, lessening their humanity, while those who reject false impressions remain free and fully human, however physically enslaved they might otherwise be. Although an Epictetian theory of volition might seem a retreat from the political sphere into the untouchable recesses of an imperceptible interiority, Webster's play reveals the threat such a radical notion of liberty might pose to a regime set on enslaving the minds of its populace. Both the Duchess' alternative way of wielding aristocratic power and Bosola's violent deposition of tyrants fall short, but through these individual responses to tyranny Webster subtly broaches a still more revolutionary notion: namely, that solidarity across class lines, sustained by a shared set of ontological assumptions about the inviolable nature of the will, might succeed – where surreptitious resistance and open revenge had failed – in displacing systemic inequity. By figuring his protagonists' quests for a more egalitarian politics as animated by more than simply personal grievances alone, Webster anchors the play's variegated modes of resistance, then, into a coherent, conditioning set of ontological predicates concerning human volition, ones which, even in their tragic failure to obtain politically, nonetheless shadow out the potentially radical import classical philosophy may hold for the dispossessed.

Although remarkably heterogeneous and drawn upon as each dramatist's particular concerns demand, the philosophies studied here serve similar dramaturgical ends as they provide deep ontological substructures to the playworlds represented, thereby conditioning along the way apprehension of the retribution narratives as they unfold in real time. The vegetative soul, ethical mean, atom, vital spirit and deepest reserves of human will emerge from diverse classical traditions, but, notably, each also uniquely centres on the last waypoint, as it were, on the border between immateriality and materiality. Each represents, therefore, a concept intelligible and not, in itself, properly sensible. These classical concepts, that is, all signify for early modern thinkers ontological realities that both undergird the observable world in the most fundamental of ways and exist just beyond the faculties of perception. As such, the writers studied here direct the perceiving subject to these concepts by means of intermediaries or proxies by which the reasoning mind may apprehend them. Thus, the vegetative soul manifests itself materially in various forms of generation such as plants or offspring; the ethical mean, an ontologically fixed point within Aristotelian theory, through embodied action within a particular social context; the atom that lies just beyond the range of perception through the finest motes, dust and dirt; the highly-refined *pneuma* that serves as interface between body and soul through the smoke that emanates from blood; and the otherwise intangible depths of human volition through the true Stoic's almost preternatural calm amid chaos and cruelty. Revenge dramatists employ such intermediaries to direct audience attention to the most rudimentary elements existing just on the cusp of materiality and immateriality. In doing so, they provide a sensible analogue to that which otherwise remains solely intelligible and integrate into their visceral, even sensational, narratives deeper ontological ground that in turn structures the playworlds they present.

As much as these plays chart the links between underlying ontologies and their common, expected material expressions, however, they also thus present radical alternatives. For the plays studied here signal the links that exist between the vegetative soul and fecundity, abstract ethical value and embodied action, atoms and particles of dust, vital *pneuma* and smoke, human volition and serene demeanour. But these plays concomitantly appropriate these doctrines in rather remarkable ways. The vegetative soul which governs the desire for all increase impels revenge when all other means of material advancement become thwarted. The ethical mean manifests itself amid a wilderness of horrors as a revenge that would otherwise register as grotesque beyond all measure. The mote provides the means for reimagining history and even time as material, capable of being 'set right' through the final retributive act. The vital spirit within the traumatised victim requires restoration, becoming part of the justification for revenge. And the passivity of an egalitarian aristocrat provides, even in its failure to elicit a timely sympathy from the oppressor, the promise of generating revolutionary solidarity across class lines. The classical doctrines represented through these plays, that is, traditionally explain how certain immaterial or faintly material components of the world translate into sensible forms. Yet, at the same time, these dramatists reveal that the materialisation of assumed ontological truths need not find expression in such uniform ways, that, quite the contrary, they might be found by the intervening, interpretative mind expressed in unconventional, even radical, ones. Through such subtle, nuanced appropriations of classical thought, revenge dramatists invite the audience to consider the ways in which underlying ontological premises get worked out in – and read into – the properties and actions of the observable world.

By drawing audience attention to doctrines centring on the intelligible but not properly sensible, revenge drama recalls the interpretative role played by the perceiving mind in providing the connective tissue between the faintest structures of the world's composition and their observable realisations as they pertain to lived experience. Revenge plays present us, then, with something of a dual action: directing minds through intermediaries toward the most fundamental theoretical structures organising the world and then articulating the process of revenge in the very terms of those structures. The effect is to reveal that what we understand as the material manifestation of a deeper ontological truth is, in fact, mediated through our subjective perception of the observed phenomenon. We cannot, for example, see the vegetative soul; we can only see a garden. If we believe the vegetative soul exists, we cannot see a garden; we can only see a garden as a manifestation of the vegetative soul. If the garden recalls to mind our ontological assumptions regarding the imperceptible world, that is, the garden as a perceived object becomes to us the *garden as an expression of the vegetative soul*. And the *garden as an expression of the vegetative soul* unites material manifestation with deeper ontological theory; what unites them is our mind, our role as the perceiving subject. Moreover, if we then see revenge articulated in terms of the vegetative soul, we must confront the variability of that ontology's import for practical life. Objective ontological ground may well exist; its instantiation as apprehended by the perceiving subject requires, however, a subjective element. The perceiving mind functions as the ligature between the deeper ontological ground and the apprehension of this ground in the observable material world itself. And in this ligature there is considerable flexibility.

Even as revenge drama reveals the various uses to which the interpreting mind may put classical doctrines of various kinds, the dramatists studied here ultimately insist upon connecting the revenging action into an ontological ground of its own, resist, in other words, asserting a merely subjective basis for retribution. In doing so, they provide a more substantive philosophical base for defying tyranny than would normally be afforded through appeals to individual grievance alone. If the mind stretches the ontological premises of classical philosophy to new, even radical, applications, such appropriations nonetheless ultimately appeal to an objective predicate. In this regard, the dramatists' subtle adaptations of such philosophies run counter to how we've traditionally considered revenge drama as operating. We've tended to figure revenge in early modern culture as subjective, as flouting an objective ontological order, as individuals elevate their personal grievances in defiance of a providentially-ordered world. But, if as I have been arguing, the dramatists studied here, in fact, reveal the flexibility of *praxis* afforded by the subjective work of the interpretative mind yet, nonetheless, lay claim through the protagonists' revenging actions to an objective ontological order, then the resistance to tyranny depicted in such plays transcends temporary and particularised grievance to instead become something that appears fundamentally rooted in the natural order itself. If the persistent assumption of an ontological order that undergirds social action seems orthodox, the idea that it could be fashioned – that it could be connected via interpretative choices to a radical resistance theory – makes it all the more revolutionary and potent. Through their unconventional appropriation of classical doctrines that treat the ontology of imperceptible yet fundamental quantities, revenge plays not only militate against the charge that vengeance stems solely from subjective desires but also present a mode of resistance to tyranny much more philosophically informed and nuanced than we've previously thought. If not unambiguously justified, retribution on the stage significantly appears in this light as part of a broader set of natural operations that extends beyond the crisis limited to a lone individual or family.

By tethering the revenge narrative itself to the very ontological concepts they invoke, revenge plays further create a sense of retribution as somehow fitting, as seeming in some measure consonant with the world as the play depicts it, and they do this, notably, by working on the audience through assumptions rather than simply through direct, overt claims to sympathy or appeals to justice alone. For those in the audience, perhaps the majority, who sympathise with the protagonists and may well approve of the final retribution, this sense of revenge's aptness accords with the visceral, even ethical, satisfactions these plays tend to offer. Yet the sort of dramaturgical effect created by linking revenge with a subtle set of ontological premises need not correspond with audience sympathy for, or approval of, the revengers or their brutal actions. For whether or not an audience shares in the emotional state or moral determinations of the protagonists, critics have long recognised how revenge plays set right – even if, in some cases, only in a contingent or qualified manner – a disordered world. The unsympathetic or morally suspect revenger, that is, still serves as 'scourge and minister', still rectifies an underlying wrong and participates in a larger providential design. By situating retribution into an ontological framework at once ubiquitous yet also simply assumed within each play, dramatists utilise the very atmosphere of their plays in order to render revenge as a reasonable and philosophically-grounded act. Whatever its emotional or ethical complications, revenge participates in a larger ecology of action in which it serves a necessary and, in its way, natural part.

If revenge drama centres on the most primal elements of social exchange and through its extraordinary cruelty and moments of sensationalism captivates audience attention, it also directs our minds to the fundamental structures of the world in a more comprehensive sense as well. In his magisterial study of revenge tragedy across genres and periods, John Kerrigan elucidates the almost elemental nature of such narratives:

> [T]he most cerebral and perplexed of revenge plays cannot escape from action as a principle [. . .] There is a sense in which theatrical 'doing' gravitates, quite naturally, towards revenge [. . .] As any director knows, it is easier for a performer to respond to something than to create events *ex nihilo*. Meanwhile, revenge is a building-block, the seed from which something larger can grow [. . .] Revenge tragedies practically construct themselves at this level, and the problem for an author is to prevent the material ramifying endlessly [. . .][42]

As he considers the dramaturgy of retribution, Kerrigan intriguingly situates revenge on the very cusp of the immaterial and material: revenge itself is a seed, something just shy of the void, but one that naturally lends itself to copious materiality, the endless ramifications inherent in reciprocity. In this respect, Kerrigan's formulation seems almost Baconian in its figuration of retribution as something that 'men's nature *runs to*',[43] as something that inevitably moves outward towards the increasingly more visible or noticeable. But through the spectacle of revenge, early modern dramatists also pointed in the other direction, using the shocks wrought by the sensational to create indraughts of air around ontological assumptions familiar in the sixteenth and seventeenth centuries, though largely lost to modern sensibilities. By doing so, the dramatists who wielded the materials of revenge not only reworked a remarkable range of rather complex classical theories in innovative, sometimes radical ways. They also elucidated the variable uses to which objective ontological ground could be put by those willing to do so in response to extreme or tyrannical circumstances.

Notes

1. 'Of Revenge', in *The Essayes or Counsels, Civill and Morall*, ed. Michael Kiernan (Cambridge, MA: Harvard University Press, 1985), 384.
2. *Elizabethan Revenge Tragedy: 1587–1642* (Princeton: Princeton University Press, 1940), 3.
3. *The Works of Thomas Kyd*, ed. Frederick S. Boas (Oxford: Clarendon Press, 1901), XXXIX.
4. *Jacobellis v. Ohio*, 84 S. Ct. 1676, 1683 (1964) (Stewart, J., concurring).
5. See Ronald Broude, 'Revenge and Revenge Tragedy in Renaissance England', *Renaissance Quarterly* 28.1 (1975): 38–58 and Linda Woodbridge, *English Revenge Drama* (Cambridge: Cambridge University Press, 2010), 5.
6. 'The Relations of *Hamlet* to Contemporary Revenge Plays', *PMLA* 17.2 (1902): 125.
7. Ibid. 143–4.
8. Bowers, *Elizabethan Revenge Tragedy*, 63–4.
9. On metadrama and revenge tragedy, see Tanya Pollard, 'Tragedy and Revenge', in *The Cambridge Companion to English Renaissance Tragedy*, ed. Emma Smith and Garrett A. Sullivan, Jr (Cambridge: Cambridge University Press, 2010), 68–9.
10. Ibid. 66, 71.
11. Lewis F. Mott, 'The Position of the Soliloquy "to Be or Not to Be" in *Hamlet*', *PMLA* 19.1 (1904): 26.
12. John W. Cunliffe, 'Nash and the Earlier *Hamlet*', *PMLA* 21.1 (1906): 193. Felix Emmanuel Schelling, *Elizabethan Drama, 1558–1642: A History of the Drama in England from the*

Accession of Queen Elizabeth to the Closing of the Theaters (Boston, MA: Houghton Mifflin, 1908), 553.

13. F. W. Moorman, 'The Pre-Shakespearean Ghost', *The Modern Language Review* 1.2 (1906): 89. Elmer Edgar Stoll, 'Shakspere, Marston, and the Malcontent Type', *Modern Philology* 3.3 (1906): 289, n. 3 and 'The Objectivity of the Ghosts in Shakspere', *PMLA* 22.2 (1907): 229.
14. Rupert Brooke, *John Webster and the Elizabethan Drama* (New York: John Lane Co., 1916), 89–90.
15. Felix Emmanuel Schelling, *Elizabethan Playwrights: A Short History of the English Drama from Mediaeval Times to the Closing of the Theaters in 1642* (New York: Harper & Brothers, 1925), 89.
16. See G. K. Hunter, 'Ironies of Justice in *The Spanish Tragedy*', *Renaissance Drama* 8 (1965): 89–104.
17. Brian Gibbons, 'Introduction', *The Revenger's Tragedy*, ed. Brian Gibbons, The New Mermaids Series, 2nd edn (New York: W. W. Norton, 1991), x.
18. See R. A. Foakes, 'Introduction', *The Revenger's Tragedy*, The Revels Plays (Cambridge, MA: Harvard University Press, 1966), xxii.
19. Rose Alden, *The Tragedy of Revenge. A thesis presented to the faculty of the Graduate School of Cornell University in partial fulfillment of the requirements for the degree of Master of Arts* (Ithaca, NY, 1920), 34.
20. Elizabeth M. Brennan, 'Introduction', *The Duchess of Malfi*, ed. Elizabeth M. Brennan, The New Mermaids Series (London: Ernest Benn Limited, 1964): xiii–xiv.
21. Katharine Eisaman Maus, 'Introduction', *Four Revenge Tragedies: The Spanish Tragedy, The Revenger's Tragedy, The Revenge of Bussy D'Ambois, The Atheist's Tragedy*, ed. Katharine Eisaman Maus (Oxford: Oxford University Press, 1995), ix–x.
22. 'The Relations of *Hamlet*', 220.
23. Bowers, *Elizabethan Revenge Tragedy*, 101, emphasis added.
24. 'Of this inherited complexity, which it so makes over, *Hamlet* is the astonishing consummation,' asserts Peter Mercer,

concluding, 'It is not, of course, just another revenge play [. . .] [T]he structure it so radically transforms [. . .] remains of the highest relevance to the play. Hamlet is born from that structure – however strange the labour' (*Hamlet and the Acting of Revenge* [Iowa City: University of Iowa Press, 1987], 7). Harold Bloom provides a unique twist to this critical tendency when he asserts, without elaboration, that '*Hamlet* is part of Shakespeare's revenge upon revenge tragedy, and is of no genre' (*Hamlet: Poem Unlimited* [New York: Riverhead Books, 2003], 3).

25. Stevie Simkin, 'Introduction', *Revenge Tragedy* (New York: Palgrave Macmillan Limited, 2001), 5.
26. On Hamlet's killing of Claudius as 'unplanned reflex', see Ruth Stevenson, '*Hamlet*'s Mice, Motes, Moles, and Minching Malecho', *New Literary History* 33 (2002): 443.
27. Augustus Schlegel, 'Course of Lectures on Dramatic Art and Literature', in Hamlet: *Critical Essays*, ed. Joseph G. Price (New York: Garland Publishing: 1986), 217.
28. Ibid. 218.
29. William Hazlitt, 'Characters of Shakespeare's Plays', in Price (ed.), Hamlet: *Critical Essays*, 214.
30. Samuel Coleridge, '*Hamlet*', in *Notes and Lectures upon Shakespeare and some of the Old Poets and Dramatists: With Other Literary Remains of S. T. Coleridge*, vol. 1 (London: William Pickering, 1849), 207–8.
31. See Margreta De Grazia, 'Teleology, Delay, and the "Old Mole"', *Shakespeare Quarterly* 50.3 (1999): 257.
32. A. C. Bradley, *Shakespearean Tragedy: Lectures on* Hamlet, Othello, King Lear, Macbeth, 3rd edn (New York: St Martin's Press, 1992), 88.
33. Lawrence J. Ross, 'Introduction', *The Revenger's Tragedy*, ed. Lawrence J. Ross, Regents Renaissance Drama Series (Lincoln: University of Nebraska Press, 1966), xx.
34. Antonin Artaud, 'The Theater of Cruelty', in *The Theater and Its Double*, trans. Mary Caroline Richards (New York: Grove Press, 1958), 86.
35. Ibid. 90.

36. Ibid. 92.
37. Ibid. 99.
38. Carol Thomas Neely, *Distracted Subjects: Madness and Gender in Shakespeare and Early Modern Culture* (Ithaca, NY: Cornell University Press, 2004), 49–50.
39. Catherine Belsey, 'Shakespeare's Sad Tale for Winter: *Hamlet* and the Tradition of Fireside Ghost Stories', *Shakespeare Quarterly* 61.1 (2010): 25.
40. Ibid. 5.
41. David Roberts, 'The Play within the Play and the Closure of Representation', in *The Play Within the Play: The Performance of Meta-Theatre and Self-Reflection*, ed. Gerhard Fischer and Bernhard Greiner (New York: Rodopi, 2007), 38.
42. John Kerrigan, *Revenge Tragedy: Aeschylus to Armageddon* (Oxford: Oxford University Press, 1996), 4–5.
43. Bacon, 'Of Revenge', 384.

CHAPTER 1

OECONOMIA AND THE VEGETATIVE SOUL: THOMAS KYD'S NATURALISATION OF REVENGE IN *THE SPANISH TRAGEDY*

The Spanish Tragedy was one of the early modern theatre's most enduringly popular plays and even the most resistant of Thomas Kyd's critics have had to acknowledge the undeniable emotional appeal, the sheer dramaturgical force, which invigorates this early revenge narrative. Few, however, even among his more receptive readers, would be inclined to praise Kyd as a deft classicist, let alone one who subtly marshals the materials of ancient philosophy as a means of shaping the profound theatrical effects for which he is more generally appreciated. In this regard, Kyd has never fully recovered from Thomas Nashe's blistering attack delivered in his preface to Robert Greene's *Menaphon* (1589). Surveying contemporary writers and bemoaning upstarts with little apparent learning, Nashe excoriates those who 'leave the trade of Noverint whereto they were borne, and busie themselves with the indevors of Art', an opening salvo likely directed at Kyd, a scrivener's son who practised the trade before turning dramatist and translator.[1] Much of Nashe's ensuing critique takes specific issue with authorial misapprehension of classical literature, and the portrait that emerges is of a poet of little facility with ancient texts and ideas.

When Nashe scoffs how 'English Seneca read by candle light yeeldes manie good sentences,' he presumably mocks Kyd's rendering of 'ad lumina' ('until dawn') as 'by candlelight' in his edition of Torquato Tasso, and also suggests such an author of limited capacity remains dependent on vernacular editions of classical texts.² Nashe's sketch depicts a parvenu of small knowledge but unbounded enthusiasm for ancient literature. 'If you intreate him faire in a frostie morning,' Nashe maintains, 'he will affoord you whole *Hamlets*, I should say handfulls of tragical speeches.' With a passing allusion to the 'Kidde in Aesop', likely a forced pun on Kyd's own name, Nashe turns to inveigh against those who would, as Kyd does in *The Spanish Tragedy*, 'thrust Elisium into hell', another apparent muddling of classical sources. Out of their element, dependent upon vernacular editions, quite possibly imprecise in their own translations, excessive, even slavish, in their devotion to Seneca, and confused regarding the details of classical narrative, the targets of Nashe's invective, of whom Kyd seems paramount, become mere interlopers characterised by their 'home-born mediocritie'.³ Nashe's stinging critique has undoubtedly left its mark on Kyd's reputation as a handler of classical material, and few today would credit the dramatist with subtle erudition or expect to find the nuanced appropriation of classical philosophical ideas at work in his engagingly lurid potboiler.

But is Kyd really such a mediocrity as a classicist and an appropriator of ancient texts and ideas? Does the evidence substantiate this picture of Kyd as an enthusiastic, undeniably popular author but one whose theatrical success exists in contrast to, perhaps in spite of, his confused use of classical content? In addition to Nashe's satire, Kyd's reputation as a thinker has been tarnished by the kinds of critical reception of *The Spanish Tragedy* briefly outlined in the introduction, and if his play has received greater appreciation among more modern critics, scholarship has still left largely intact the underlying assumption of Kyd as an adept, savvy playwright but one of limited classical and philosophical learning. To be sure, there are notable exceptions to this enduring trend, and in recent years sensitive readers have begun, if modestly, to correct the picture. Eugene Hill and Zackariah Long have done much to re-evaluate Kyd's clever appropriation of Senecan and Virgilian sources.[4] Where G. K. Hunter, in a brief piece, has recently uncovered Kyd's indebtedness to Tacitus, Frank Ardolino has likewise newly traced the dramatist's reliance on Apuleius.[5] And in an influential reading of Kyd's *Cornelia*, Curtis Perry has persuasively situated Kyd's work as one that teases out the implications of classical republicanism for the author's own cultural moment.[6] As these emerging though isolated strands of critical inquiry have begun to suggest, assumptions about Kyd's failures as a classicist may well have been misguided, his limitations overstated, as this popular playwright reveals himself to be, in fact, an astute manipulator of multiple, often unexpected, strands of classical thought. Indeed, we might go even further still and think of the much-lauded performative force of his early revenge play as emerging in large measure from this very capacity to learnedly and imaginatively refashion his era's received classical ideas.

The other scattered references to Kyd by his contemporaries – references often interpreted as simply indicative of the author's popularity – in fact signal an author of some estimation, a writer frequently aligned with those of marked, or at least respectable, classical learning, suggesting others perceived in Kyd the presence of no mean intellect. Francis Meres, for instance, lists Kyd as among 'our best for Tragedie' and places him in the company of 'Lord Buckhurst, Doctor Leg of Cambridge, Doctor Edes of Oxford, master Edward Ferres, the Authour of the Mirrour for Magistrates, Marlow, Peele, Watson [. . .] Shakespeare, Drayton, Chapman, Decker, and Benjamin Jonson'.[7] John Bodenham's

Bel-vedere or the Garden of the Muses (1600), an anthology of commonplaces billed as an 'Abstract of knowledge, Briefe of Eloquence'[8] and compiled by a man identified as 'Art's lover, Learning's friend',[9] cites Kyd no fewer than twenty-eight times, second only to Shakespeare and approximately four times as much as Marlowe or Jonson. What's more, Robert Allott's *England's Parnassus* (1600), which purports to collect 'flowers of Learning' from authors 'affronted' by 'dull ignorance', likewise quotes heavily from Kyd, with at least twenty-one identified passages drawn from his translation of *Cornélie* alone.[10] And, most famously, Ben Jonson references 'sporting Kid' while placing him in the company of Lily and Marlowe, just a few lines after invoking Chaucer, Spenser and Beaumont, in his dedicatory poem to Shakespeare in the First Folio.[11] For someone satirically deemed a home-borne mediocrity with a limited command of classical material, Kyd certainly keeps exalted, rather learned, company, and it seems a kind of critical prejudice, traceable to Nashe's initial sketch, to explain these other valuations of Kyd as mere concessions to a popular but not especially learned author rather than as indicators of the credit he earned as a sharp and original mind in his own right.

This disposition to allow Nashe's satire to obscure appreciation of Kyd's intellectual facility and, more particularly, his subtlety in adapting classical material – a tendency that has profoundly conditioned reception of *The Spanish Tragedy* – is perhaps best exemplified in the critical response to Thomas Dekker's mention of Kyd in *A Knight's Conjuring* (1607). In the ninth chapter, Dekker imagines poets congregating in the 'Fieldes of Joye', the Elysian green, and he explains how, 'In another companie sat learned Watson, industrious Kyd, ingenious Atchlow, and [. . .] inimitable Bentley'.[12] Here, yet another contemporary of Kyd's places the dramatist among the learned and accomplished, but Dekker's use of 'industrious' has served, more often than not, to *diminish* Kyd's reputation as a serious thinker and savvy reader of classical texts. Even at their most charitable, critics have taken the term as pointing to 'the sheer number of [Kyd's] works', but, less charitably, most have understood the term 'as a backhanded compliment meaning "prolific but prosaic"',[13] and the emergent picture of Kyd has been one, as Nashe would well like, of a hardworking but plodding author, certainly not distinguished by his erudition. But in Dekker's day, 'industrious' signified something rather different, often connoting a quick and perceptive intellect. As the *OED* notes, 'industrious' meant 'characterised by or showing intelligent or skillful work; skilful, able, clever, ingenious'.[14] While the term was periodically linked with studiousness, the sense of plodding or prosaic labour didn't inhere in the word itself. On its own, 'industrious', in fact, suggested to Dekker's contemporaries a keen, agile mind. 'Industrious', as Thomas Elyot defines it in his *Dictionary* (1538), refers to 'he that is wytty and actyve',[15] and in *The boke named the Gouernour* (1537), Elyot expounds on this sense of the word, painting a picture of the industrious as quite the opposite of the slow-witted but earnest student labouring over material beyond his ken. Indeed, explicitly setting those who struggle in contrast with the industrious, Elyot notes how in 'those thinges, in whome other men travayle, a person industrious lyghtly and with facilitie spedeth'. If Elyot's industrious man exhibits a notably agile mind – he 'perceyueth quickely', 'counsayleth spedily', and 'sonest exployte[s]' that which is 'expedient' – he also appears remarkably *adaptive*, for he combines 'wytte and experiēce' in order to 'inventeth freshely' and find 'new wayes and meanes to bryng to effecte that he desyreth'.[16] Free of the derogatory sense later criticism has read into it, Dekker's 'industrious' points us towards someone who perceives quickly but also invents freshly, craftily understanding the material at hand and soonest exploiting it.

If, as I have been suggesting by way of introduction, Kyd's contemporaries perceived in the author of *The Spanish Tragedy* an agile mind capable of keeping company, at least in print, with the era's learned authors, then Nashe's satire appears less like a normative statement about an inept parvenu and more like a reaction against an inventive writer who authorises his own social mobility, in part, by appropriating classical texts. At first glance, the different strands of Nashe's criticism seem of a piece and, taken at face value, lend themselves to the image of Kyd as an author, however popular with the masses, with at best a tenuous grasp of classical texts and ideas. For if the principal target of Nashe's attack indeed mishandles his sources, then the satire retains a certain coherence: the upstart author gets things wrong, and this makes his pretensions more glaring. But if the author in question – widely lauded by his peers and frequently included in the ranks of the best, most learned authors – adapts his sources rather cleverly, then this emphasis in Nashe's attack on social mobility seems quite curious. Why, after all, articulate disdain for an intermeddling tradesman by focusing so heavily on his engagement with classical texts? In addition to Kyd's reputation among his peers, Nashe's own argument provides warrant for such scepticism toward his central charge against the playwright. For the satirist not only embarrassingly misses Kyd's reliance on Virgilian, not Senecan, precedent for placing Elysium within hell but also, when going out of his way to mock via a pun, erroneously ascribes to Aesop a story derived, in fact, from Spenser. Nashe's errors undermine his own critique of Kyd's command of classical material. More importantly, they also expose his deep investment in attacking the playwright's inventive use of classical texts in his theatrical endeavours, the very mechanism for his social mobility. Nashe criticises Kyd's handling of classical sources, that is, because they potentially provide authority for the writer's own aspirations, aspirations Nashe finds especially distressing. In this, the satirist, I would argue, paradoxically points toward the same defining trait suggested by Dekker's 'industrious' (and perhaps even Jonson's 'sporting') by drawing attention, albeit in his own uniquely negative way, to Kyd's inventiveness, his propensity toward adapting classical materials in innovative ways.

To what end, though, does Kyd 'invent freshly' and how might we see his deft appropriation of classical sources at work in his most famous play? In my introduction, I charted the ways preconceptions of revenge tragedy as a genre can serve to delimit the kinds of philosophical concerns considered as germane to such plays. A similar critical blind spot can occur when we too readily dismiss Kyd's handling of classical texts and ideas as that of a riveting, but not particularly well-versed or nuanced, popular author. In this chapter, I intend to show how the lauded dramaturgical potency of Kyd's play and his overlooked engagement with elaborate ontological notions drawn from classical philosophy, yet very much current within his own culture, are in fact of a piece. Indeed, the same sorts of things we see in Nashe's critique – the transgression of social boundaries, the employment of classical precedent as means of authorising such mobility – inform Kyd's work in the theatre itself, and closer examination quickly reveals how the central *agon* of Kyd's play notably emerges from an expansive philosophical substructure readily available to his original audiences. As surprising as it might seem given Kyd's ostensibly limited classicism as well as the genre's reputation for predominantly centring on matters of law, politics and religion, Kyd cleverly situates his play's revenge narrative within a complex, though accessible, ontological framework that will, in essence, naturalise the brutal retributive acts of the play's distraught protagonist.

Literary scholars have long recognised the dramatic tensions of Thomas Kyd's *The Spanish Tragedy* as arising from the class antagonisms between its central players. Locating

Hieronimo and Horatio as members of the 'middling sort', a category roughly tantamount to the middle class, Kyd sets the Knight Marshal and his son in conflict with an entrenched aristocracy jealous to retain its own privileged insularity. But Kyd also imagines his protagonists collectively as an ambitious household, a fact only glanced at in existing criticism, and presents their success as informed by prudent *oeconomia*, or household management, a practical philosophy ubiquitous in Kyd's culture and one undergirded, as we will see, by a rich intellectual history of its own. Shrewd *oeconomia* enables the middling sort to advance their station in life, but it also, when particularly successful, leads to the higher strata of the middling sort pressing against (and threatening to unsettle) aristocratic prerogative. Kyd's interest in the workings of *oeconomia* is evinced both here and in his translation of Torquato Tasso's *Padre di famiglia*, or *The Householder's Philosophy*. As suggested by his translation's title, Kyd attends to the philosophical predicates of *oeconomia*, and the class conflicts in *The Spanish Tragedy* have, as it were, deeper roots than we have previously understood.

Perhaps most astonishing is how the Aristotelian tripartite soul permeates Kyd's drama and shapes the *oeconomia* that gives rise to the play's central tensions. Cartesian dualism simplified matters by subsuming the soul's lesser capacities within a mechanistic materialism, but Kyd's contemporaries imagined a more variegated psychology.[17] The Aristotelian tripartite soul, comprised not only of the rational and animal faculties but also the vegetative, provided the prevailing psychological paradigm for late sixteenth-century England. The vegetative faculty governed all reproduction, nutrition and growth; it was the essential component, quite literally the *sine qua non*, of all life. As the source of all development and growth, the vegetative principle – or, as Kyd renders it in *The Householder's Philosophy*, the 'faculty of getting' – represents for Kyd both ontological reality and social possibility. By presenting ambition, the latent desire for growth and advancement, as the natural product of a human psychology informed by Aristotle, Kyd reveals both the artificiality of socially constructed class hierarchy and a legitimised rationale for middling aspiration. More significantly, however, he imaginatively depicts revenge as not simply irrationally brutish, or, conversely, highly calculative, but also as *instinctively* reproductive, a mode of production that functions as an outlet for thwarted material fecundity. In this way, the very shaping predicates, the ontological assumptions, which imbue Kyd's play exert their own performative force, operating both in central scenes and around the edges to condition, by turns overtly and subtly, reception of the play's central revenge narrative, as revenge, aligned with shared ideas about how the world functions on its most fundamental levels, becomes naturalised, figured, that is, as consonant with other expressions of this most organic of impulses animating the play's world.

On The Middling Sort and Household Oeconomia *in* The Spanish Tragedy

As part of a dramaturgical strategy that will shape the play's central conflicts and, in turn, influence the kind of conditioning ontological framework he will choose to create for his play, Kyd situates Hieronimo and Horatio as rising members of the 'middling sort', marking them as outside the aristocratic echelon their innate ambition prompts them to challenge. Keith Wrightson observes that 'from the last third of the sixteenth century [. . .] a specific vocabulary of informal social description emerges into prominence, a set of terms called the language of "sorts" [. . .] [that] appears primarily to express an essentially dichotomous perception of society'.[18] This method of articulating a 'dichotomous perception of society' provides definition by contrast, identifying the middling sort not only by revealing who they are but more often indicating who they are *not*. 'Though not a middle class, but like the middle class,' Theodore Leinwand argues, 'they make it easier for us to determine with whom they did or did not identify than with what.'[19] Writing before Wrightson and Leinwand, C. L. Barber identifies Hieronimo and Horatio as belonging to what we might now recognise as this 'middling sort'. Hieronimo, Barber argues, has 'a very clearly-defined social position that makes him an appropriate figure for a middle-class London audience to identify with. He is not a member of the high nobility but a high civil servant'.[20] He is, therefore, 'the sort of man Kyd would look up to, himself the son of a scrivener, and a client of a noble family who respected learning'. Barber anticipates Wrightson and Leinwand here, arriving at this 'clear' delineation by setting Hieronimo against 'the high nobility', a category into which he clearly does not fit.

Kyd imagines the play's central conflicts as occurring not simply between the aristocracy and a middling individual, however, but as between the aristocracy and a middling *household*, figuring, therefore, the frustrations to social advancement wrought by Lorenzo as denying the very progress invited by the discourses of *oeconomia*. Barber adumbrates without further explication this subtext when he argues the king thinks of Hieronimo and Horatio 'as a "house"; the ransom [for Balthazar] is the kind of reward which could make a substantial difference to their fortunes'. Discussing the 'social division and contention [that] pervades Kyd's play', James Siemon more thoroughly examines the limitations of father and son as indicative of their conjoined plight, rooted in their shared social stratum:

> Hieronimo himself, of unmentioned antecedents and doubtful finances, occupies a house too small for the captured Portuguese train, and appears to be the only major character with a career and the accompanying daily professional

responsibilities that must be followed whether he will or no. While his own success in rising from petty correigedor to Knight Marshal may suggest the openness of the Spanish court to the talented individual, the fate of his son Horatio reveals both of them to be caught in the structural inequities of court life.[21]

Despite their particular individual circumstances, Hieronimo and Horatio together occupy a frustrating middling space, existing with Isabella as a household limited in means yet possessing ambition for advancement. Rising and talented yet daily labouring and occupying 'a house too small' for the captured Portuguese prince, the protagonists may be ambitious, but they have also become functionally static, lacking the promise of any additional advance beyond their present condition. This, it would seem, is the particular dilemma of middling success, but such a situation becomes especially acute for Hieronimo and Isabella once Horatio is killed, a scenario the third addition of the 1602 quarto further develops when Hieronimo describes Horatio as 'the very arm that did hold up our house. / Our hopes were storèd up in him [. . .]'. Hieronimo, Isabella and Horatio together dramatise the challenges of holding up one's house, of seeking future advancement through prudent management in an uncongenial environment. With 'the ethic of household management, or *oeconomia*, newly popular with the "middling sort" of the population',[22] *The Spanish Tragedy* draws on a discursive field familiar to its audience but, notably, depicts *oeconomia* as useful only to a point, as the promise of social advancement remains starkly delimited by existing social hierarchies.

Kyd's *The Householder's Philosophy*, his 1588 translation of Torquato Tasso's minor treatise *Padre di famiglia*, reveals both his interest in *oeconomia* and his understanding of society as shaped by class antagonism, as fraught with the social stratification that is and the social mobility that could, in theory, be. It also tellingly makes manifest the dramatist's interest in the way ontological assumptions about the fundamental nature of the universe give shape to the very real, material conditions of lived experience. Prominent among domestic management manuals of the late sixteenth century, Tasso's treatise is a 'humanistic work outlining the universal principles of cosmic ordering underlying metaphysical and material worlds rather than detailing pragmatic tasks'.[23] Neither a simple, practical guide to daily domestic life nor a mere recitation of abstract philosophy, the treatise directs attention to the ways ontological assumptions about the natural order of the world find instantiation in the social commerce of everyday life. What's more, Kyd's translation reveals a distinct concern with the concrete realities of social stratification and the economic disparities that both impinge on and yet define one's household. While Kyd's subtitle may promise he will 'perfectly and profitably' put forward 'the true *oeconomia* and forme of housekeeping', it does not promise an exact rendering of Tasso's original. In fact, Kyd's deviations from the original text signal an authorial bias toward a more equitable system where merit, not privilege, governs. The railings against usury, for example, stem entirely from Kyd's own additions and seem to reflect his distaste for oppressive economies.[24] The translation may be stylistically uneven, but Kyd consistently makes the case that lack of 'clothing, purse, or birth need not preclude true nobility, which should be measured by richness of action, comeliness, utterance, judgment, and argument – as if such capacities might arise like Horatio's virtues independently of social and material conditions'.[25] The 'universal principles of cosmic ordering' of Kyd's translation, then, pertain directly to the distinctly fiscal, or material, differentiations between society's strata, with the translator exhibiting distaste for when such differentiations become arbitrarily or artificially established. For while Kyd imagines these material differentiations separately from his definition of true 'nobility', he nonetheless, by doing so, depicts the inherent capacities for self-improvement as continually set against the material advantages of the recognised 'nobility' of the world as presently constituted. The society Kyd inhabits, the one he reflects in his translation of *The Householder's Philosophy*, and the one he creates in *The Spanish Tragedy* are all ordered by the dialectic implied in this contrast between privilege and merit, between entrenched power and labouring aspirants. Indeed, since Kyd thinks of the capacities for self-improvement as arising 'independently of social and material conditions', as emerging from a deeper set of ontological predicates undergirding the natural order as a whole, it is worth asking from *where* such capacities derive.

The Vegetative Faculty and the Roots of Oeconomia *in Early Modern England*

The Aristotelianism still dominant in Kyd's day and the Cartesian dualism that would eventually supplant it differ significantly on this point, and to understand *The Spanish Tragedy*, we must, therefore, look past Descartes' rejection of the vegetative soul to the Aristotelian concept of a fundamental drive to self-perfection inherent to all living things. In his survey of late Aristotelianism and the rise of Cartesian dualism, Dennis Des Chene observes that 'the divorce of the vegetative soul and its functions from the sensitive and rational souls [. . .] was effected by Descartes'.[26] He continues: 'the operations of the Cartesian soul have no intrinsic relation to nourishment, growth, or reproduction. Its sensations and passions are [. . .] "instituted" by God so as to provide a guide to life [. . .] The Aristotelian soul, it would seem, requires no such institution [. . .] [T]he soul, by way of its vegetative part, is *in* the organs of generation, and through its powers immediately acts on and is acted on by them'. Indeed, Des Chene treats the removal of the vegetative soul as one of the defining characteristics of Cartesian psychology. For Descartes 'insists upon sensation and passion as evidence of the strongest sort for the "intimate union" of soul and body [. . .] The result is that thought is severed *only* from the *vegetative* functions, not the sensitive'. In Kyd's England, however, the vegetative capacity had yet to be severed from the soul's functions. Fundamental to all life, the vegetative soul had 'three powers: nutrition, growth (or augmentation), and generation'.[27] The concept of growth as being a type of augmentation derives itself from Aristotle's idea that 'self-change' is the 'one criterion for being alive' and that 'spontaneous movement directed to self-perfection is characteristic of life'.[28] As Franciscus Suarez observes, non-living things do not act 'so as to acquire what is needed to perfect themselves' whereas 'living things are those that have this power of moving and perfecting themselves by virtue of something intrinsic'.[29] Thus, Aristotelian writers argue that even plants, which lack 'sense and locomotion', still 'live and have souls', since they move (even if imperceptibly) as they reproduce, attain nourishment, and grow.[30] Though the function occurs more subtly in plants, the vegetative soul operates in all life, and its hallmark is this fundamental instinct towards self-perfection.[31]

In tracing signs of reproduction, nutrition and growth back to the vegetative faculty, the writers of Kyd's day drew attention to a function of the soul responsible for the subtlest instantiations of material form, and such investigation naturally invited inquiry into the materiality of the vegetative soul itself. How, after all, should one apprehend this imperceptible but fundamental component of all life? In an early seventeenth-century text, Pierre Charron asserts 'the vegetative and sensitive [soul] of Plants and Beasts, is, by the opinion of all, altogether materiall' and that it exists 'in the seed, for which cause it is likewise mortall'.[32] But such materialism and its coincident mortalism, while perhaps permissible for lower orders of the soul, could invite problematic speculation regarding the soul's higher functions. As William Hill explains in *The infancie of the soule* (1605), Plato understood the soul as 'bodilesse and spirituall', but Galen – after lengthy consideration of the vegetative faculty and the way heat affects the soul's powers – was 'brought [. . .] into a confusion' and 'could not receave' the immateriality of the soul without qualification.[33] Confronted with such an intractable problem, rife with unsettling implications, many authors simply depicted the vegetative faculty – whatever its precise status in itself – as something of a last waypoint between immateriality and materiality. In *The second part of the French academie* (1594), Pierre de La Primaudaye remains content to observe that 'the seede is a body that hath in it selfe a vegetative soule',[34] and Helkiah Crooke, writing in *Mikrokosmographia* (1615), avers as well that the 'vegetable soul [. . .] lyeth potentially in the seed, diffused equally through the whole masse'.[35] Whether represented as material, immaterial, or as something altogether more ambiguous in its own composition, the vegetative soul existed at the very origins of embodied forms and persistently appeared as subtending the most basic components of the known world in the late sixteenth and early seventeenth centuries.

Kyd's contemporaries were keen to understand just how this vegetative soul – ubiquitous but not, in itself, perceptible – manifested itself in embodied forms, and the conundrum was popular enough to appear in a wide range of treatises.[36] But beyond tracing the ways in which the imperceptible faculty manifested itself in material form, most writers tellingly used the doctrine of the vegetative soul – hardly a recondite theory known only to a few – as the basis for analogies designed to explain other unfamiliar or complex material. Most significantly, the clergy frequently perceived in the vegetative faculty a ready trope for illustrating the distinction between different types of faith, clarifying pastoral exegesis, and even explaining the doctrine of justification,[37] and, since eternal ramifications were thus at stake, its role in providing clarity cannot be overstated. The vegetative soul's common deployment as a versatile metaphor suggests a notable currency to the doctrine among early modern audiences who could be expected to understand such allusions with little effort. Moreoever, whatever their various purposes when invoking the vegetative faculty, Kyd's contemporaries often expressed this doctrine which undergirded *oeconomia* in terms of increase, productivity, expansion and self-preservation, setting the stage for its more symbolic appropriation by still others. When La Primaudaye observes how the vegetative soul encompasses 'the vertue of nourishing, of augmenting or growing, and of engendering', he provides the standard descriptive phrase for explaining the faculty in the period, and he then emphasises its role as '*profitable* for the nourishment of the bodie'.[38] Redolent of the language of acquisition, this sense that the vegetative soul governs that which is profitable for a person frequently finds expression as that which will not only 'nourish' but also 'increase' the body.[39] Such language was commonplace in the era: profitable and leading to increase, the vegetative faculty acquires in order to preserve and sustain. Describing a corporeal process of growth and development, early modern authors attempting to explain the vegetative soul frequently deployed a vocabulary, then, of acquisition, increase and preservation that not only informed the concept of *oeconomia* but also, by its very nature, lent itself to ever-broadening application.

In light of this, perhaps it is little wonder that early modern poets perceived in the vegetative faculty a trope useful for articulating expansive ambition and the impulse to preserve one's condition in life. Literary scholars will be most immediately familiar with Andrew Marvell's own version of imperial ambition in 'To His Coy Mistress' where he imagines how his 'vegetable love should grow / Vaster than empires, and more slow' (ll.11–12),[40] but perhaps the most salient poetic reflections on the vegetative soul and its role in growth and development may be found in John Davies' 'Of the Soule of Men, and the Immortalitie thereof'. Entered in the Stationers' Register in 1599, Davies' poem meditates on the 'effects diversified' of the soul, beginning with what the marginal gloss terms its 'vegetative or quickening power' (l.936).[41] What's more, Davies explicitly charts the relationship between the soul's vegetative function and *oeconomia*:

> Her quickning power in every living part
> Doth as a Nurse, or as a Mother serve;
> And doth employ her *Oeconomicke* Art,
> And busie care, her houshold to preserve.
> [. . .]
> This power to Martha may compared bee,
> Which busie was the household things to do;
> Or to a Dryas living in a Tree,
> For even to Trees this power is proper too.
>   (ll.937–40, 945–8)

Significantly, in Davies' poem, the vegetative soul functions as Nurse or Mother and employs her '*Oeconomicke* Art' entirely for the purpose of *preserving her household*. Davies makes explicit the common understanding that reproduction, nutrition and growth are, logically, the essence of preservation; the vegetative soul gives rise to *oeconomia*, and it is through *oeconomia* that one preserves the household. Thus, Davies moves the reader from Martha, symbolic of busy activity, to a Dryas, the very animating essence of the tree. Davies invokes the Dryas to reveal that trees, too, have this vegetative faculty. But the image simultaneously emphasises *oeconomia* not simply as an activity but also as the latent essence of survival, of remaining alive and, ideally, thriving in an often inhospitable world.

The vegetative faculty likewise informs Tasso's original treatise on *oeconomia*, and Kyd's translation tellingly depicts this latent, instinctive drive towards advancement as 'the faculty of getting', a rendering that further suggests his work as interested not only in social delineation and class antagonism but also in the traversal from underlying ontological theory to embodied experience and social application. Kyd's translation notes that:

> The facultie of getting may be *Natural* and not *Naturall*: *Natural* I call that which getteth the living out of those thinges that hath beene brought forth by Nature for mans use and service: and forasmuch as nothing is more naturall then nourishment, which the Mother giveth to her Childe, most naturall above the rest must that gayne needes be that is had and raised of the fruits of the earth, considering that the Earth is the naturall and universall Mother of us all.[42]

Similar to Davies describing the vegetative soul 'as a Nurse or as a Mother', Kyd's explication of the 'faculty of getting' depicts the earth as 'the naturall and universall Mother of us all'. Here, Kyd stresses the earth's fecundity, connecting it to the 'faculty of getting' designated for increase and growth (for 'nothing is more natural than nourishment') and figuring it as vegetative ('for most naturall', therefore, are the gains derived 'of the fruits of the earth'). What in Aristotle is simple nutrition and 'nourishment' becomes glossed in *The Householder's Philosophy* as a process whereby one 'getteth the living' via nature for 'mans use and service' in order to acquire 'gayne'. *The Householder's Philosophy* is thus informed by both the Aristotelian vegetative soul and the material, economic concerns of the middling sort regarding self-preservation. When Jonathan Barry observes that 'the middling sort defined themselves in relation to households, which often formed the heart of the trading unit [. . .] but also acted as the key unit for the reproduction and security of the family',⁴³ he is noting something that Kyd's contemporaries would have thought of as both a harsh social reality and a philosophical, ontological truth as well. Ubiquitous in early modern culture and invoked by a wide range of authors including Kyd himself, the remarkably versatile trope of the vegetative soul appears a crucial context for understanding Kyd's own work, so invested as it is in representing – often through explicitly vegetative imagery – ambition and the preservation of one's household.

Middling Ambition and Aristocratic Resistance in The Spanish Tragedy

The Spanish Tragedy's opening – with its subtle yet distinct assumption of Aristotelian psychology and its ghost more preoccupied with locating his former class position and cataloguing his successes than seeking vengeance – immediately sets the stage for understanding the ensuing revenge narrative as one wherein its stymied middling protagonists redirect their natural, latent desires for advancement into a darker register upon encountering unjust suppression. Don Andrea enters and instantly conflates his assessment of his soul's condition with his social status at court:

> When this eternal substance of my soul
> Did live imprisoned in my wanton flesh,
> Each in their function serving other's need,
> I was a courtier in the Spanish court. (1.1.1–4)⁴⁴

Don Andrea's opening statement signals the play's underlying psychology, but the third line presents to the modern observer an apparent contradiction. If Kyd figures the relationship between soul and body as antagonistic, as one of prisoner to prison, then what need of the soul does the wanton flesh serve? What benefits the captive from the prison?⁴⁵ The relationship described in line three, so often misunderstood by modern readers, is not between soul and flesh but between the soul's various components: the construction here is elliptical. Prepared by 'this eternal substance', the opening clause's subject, and directed by the immediate invocation of 'function', Kyd's contemporaries almost certainly would have assumed 'each' as referencing the capacities intrinsic to the soul's substance that function co-operatively within the confines of the material body. Since the soul's capacities were often articulated as 'functions' and, for the human, all three capacities must perform co-operatively, the audience could be relied on to know just *what* must serve each other's needs. What registers as dissonant to us would have followed logically to Kyd's audience because of their shared assumptions vis-à-vis the psyche. At the outset, then, Kyd signals not only that Don Andrea represents a disembodied soul entering the stage but a soul particularly conceived within an Aristotelian context. This, quite literally, introduces Don Andrea's announcement that he was as 'a courtier in the Spanish court'.

Don Andrea frames the subsequent play not solely (or even primarily) as an angry ghost seeking revenge but as the unsettled soul of a middling courtier who exhibited a sharp awareness of class taxonomy, an innate ambition for greater status, and a knack for working around societal obstructions – until death foreclosed his natural progress, 'nipped', as it were, 'the blossoms of [his] bliss', even during 'the harvest of [his] summer joys' (1.1.12–13). Interestingly, Don Andrea's first seventeen lines employ the definition-by-opposition and the aspiration for advancement affiliated with the middling sort. Despite appearing with a personified Revenge, he articulates no initial desire for vengeance but rather obsesses over fixing in place his social rank for the audience. Setting himself against those beneath his station and then against those above him, Don Andrea describes his 'descent, / though not ignoble, yet inferior far / To gracious fortunes of my tender youth' (1.1.5–7). The litotes 'not ignoble' positions him above the lower class but 'inferior far' to his promising start in life. Don Andrea likewise exhibits an active 'faculty of getting' for he 'by duteous service and deserving love, / In secret [. . .] possessed a worthy dame' (1.1.9–10). Rapidly undercutting any suggestion of humility implicit in acknowledging his service as 'duteous', Don Andrea trumpets his love as 'deserving', despite letting slip that his loving was done 'in secret'. What's more, Don Andrea makes clear the causal connection between both his 'duteous service' and 'deserving love' and his 'possess[ing]' Bel-Imperia, signalling at once his own sense of personal merit and his natural inclination towards acquisitiveness across class lines. Ambitious in life and unsettled in death, Don Andrea enters preoccupied with his status and his worldly successes, yet he will subsequently shift his thoughts towards revenge, eventually desiring it in ever-increasing measure, as his acquisitive impulses find articulation through the ensuing play's promised catastrophe.

Don Andrea's temporary release from Hades by Proserpine, the quasi-numinous, vegetative and motivating figure behind the play, seems unsatisfactory as a solution to the underworld's bureaucratic confusion over his status in the afterlife. It makes sense, however, as a reimagined movement of the aspiring soul into an alternative outlet for ambitious energies, a means to bypass the circumscription wrought by external forces. Don Andrea's indeterminate status as lover-soldier prompts Aeacus to assign him 'to walk with lovers in our fields of love' and Rhadamanth to counter 'No, no [. . .] it were not well / With loving souls to place a martialist' (1.1.41, 45–6). After Minos forwards him to Pluto's court, Don Andrea himself articulates the social taxonomies of Hades in the language of dichotomous opposition and 'sorts'. He passes 'the foresaid fields, / Where lovers live, and bloody martialists, / But either sort contained within his bounds' (1.1.60–3). As in life where neither noble nor ignoble, Don Andrea is appropriate here for neither 'sort'. Lovers and martialists may be contained within their respective bounds, but Don Andrea, as one who straddles the two categories, remains excluded from both. When he approaches 'Pluto with his Proserpine' (1.1.76) and kneels, Proserpine becomes the prime mover of what will be the play. For at the sight of Don Andrea, 'fair Proserpine began to smile, / And begged that only she might give my doom' (1.1.78–9). As Don Andrea tells Revenge, 'Forthwith [. . .] she rounded thee in th'ear', and 'No sooner had she spoke but we were here' (1.1.81, 84). Proserpine, the daughter of Ceres who generates springtime fecundity and nourishment, provides the impetus behind the soul of Don Andrea returning to earth with Revenge by his side.[46] Her release of Don Andrea's soul 'through the gates of horn, / Where dreams have passage in the silent night' (1.1.82–3) frames the play as a dream vision reflective of Don Andrea's dual concerns of class stratification and social (im)mobility. Don Andrea's dream – that is, the body of *The Spanish Tragedy* – suggests his own insatiable desire for increase, for he begins with no discernible inclination towards revenge and concludes the play invoking eternal wrath upon his enemies. The play's framing figures revenge, then, as the avenue by which stifled energies of self-autonomy and advancement find darker expression, as Kyd, from the very outset, begins to naturalise the impulse toward retribution by aligning it with a deeper, unseen motivating force that will continue to run at odds with the entrenched social hierarchy which dominates the world of the play's fictitious court.

After the Induction, the play's opening dispute over the captured Balthazar pits middling against aristocratic, merit versus rank, but also establishes Hieronimo and Horatio's fortunes as inextricably intertwined due to their shared middling household. Kyd develops the central conflict of his play, that is, through the glaring contrast that exists between the theory of *oeconomia*, undergirded by the era's ontological assumptions about the vegetative soul, and its limited purchase within the actual, material realities of the court as constituted. The King tells Balthazar, 'Young prince, although thy father's hard misdeeds [. . .] Deserve but evil measure at our hands, / Yet shalt thou know that Spain is honourable' (1.2.134–7). A privilege extended to royalty, this severance of father and son's worth allows the Spanish King to treat Balthazar individually, 'for in our hearing thy deserts were great, / And in our sight thyself are gracious' (1.2.149–50). Thus we have the paradox of aristocratic privilege: on account of his birth Balthazar is afforded the right to be evaluated on his own terms, in this case as one separate from his royal father. Balthazar gets to receive kingly munificence freely, and then exert himself afterwards: 'I shall study to deserve this grace' (1.2.151). This aristocratic privilege stands in marked contrast to the King's conflation of Hieronimo and Horatio's status and its continual dependence upon performance. Identifying Hieronimo by his civil function, the King addresses his first lines to him, 'Knight Marshal, frolic with thy king, / For 'tis thy son that wins this battle's prize' (1.2.96–7), and then claims, 'Hieronimo, it greatly pleaseth us / That in our victory thou have a share, / By virtue of thy worthy son's exploit' (1.2.124–6). To make the linkage between father and son's fortunes wholly unmistakable, Kyd has the King reverse the trajectory of influence later when he promises, 'Content thee, Marshal, thou shalt have no wrong, / And for thy sake thy son shall want no right' (1.2.173–4). When Hieronimo angles for Horatio's advancement, he is 'enforced of nature [. . .] [to] plead for young Horatio's right' (1.2.168–9) by affection but also by the reality – articulated often by the King – that both their fortunes rise or fall together. Hieronimo is thus 'enforced of nature' by the imperatives, to use Davies' phraseology, of his '*Oeconomicke* art', his 'household to preserve' (l. 940). This accounts for why the King reassures the Knight Marshal that *he*, not Horatio, 'shalt have no wrong' in the settlement of Horatio's dispute with Lorenzo.

Although the King presents his adjudication as according with the claims of merit, the unequal, artificially constructed social positions – not the martial exploits of Horatio and

Lorenzo – influence significantly the division of Balthazar's ransom and goods. The King begins equitably enough by noting 'You both deserve and both shall have reward' (1.2.179). He assigns horse and weapons to Lorenzo and ransom to Horatio, mediating competing claims in a manner that leads some to think him 'generously mindful of his obligations to his subjects, painstakingly judicious, and politically astute'.[47] However, while Kyd may indeed leave the King's motives ambiguous, his actions remain unmistakably shaped by the pressures of class competition. As the King concludes his division of the goods, he turns to Lorenzo and explains:

> But nephew, thou shalt have the prince in guard,
> For thine estate best fitteth such a guest;
> Horatio's house were small for all his train.
> Yet in regard thy substance passeth his,
> And that just guerdon may befall desert,
> To him we yield the armour of the prince. (1.2.185–90)

Confronted with Horatio's undeniable merit publicly displayed twice in procession, the King must publicly assure that 'just guerdon may befall desert'. In contrast, however, Lorenzo receives the King's generosity freely, not by merit but because of his 'estate'. Indeed, in awarding Balthazar's armour to Horatio, the Spanish King seems to dilute his praise of the Knight Marshal's son by linking the award, in part, to Lorenzo's possession of more wealth, of greater 'substance'. The conflicting ambitions of an established family and a rising one force the King to strike an uneasy balance between a middling household and a privileged aristocrat. Kyd gives us a court in which the success of civil servant and soldier encroaches on the honours distributed by rank – and vice versa. Spain, it would seem, rests precariously on the faultline running between Hieronimo and Horatio's house and Lorenzo's estate. The King remains diligently aware of this faultline for he tellingly concludes his mediation by bypassing both Lorenzo and Horatio. Neither Lorenzo nor Horatio is given a voice here, despite the fact that the adjudication centres on their claims to honour. Instead, the King seeks affirmation for his decision (perhaps because neither soldier, from his perspective, could be pleased with it fully) from the subjected and powerless, yet nonetheless royal, Balthazar: 'How likes Don Balthazar of this device?' (1.2.191). Thus, the King publicly affects equanimity while still governing his decision by the pressures of an arbitrary aristocratic privilege.

By threatening the royal Balthazar with subjugation to Horatio, Kyd unsettles the justifications for class hierarchy by using the philosophical predicates of *oeconomia*. *The Householder's Philosophy*, for example, addresses the delineation between master and servant and then shifts to explain how the spoils of war should be divided. Tasso identifies a clear hierarchy rooted in Nature when he explains that 'it also seemes that Nature hath engendred not onely bruite Beasts for the service of Man, but hath framed men, that are apt to obey, to serve those whom also she hath framed to commaund' (p. 276). It might seem that Tasso's division of men into two categories (namely, those 'framed to commaund' and those 'apt to obey') justifies class hierarchy, but he leaves indeterminate just how, exactly, these two categories might be implemented socially. Indeed, the very rootedness of this framing in Nature posits a distinct egalitarian strain, for it ignores as irrelevant any material factors such as wealth or status.[48] Moreover, immediately after this delineation, Tasso observes that 'Whatsoever is gotten or obtained in the warres being just, the same may also bee tearmed naturall gayne' (p. 276). As we have already seen, *The Householder's Philosophy* approvingly mentions 'naturall gayne', citing its relation to the fundamental impulse of the 'faculty of getting'. Thus, Tasso tells us there are men apt to obey, men framed to command, and the spoils of war may be deemed 'naturall gayne', the acquisition wrought by the 'faculty of getting'. Balthazar notes the unsettling of social order made possible by just such a formulation later in *The Spanish Tragedy* when he admits, 'by my yielding I became [Horatio's] slave' (2.1.123). When Balthazar, one socially framed to command, becomes the 'naturall gayne' of Horatio, one socially framed to serve, the aristocratic, royal system of privilege becomes threatened. In Horatio's defeat of Balthazar, natural merit quite literally unseats royal status. The King, therefore, must point to Horatio's inadequate household and use Lorenzo's estate to trump merit, returning things to their 'proper' (but, to Kyd, not necessarily natural) order. The King's decision underscores the artificiality of aristocratic privilege, for it eschews Nature's framing of Balthazar and Horatio in favour of their socially predetermined class positions.

The Faculty of Getting: Instantiating the Vegetative Faculty

Subsequent to this opening dispute, Kyd suggests Hieronimo's house as contiguous to, but not incorporated within, the aristocracy by emphasising it has a pleasure garden, transgressively marking it (beyond its actual status) with aristocratic trappings. Kyd takes pains to establish Hieronimo's garden as one designed for pleasure, not utility. Bel-Imperia arranges her rendezvous with Horatio to be in 'thy father's pleasant bower' (2.2.42). Horatio states that since 'in darkness pleasures may be done, / Come, Bel-Imperia, let us to the bower; / And there in safety pass a pleasant hour' (2.4.3–5). And Hieronimo himself declares in the recognition scene, 'This place was made for pleasure not for death' (2.5.12). Hieronimo's garden is paradoxically situated between labour and leisure, then, as it supplies the *otium* wrought by *negotium*, even as it operates as daily testimonial to the fruitfulness of Hieronimo's labour. Attached to Hieronimo's middling household it functions as a semi-private (but, therefore, semi-public) exhibition of his *oeconomic* facility and his exalted status within the middling strata. Kyd's notable emphasis on Hieronimo's garden as one for pleasure brings into sharper focus the central class conflict of the play by materially marking, via the vegetative trope, the Knight Marshal's natural, innate aspirations for advancement, aspirations, that is, that actively propel him toward the coterie that actively excludes him.

By drawing on the pleasure garden *topos* for the most pronounced moments of class antagonism, Kyd not only places vegetative fecundity quite literally centre stage but also employs a potent image of status differentiation. The garden took many forms in early modern English society, but the pleasure garden only made its appearance in England in the mid-sixteenth century and was a distinct marker of aristocratic leisure. Delineating the types of gardens and their roles throughout Europe, A. G. Morton notes that 'the private garden [. . .] became the fashion and pride of Renaissance princes and wealthy families' and differed remarkably from the medieval garden which was 'essentially utilitarian in lay-out, contents, and intention'.[49] While such a link between the aristocracy and the pleasure garden had a lengthy Continental history, the pleasure garden's ascendancy among the upper class in England took place in the middle of the sixteenth century. Roy C. Strong painstakingly charts the development of the English pleasure garden, noting that the most significant development in Renaissance gardening after 1580 'was that the pleasure garden became an essential adjunct of the great house'.[50] Strong observes that 'the earliest and longest description of an Elizabethan pleasure garden comes in a letter by Robert Laneham narrating the entertainments given by Robert Dudley, Earl of Leicester, for Queen Elizabeth I in July 1575 at his castle at Kenilworth in Warwickshire'.[51] At the time of *The Spanish Tragedy*, then, the pleasure garden figured as a relatively recent marker of aristocratic status in

England, a recreational (and not simply functional) space for the well-to-do.[52]

Kyd introduces the garden through Bel-Imperia, who seeks to use it, in part, for her own transgressive rejection of hierarchical strictures, a rejection prompted by her own restricted position and one that establishes her variance with the men of her social class. As sister to Lorenzo and daughter to the Duke of Castile, Bel-Imperia actively seeks to marry downward a second time. Despite her previous union with Don Andrea, however, her attraction down the social hierarchy seems unthinkable among the aristocrats. Balthazar imagines his failure in wooing Bel-Imperia as one of material worth, that his 'presents are not of sufficient cost, / And, being worthless, all [his] labour's lost' (2.1.17–18). Consequently, he envisions his noble status as possibly saving his cause, but only momentarily: 'Yet might she love me to uprear her state; / Ay, but perhaps she hopes some nobler mate' (2.1.25–6). When Pedrigano finally reveals Horatio as her new love, Kyd adds stage direction to emphasise the shock, for 'Balthazar starts back' (2.1.78–9). To be sure, Balthazar lacks imagination, but even Lorenzo seems surprised, exclaiming 'What, Don Horatio, our Knight Marshal's son?' (2.1.79). His incredulous response reflects his disdain for this upstart middling civil servant by shifting into the royal 'our' and categorising Horatio by his father's civil profession. Bel-Imperia's active pursuit of Don Andrea, then Horatio, confounds the aristocratic men who anticipate her looking equal to, or above, her own station.

One might expect 'the faculty of getting', the impulse to preserve and advance oneself via prudent management, would direct Bel-Imperia into quite a different trajectory, towards someone who *could* 'uprear her state', for example, or, at the very least, one who would maintain her current status. To be sure, if Bel-Imperia appears too easily attracted down the class hierarchy, it may well be the effect of Kyd's own middling perspective, the authorial fantasy of an accessible aristocratic woman. But Bel-Imperia's position within the play's own milieu is itself unique and accords well with the drive for reproduction, growth and nutrition. For as Bel-Imperia flouts the boundaries of such class divisions, she also defies expectations of female complaisance. She expresses autonomous desire of a different sort, a self-determining ambition to resist a forced union. Situated in aristocratic privilege yet in subjection as a marriageable woman, Bel-Imperia repudiates the strictures imposed by both father and brother. Instead, her impulses for growth and nourishment shift towards autonomy rather than class escalation. Her downward selection of lovers remains an expression of ambitious growth precisely because it is a *selection*. Building on Frank Whigham's argument that Bel-Imperia's 'sexual relations are certainly murderous, not literally of her superiors, but of their sustaining ideology', Ian McAdam notes that she challenges 'gender (and class) restrictions by refusing to allow her father and uncle to use her as a valuable commodity in the royal marriage market of Europe'.[53] When we remember the play is framed by the conscripted and circumscribed Proserpine, powerless against her abduction and choiceless in her mate, the impulse of Bel-Imperia to woo according to her own determination appears liberating, a 'faculty of getting' that acquires something beyond the scope of her established lot. Indeed, as a secure aristocrat but entrapped woman, Bel-Imperia has little else she needs to get other than freedom to act on her own terms.

Bel-Imperia courts Horatio as both a means to acquire her autonomy and a vehicle to advance her revenge, two types of 'getting' that Kyd imbues with images of preservation and, finally, vegetative growth. Bel-Imperia easily conflates revenging Don Andrea and loving Horatio in a remarkable synthesis of what would ordinarily seem contradictory, conflicting impulses:

> But how can love find harbor in my breast
> Till I revenge the death of my beloved?
> Yes, second love shall further my revenge.
> I'll love Horatio, my Andrea's friend,
> The more to spite the prince that wrought his end. (1.4.64–8)

At this point in the play, we have only been promised Bel-Imperia's revenge on Balthazar (indeed, there is nothing else yet *to* revenge). Significantly, Kyd links Bel-Imperia's first articulation of revenge with her first affirmation to love Horatio. The relationship between the impulses to love and revenge in Bel-Imperia appears, therefore, symbiotic. Revenge keeps love viable, enables love to 'find harbor in [her] breast'. And love, likewise, propels and sustains vengeance, for it shall 'further' revenge 'the more to spite the prince that wrought [Andrea's] end'. The circular interplay of preservation or nourishment (of autonomy in love) and acquisition or advancement (of her vengeful designs) creates in Bel-Imperia a nuanced expression of *oeconomic* principles. She seeks to bring both love and revenge to fruition at the same time, and Kyd immediately makes explicit the vegetative trope, the image of cultivation, for each. For Bel-Imperia vows to use Horatio to spite Balthazar to make the latter 'reap long repentance for his murd'rous deed' (1.4.72). And when Bel-Imperia drops her glove in front of Horatio and Balthazar, the former retrieves it, observing, 'I reaped more grace than I deserved or hoped', initiating the rivalry between the two men (1.4.103). At the precise moment when Horatio 'reaps' grace from Bel-Imperia, Balthazar begins the process of 'reap[ing] long repentance'. In the language of harvesting, Kyd articulates Bel-Imperia's dual projects of preserving her autonomy and advancing her vengeful ambitions.

Shortly thereafter, as Horatio and Bel-Imperia approach the garden, Bel-Imperia alone intuits danger, articulating her unease as a function of her soul, a statement that will acquire additional resonance in the ensuing scene as the conflicting ambitions of the two lovers become more apparent. Bel-Imperia's reactions to Horatio's wooing reveal that her apprehensions lie in the incompatibility of her project for autonomy and Horatio's project to acquire her. Tellingly, Bel-Imperia seems notably more comfortable figuring the courtship in martial terms and baulks when Horatio shifts into the language of acquisition mediated by vegetative imagery. In a series of cantilevered syllogisms, Bel-Imperia deftly moves Horatio away from birdsong to a counterfeiting Cupid, and then from Venus to the martial dominance of Mars. She notes, 'And where Mars reigneth there must needs be wars' (2.4.35). Most at ease while acknowledging the power dynamics of wooing, Bel-Imperia operates comfortably within a discourse self-consciously allusive of tension and the pursuit of supremacy. She demurs, however, with Horatio's transition to more pastoral rhetoric in which he envisions attaining mastery over her:

> *Horatio:* Then thus begin our wars: put forth thy hand,
> That it may combat with my ruder hand.
> *Bel-Imperia:* Set forth thy foot to try the push of mine.
> *Horatio:* But first my looks shall combat against thine.
> *Bel-Imperia:* Then ward thyself. I dart this kiss at thee.
> *Horatio:* Thus I retort the dart thou threw'st at me.
> <div align=right>[<i>They kiss.</i>]</div>
> *Bel-Imperia:* Nay then, to gain the glory of the field,
> My twining arms shall yoke and make thee yield.
> *Horatio:* Nay then, my arms are large and strong withal;
> Thus elms by vines are compassed till they fall.
> *Bel-Imperia:* O, let me go, for in my troubled eyes
> Now may'st thou read that life in passion dies. (2.4.42–9)

On one level, these may be playful lines spoken among lovers closing the physical space between them. Here, the pushing of middling on aristocratic takes on an amorous, erotic quality. Yet Kyd imbues the language with more than sexual tension by highlighting the contest for power implicit in *this* courtship. Bel-Imperia imagines her 'gain' as the product of her arms that 'yoke' Horatio and 'make [him] yield'. Horatio twice invokes 'combat', the means by which he forced the King's favour (through his own 'naturall gayne' of Balthazar) and won Bel-Imperia's notice, and Bel-Imperia entreats Horatio to 'try the push of' her foot as she both invites him closer and holds him at bay. Suggestive of her concomitant desire to have Horatio without him necessarily having her, this ploy frames the clearest articulation of the actual nature of Bel-Imperia's misgivings. For at the very moment Horatio leaves the martial for the arboreal, the character of his ambition (and the reason for her distrusting it) becomes clear. Horatio figures his attainment of Bel-Imperia with a threefold image of vegetative growth, circumscription and the levelling of distinction, for he compares the embraced Bel-Imperia to 'elms by vines [. . .] compassed till they fall'. Bel-Imperia, as we have seen, recoils at being 'compassed' and erupts once again with her doubts, this time noting that her own self-preservation is at stake. For she pulls away, telling Horatio that in her eyes he 'may read that life in passion dies'. While Horatio will make this into a sexual pun, Bel-Imperia envisions the stifling of her own life under the passion of Horatio, an appropriation of Horatio's own metaphor that drops an elm with choking vines. Where Horatio sees this felling of Bel-Imperia as the levelling of distinction (and analogous to the combat through which he unseats the socially superior), Bel-Imperia recognises this as a very real kind of death.

In the *scelus*, or great crime, of *The Spanish Tragedy* immediately subsequent to this scene, the aristocratic villains violently suppress the lawful – indeed, as we have seen, natural – 'getting' of Horatio, a deed conspicuously full of ironic allusions to the vegetative tropes used to describe middling ambition. By having Horatio woo Lorenzo's sister, Kyd once again portrays a threat to an aristocratic order that requires a virtually hermetic structure to retain its identity. Consequently, Lorenzo penetrates the arbour by bribing Pedrigano, by wielding his greater 'substance' to frustrate Horatio's ambition. When the villains murder Horatio, Kyd juxtaposes the overwhelming force wrought by Lorenzo's wealth with variant permutations of the metaphor linking the vegetative and the ambitious. Taken by surprise and outnumbered, Horatio poses little threat of successful resistance. His hanging could seem entirely superfluous, especially since Kyd clearly establishes Horatio's death as caused by stabbing:

>*They hang him in the arbour.*
>*Horatio*: What, will you murder me?
>*Lorenzo*: Ay, thus, and thus! These are the fruits of love.
>*They stab him.* (2.4.54–5)

While Hieronimo later notes that Horatio was slain by a cord (3.13.175), the scene itself presents evidence to the contrary, as Lorenzo kills Horatio by stabbing, not hanging, him. Able to talk, Horatio clearly hangs in such a way not intended as fatal in itself. Kyd graphically underscores this when Lorenzo, in response to Horatio's question ('What will you murder me?'), punctuates his answer ('Ay, thus, and thus!') with coincident thrusts of his blade. The hanging of Horatio in the arbour functions not simply as a means of murder, then, nor as a method of subduing resistance but also as a vehicle by which Kyd emphasises the figurative connection between Hieronimo's child and garden. Both extensions, or outgrowths, of Hieronimo's own identity and household, Horatio and the garden symbolise the Knight Marshal's ambition.[54] Moreover, the garden and Horatio's grotesque position within it in the *scelus* scene also become the means for Lorenzo's sarcastic sneering at the son's ambition as well. For in case we missed the emphasis on extending one's reach beyond one's allotted station in life, Kyd concludes this scene with Lorenzo's quip, 'Although his life were still ambitious proud, / Yet is he at the highest now he is dead' (2.4.60–1). Lorenzo equates Horatio's ambitious life to his corpse's physical elevation among the boughs of his father's arbour. The same Horatio who sought to fell Lorenzo's sister like an elm is ironically raised among the trees to his death, iconic of the violent suppression of his own ambition.

Revenge as Vegetative Impulse

In the aftermath of Horatio's death, Kyd markedly anchors Hieronimo's impending revenge into the ontological assumptions that have been pervading the playworld to this point, naturalising the Knight Marshal's grief and reaction to it as clearly of a piece with the play's larger ecology of action. Hieronimo's dirge for the slain Horatio immediately signals a shift in his own ambitious energies and tacitly figures his revenge as a modified application of the vegetative faculty. Though operating rationally through his imaginative, Latinate rhetoric and emotionally through his effusions of anguish, Hieronimo desires a scenario where rational and sensitive functions dissipate, leaving him just this side of complete death with only his impulse to revenge Horatio remaining. In the dirge, Hieronimo calls three times for herbs, the very first line reading 'let someone mix for me herbs which the beautiful spring brings forth' (2.5.67–8).[55] He then promises that he will 'gather whatever herbs the sun brings forth' and concludes he will 'drink [. . .] whatever herbs' may ease his grief (2.5.71–4). Interestingly, Hieronimo turns to the vegetative to heal his pain by suppressing the soul's other, non-vegetative functions. He seeks a medicinal draught 'which will bring oblivion to our minds' and will try any remedy 'until all feeling dies at once in [his] dead heart' (2.5.69–70, 74–5). Kyd's Latin here is telling. He has Hieronimo seek oblivion for his and Isabella's 'animis', that is, their rational souls, and then imagines the extinction of his 'sensus', his power of perceiving or sensing.[56] In short, while three times imagining a herbal concoction (and twice a mysterious feminine force that supplies it), Hieronimo desires the comforting annihilation of two of the soul's three functions. As he begins to imagine joining Horatio wholly in death, he draws back 'in case then no revenge should follow your death' (2.5.80). After imagining the absence of the rational and sensitive functions of the soul, Hieronimo eschews complete death in favour of a continuing impulse towards revenge. By concluding with 'sequatur', a word meaning not only 'to follow' but also 'to follow naturally', 'succeed', or 'ensue',[57] Hieronimo's dirge again suggests revenge as a sequential outgrowth or conclusion to a matter. Ensuing naturally and deriving from something beyond the rational or sensitive capacities only, revenge, it would seem, emerges from Hieronimo's redirected energies towards creation and growth. Indeed, right after the dirge, the personified Revenge underscores the underlying vegetative trope by responding to Don Andrea's impatience: 'Thou talk'st of harvest when the corn is green', and, again, 'the sickle comes not till the corn be ripe' (2.6.7, 9). Here, Revenge echoes not only Bel-Imperia's intent to make Balthazar 'reap long repentance' but also the Latin dirge's underlying psychology, tacitly affiliating vengeance with vegetative fruition.[58]

After figuring revenge as a function of the vegetative soul during Hieronimo's dirge and re-emphasising (through Lorenzo's machinations in the third act) the entrenched power structure Hieronimo opposes, Kyd uses the Don Bazulto subplot to further suggest revenge as a type of gain acquired in the face of opposition and fed, in part, by the deepest undercurrents of the human psyche. Hieronimo witnesses Don Bazulto's grief and marvels that 'love's effects so strives in lesser things', that 'love enforce[s] such mood in meaner wits', and that it 'express[es] such power in poor estates' (3.13.99–101). Observing the inverse relationship between the power afforded by social class and that by love, Hieronimo ruminates on the undercurrents of his own psyche that move him towards revenge. Contrasting the 'lesser waters [that] labor in the deep' to the raging of the sea's 'upper billows' (3.13.104–5), Hieronimo evokes an image of 'an elemental power sought by the human revenger'[59] right before aligning vengeance with acquisition and turning once more to Proserpine. Hieronimo sees revenge as acquisition or gain, for he imagines Don Bazulto and himself going to Hades and 'in this passion [. . .] getting by force' the means of vengeance (3.13.109–11); consequently, he will endure, 'Till we do gain that Proserpine may grant / Revenge on them that murderèd my son' (3.13.120–1). As Kyd moves Hieronimo's imagination from the earthly court he currently inhabits with Don Bazulto to that of Proserpine, he shifts the play's focus from the turbulent surface, the 'upper billows', to the deeper recesses of the soul that generates revenge. For, here, Hieronimo's passion runs deeper than mere emotive excess and into the lesser waters of his psyche, the ones that govern 'getting' and 'gain' and find communion with the motivating, vegetative impulse figured in Proserpine.

What I am suggesting is that the vegetative faculty that gives rise to the middling sort's lawful attainments of the play's first half, also promotes the revengers' ambitions in the second but does so in a different register, as Kyd figures revenge as an altered type of 'getting' within (and against) an increasingly vicious milieu, one where aristocrats such as Lorenzo violently seek to 'hold their own' (3.4.43). Revenge, in *The Spanish Tragedy*'s denouement, becomes one of a number of expressions of household *oeconomia*, a form of propagation and extension of one's self via alternative means when lawful attempts to advance become retarded. As such, revenge functions as a subset of the vegetative capacity, a method for the powerless or marginalised to reproduce their influence (and, ideally, something of their likeness) in the society that has robbed them of both identity and hope. The culminating effect of Kyd's artistic manipulations of his culture's shared ontological assumptions reveals how the desire for advancement, intrinsic by nature to each individual, *will* find outlet – even if it must do so negatively. In short, Kyd shifts the concept of continuing one's existence through progeny and legacy into a darker register. Unleashing their creative energies on a courtly milieu inattentive to their unrest, Kyd's revengers forever alter the landscape by puncturing the secure spaces surrounding the court with irremediable absences. What appears to many critics as cunning rationality, a studied waiting for opportunity, mixed with irrational excess is also an altered form of natural outgrowth and a management of one's condition. Kyd's ironic inversion of the latent principle of reproduction and preservation helps explain why, as Scott McMillin astutely points out, Hieronimo draws from Seneca 'passages [that] have nothing literally to do with revenge' but rather 'share an unusual idea about "safety" or "preservation" which obviously concerns [him]'.[60] Making their final desperate acts unalterable and irrevocable, Hieronimo, Bel-Imperia, and Isabella guarantee the perpetuation of their influence, and something of their likeness, indefinitely into the future.

Take for instance Isabella's destruction of the arbour, the most salient instance of revenge as the creation of an eternal, immutable absence in the play. Distraught, constrained and unable to reach the murderers themselves, Isabella resolves to 'revenge myself upon this place', what she later terms the 'accursèd complot of my misery' (4.2.4, 13). Kyd figures Isabella's project as one of utter annihilation:

> Down with these branches and these loathsome boughs
> Of this unfortunate and fatal pine!
> Down with them, Isabella, rend them up
> And burn the roots from whence the rest is sprung!

> I will not leave a root, a stalk, a tree,
> A bough, a branch, a blossom, nor a leaf,
> No, not an herb within this garden plot –
> Accursèd complot of my misery.
> Fruitless forever may this garden be,
> Barren the earth, and blissless whosoever
> Imagines not to keep it unmanured! (4.2.6–15)

Isabella's whole project here is the creation of absence, the void without which her continuing impact on her environment, however limited in scope it may be, is impossible. Not only must the earth remain fruitless and barren but so, too, must the human mind preserve a sense of absence, for Isabella extends her curse even to those potentially interested in the future cultivation of this space. The negative formulation of her curse – 'whosoever imagines not to keep it unmanured' – further suggests that she seeks to create an absence, a perpetual hole, continuing indefinitely into the future. Her concern is not simply that someone might imagine manuring this plot of land, but rather that someone might *not* imagine to keep it *un*manured. In other words, she seeks the continual reinforcement of negation, the perpetual remembrance that this is a barren space that must remain incontrovertibly barren. Indeed, so total is Isabella's proposed and enacted annihilation that she even imagines the complete absence of people inhabiting the space, since 'passengers, for fear to be infect, / Shall stand aloof' (4.2.20–1).

By cursing and destroying both womb and garden, the two sites of Hieronimo's fruitful reproduction in which his seed(s) took root and expanded his household, Isabella renders his revenge as necessary, the only means left of making his lasting mark in Spain. Isabella explicitly figures her destruction of the garden as part of her desire for Hieronimo to act. After tearing down the arbour, she doubly curses Hieronimo, apostrophising: 'Hieronimo, make haste to see thy son', and, again, 'Make haste, Hieronimo, to hold excused / Thy negligence in pursuit of their deaths, / Whose hateful wrath bereaved him of his breath' (4.2.24–6, 29–31). After faulting Hieronimo's 'negligence', Isabella concludes 'and as I curse this tree from further fruit, / So shall my womb be cursèd for [Horatio's] sake' (4.2.35–6). That Isabella curses both womb and tree after bemoaning Hieronimo's torpor suggests she sees both as vehicles for his 'faculty of getting' and his *oeconomic* energies, for she simultaneously shuts down their fruitfulness and links the destruction of each with her call for Hieronimo to act anew.

Once Hieronimo's wife and garden no longer exist, Kyd has the Knight Marshal employ his 'fruitless poetry [. . .] though it profit the professor naught' (4.1.72–3) to enact his revenge, a destruction as absolute as Isabella's and one equally figured as a type of reproduction through the creation of absence. In this case, however, Hieronimo, in a manner analogous to his earlier advocacy for Horatio's advancement, seeks to reproduce his own likeness and implant it thoroughly in the court by creating in his adversaries the sense of negation and loss he himself experiences. After exposing the reason for his revenge, Hieronimo turns to his audience:

> Speak, Portuguese, whose loss resembles mine:
> If thou canst weep upon thy Balthazar,
> 'Tis like I wailed for my Horatio.
> And you, my lord, whose reconcilèd son
> Marched in a net, and thought himself unseen,
> And rated me for brainsick lunacy,
> With 'God amend that mad Hieronimo!' —
> How can you brook our play's catastrophe? (4.4.114–21)

Hieronimo revels in the mimetic effects of his revenge by anticipating the Portuguese king's weeping, something he correlates to his own wailing for Horatio. Likewise, Hieronimo anticipates how the Duke of Castile will 'brook our play's catastrophe', offsetting the Duke's impending reaction with a recitation of his own response to personal trauma, namely, his feigned madness and clever machinations. The deaths of Lorenzo and Balthazar may satisfy justice but they also transform Castile and the Portuguese King into fathers of slaughtered sons, transposing Hieronimo's likeness onto them. To the two Kings and Castile, Hieronimo subsequently asserts that 'As dear to me was my Horatio / As yours, or yours, or yours, my lord, to you' (4.4.169–70). On one level, this vengeance forces a type of parity between Horatio, Lorenzo and Balthazar. Yet Hieronimo's revenge is not only one of equalisation but also one of mimesis, or reproduction, a fact that becomes even clearer in the play's final moments. For while the deaths of Lorenzo and Balthazar may seem to satisfy justice, the killing of Castile seems superfluous – until one compares the effects of such an action. For Hieronimo explains his first two killings, by pointing to Horatio's body and saying 'Here lay my hope, and here my hope hath end' (4.4.90). Then, immediately after Hieronimo – in one fluid motion – kills Castile and himself, the King of Spain mourns, 'My brother, and the whole succeeding hope / That Spain expected after my decease!' (4.4.203–4). The Knight Marshal's slaying of Castile robs the Spanish King of the 'whole succeeding hope' of himself and his nation, recreating in the King Hieronimo's hopeless image by making him bereft of his successor. By the end of this scene, the Knight Marshal has created in the two Kings two Hieronimos, establishing his perpetual presence at court by puncturing it with irremediable absences.

We see something of this insatiable desire to recreate loss with Don Andrea's final resumption of centre stage when he depicts revenge as a concomitantly complete yet unfinished expression of ambition. His first words as he reclaims the audience's attention are, 'Ay, now my hopes have end in their effects, / When blood and sorrow finish my desires' (4.5.1–2). Don Andrea more narrowly locates his delight in his soul, as part of his fundamental psychology, and returns his thoughts to Proserpine and the division of sorts:

> Ay, these were spectacles to please my soul.
> Now will I beg at lovely Proserpine,
> That by the virtue of her princely doom
> I may consort my friends in pleasing sort,
> And on my foes work just and sharp revenge. (4.5.12–16)

Despite having previously labelled his desires as finished (and, in the Induction, having displayed no inclination at all towards revenge), Don Andrea here exhibits insatiable desire, culminating in the play's final line envisioning 'endless tragedy' (4.5.48). As Kyd draws his play towards this endless conclusion, he reminds us that Don Andrea's revenge operates pleasurably on his soul, stems from the motivating acquiescence of Proserpine, and will ensure the eternal distinction between his friends and foes. While the latter consist entirely of the aristocracy, the former are entirely from the middling sort, with the exception of Bel-Imperia, who, as we have seen, encounters proscription and oppression in her own unique situation. As Don Andrea delights in his soul at the revenge initiated by Proserpine, he imagines a continuation of such delight, that he may 'consort [his] friends in pleasing sort'. Kyd conflates here the pleasure of Don Andrea's soul wrought by revenge and the pleasure the ghost imagines awaiting him in eternity, a utopian vision where his aristocratic foes remain forever subordinate to his power and his own circle of equals (including, notably, Bel-Imperia) receive unending favour.

The Spanish Tragedy, of course, is informed by other aspects of early modern psychology beyond the Aristotelian vegetative soul. The rational calculus found in the play's stratagems is very real; so, too, are its emotive excesses for which Kyd was famous (and, subsequently, famously derided). But Kyd's appropriation of classical ideas, specifically that found in his culture's tripartite psychology, reveals to our post-Cartesian minds how cleverly the author sought to use existing natural philosophy, conjoined with the pathos of his drama, to fashion a pervasive, conditioning philosophical context in which revenge appears a natural, apparently organic, part, all in the service of suggesting the importance of a more egalitarian politics. Interested in the very real, material advancement among the middling sort, Kyd articulated not simply the sententious imperatives common to the discourses of *oeconomia* but also the potent philosophical predicates informing those discourses. By emphasising the most universal yet most often overlooked and minor of the soul's faculties, Kyd found a useful vehicle for depicting the particular condition of the middling sort; by turning to the part of the soul at once immaterial yet also responsible for all material reproduction and increase, he likewise found an apt means for tethering his revenge narrative into a recognisable ontological frame, weaving retribution, in this way, into the very fabric of his playworld's most fundamental structuring principles. The *oeconomia* of *The Spanish Tragedy*, and particularly the play's engagement with the vegetative soul's capacity for reproduction, growth and nutrition, suggests revenge as not merely sensationally brutish but also coherent, the natural outgrowth of a middling sort circumscribed by an artificial yet entrenched system of preferment and advancement.

By appropriating the concept of the vegetative soul in order to help structure his play's central conflicts, Kyd attends to one of the most rudimentary components understood in his age as subtending all of life, and he shrewdly creates thereby a fully-realised, conditioning philosophical system for the world his characters inhabit. The vegetative soul, ubiquitous yet imperceptible, existed in the minds of early modern thinkers right at the boundary between immateriality and materiality.

Early modern audiences of all kinds understood this faculty as manifesting itself in many forms. As Kyd invokes, by turns subtly and overtly, the classical doctrine of the vegetative soul to convey notions of ambition and *oeconomia*, he also draws on the concept to shape his depiction of revenge itself, aligning the process of retribution with the premises of this familiar underlying system, one accepted, in so many other registers, as informing the daily operations of life. In doing so, Kyd figures revenge as fitting, as consonant with how the world as constructed in the play functions at its most fundamental levels, and provides, as a result, deeper ontological ground for retribution than might be found in appeals to sympathy or notions of justice alone. Through all of this, Kyd does more than simply reveal himself as an inventive handler of classical texts and ideas of considerably greater sophistication than Thomas Nashe or his harsher critics might have it. He also reveals the capacity of the theatre, even at its most brutal, to do intricate philosophical work, and, more specifically, to appropriate the most subtle, refined ontological assumptions of the age and marshall them for unconventional, even radical, ends.

Notes

1. Robert Greene, *Menaphon Camillas Alarum to Slumbering Euphues, in His Melancholie Cell at Silexedra* (London, 1589), 3r.
2. Ibid. 3r. On Nashe's gibe as a critique of Kyd's 'ad lumina', see Lukas Erne, *Beyond The Spanish Tragedy: A Study of the Works of Thomas Kyd* (Manchester: Manchester University Press, 2001), 150.
3. Greene, *Menaphon Camillas*, 3r.
4. Eugene Hill, 'Senecan and Virgilian Perspectives in *The Spanish Tragedy*', *English Literary Renaissance*, 15.2 (1985): 143–65; Zackariah C. Long, '*The Spanish Tragedy* and *Hamlet*: Infernal Memory in English Renaissance Revenge Tragedy', *English Literary Renaissance* 44.2 (2014): 177–8.

5. G. K. Hunter, 'Tacitus and Kyd's *The Spanish Tragedy*', *Notes and Queries* 47.4 (2000): 424–5; Frank Ardolino, '"Author and Actor in This Tragedy": The Influence of Apuleius's *The Golden Ass* on Kyd's *The Spanish Tragedy*', *Medieval & Renaissance Drama in England* 27 (2014): 110–31.
6. Curtis Perry, 'The Uneasy Republicanism of Thomas Kyd's *Cornelia*', *Criticism* 48.4 (2006): 535–55.
7. Francis Meres, *Wits Common Wealth* (London, 1634), 626.
8. R. Hathway, 'Of the Booke', in John Bodenham, *Bel-vedere or the Garden of the Muses* (1600), n.p.
9. Anthony Munday, 'To his loving and approved good Friend, M. *John Bodenham*', in Ibid. n.p.
10. Robert Allott, *England's Parnassus* (London, 1600), A4. See also, Arthur Freeman, *Thomas Kyd: Facts and Problems* (Oxford: Clarendon Press, 1967), 167.
11. 'To the memory of my beloved, The AUTHOR MR. WILLIAM SHAKESPEARE: AND what he hath left us', in William Shakespeare, *Mr. William Shakespeares Comedies, Histories, & Tragedies Published According to the True Originall Copies*, ed. Henry Condell (London, 1623).
12. Thomas Dekker, *A Knights Conjuring Done in Earnest: Discovered in Jest* (London, 1607), K2.
13. Clara Calvo, 'Thomas Kyd and the Elizabethan blockbuster: *The Spanish Tragedy*', in Ton Hoenselaars, *The Cambridge Companion to Shakespeare and Contemporary Dramatists* (Cambridge: Cambridge University Press, 2012), 20.
14. *OED*, s.v. 'industrious'.
15. Sir Thomas Elyot, *The dictionary of syr Thomas Elyot knyght* (London, 1538).
16. *The boke named the Gouernour* (London 1537), 82v.
17. Throughout, I employ 'psychology' to denote the pre- and early modern study of the soul, or *psuchê*.
18. Keith Wrightson, '"Sorts of People" in Tudor and Stuart England', in *The Middling Sort of People: Culture, Society, and Politics in England, 1550–1800*, ed. Jonathan Barry and Christopher Brooks (New York: Palgrave Macmillan, 1994), 44–6.

19. Theodore B. Leinwand, 'Shakespeare and the Middling Sort', *Shakespeare Quarterly* 44 (1993): 292.
20. C. L. Barber, *Creating Elizabethan Tragedy: The Theater of Marlowe and Kyd*, ed. Richard P. Wheeler (Chicago: University of Chicago Press, 1988), 135, 136, 139.
21. James R. Siemon, 'Sporting Kyd', *English Literary Renaissance* 24 (1994): 556, 32-3.
22. Wendy Wall, *Staging Domesticity: Household Work and English Identity in Early Modern Drama* (Cambridge: Cambridge University Press, 2002), 5.
23. Ibid. 35.
24. F. S. Boas, *The Works of Thomas Kyd* (Oxford: Clarendon Press, 1901), lxiii–lxiv. See also Erne, *Beyond* The Spanish Tragedy, 146–50, 217–20.
25. Siemon, 'Sporting Kyd', 571.
26. Dennis Des Chene, *Life's Form: Late Aristotelian Conceptions of the Soul* (Ithaca, NY: Cornell University Press, 2000), 5-6, 169 (emphasis mine).
27. Ibid. 134.
28. Ibid. 55.
29. quoted in Ibid. 55.
30. Ibid. 57.
31. Rosamond Kent Sprague explains that for Aristotle, plants exhibit 'aspiration' and, 'like other Aristotelian entities, are controlled by teleology' ('Plants as Aristotelian Substances', in *Aristotle: Critical Assessments*, ed. Lloyd P. Gerson, vol. 2 [New York: Routledge, 1999], 362).
32. Pierre Charron, *Of wisdome* (London, 1608?), 27.
33. William Hill, *The infancie of the soule* (London, 1605), C2v.
34. Pierre de La Primaudaye, *The second part of the French academie* (London, 1594), Bbv.
35. Helkiah Crooke, *Mikrokosmographia* (London, 1615), 221, V3r.
36. See Ibid. 657; La Primaudaye, *The second part*, 339; John Rastell, *A new boke of purgatory* (London, 1530), f3r-f3v; and Jean Huarte, *Examen de ingenios* (London, 1594), 34-5.

37. See Miles Mosse, *Iustifying and sauing faith distinguished from the faith of the deuils* (London, 1614), 39; Thomas Adams, *The happines of the church* (London, 1619), 428; William Pemble, *Vindiciae fidei, or A treatise of iustification by faith* (Oxford, 1625), 193, respectively.
38. La Primaudaye, *The second part of the French academie*, Yr, 337.
39. Huarte, *Examen de ingenios*, 35.
40. *Andrew Marvell: The Complete Poems*, ed. Elizabeth Story Donno (New York: Penguin Books, 1987), 50–1.
41. *The Poems of Sir John Davies*, ed. Robert Kruger (Oxford: Clarendon Press, 1975).
42. Thomas Kyd, *The Housholders Philosophie: Wherein is perfectly and profitably described, the true oeconomia and forme of housekeeping* (1588). Rpt. in *The Works of Thomas Kyd*, ed. F. S. Boas (Oxford: Clarendon Press, 1901), 275.
43. 'Introduction', *The Middling Sort of People*, 2.
44. All quotations come from Thomas Kyd, *The Spanish Tragedy*, ed. David Bevington (Manchester: Manchester University Press, 1996).
45. On the perplexing nature of the play's opening image, see Eugene Hill, 147.
46. On Proserpine's role here and its relation to the 'mythologizing literalisation of the seasonal cycle', see Lisa Hopkins, 'What's Hercules to Hamlet? The Emblematic Garden in *The Spanish Tragedy* and *Hamlet*', *Hamlet Studies* 21 (1999): 118.
47. James T. Henke, 'Politics and Politicians in *The Spanish Tragedy*', *Studies in Philology* 78 (1981): 354.
48. Thus, we are earlier told that 'hee that is borne to obey, were hee of Kings bloode, is neverthelesse a servant, though he be not so reputed' (262).
49. *History of Botanical Science: An Account of the Development of Botany from Ancient Times to the Present Day* (New York: Academic Press, 1981), 151.
50. *The Renaissance Garden in England* (London: Thames and Hudson, 1979), 45.
51. Ibid. 50.

52. On the garden's role in 'extend[ing] royalty to ordinary men', see Terry Comito, 'Renaissance Gardens and the Discovery of Paradise', *Journal of the History of Ideas* 32 (1971): 501.
53. '*The Spanish Tragedy* and the Politico-Religious Unconscious', *Texas Studies in Literature and Language* 42 (2000): 45.
54. See Vin Nardizzi, '"No Wood, No Kingdom:" Planting Genealogy, Felling Trees, and the Additions to *The Spanish Tragedy*', *Modern Philology* 110.2 (2012): 210–15.
55. All translations are from Bevington, except where noted.
56. C. T. Lewis, *An Elementary Latin Dictionary* (Oxford: Oxford University Press, 1997), *s.v.* 'anima', *s.v.* 'sensus'.
57. Ibid. *s.v.* 'sequator'.
58. Lisa Hopkins concludes that 'it is precisely on this complex of images of husbandry and of the seasonal cycle that Revenge draws when he attempts to reassure Andrea [. . .] Even if events seem to outrage the customary logic of human growth and progression by killing the children before the eyes of their parents, Revenge seems still to see them as contained within an appropriate framework of cultivation and fruition' ('What's Hercules to Hamlet?', 123).
59. Scott McMillin, 'The Figure of Silence in *The Spanish Tragedy*', *ELH*, 39.1 (1972): 45.
60. 'The Book of Seneca in *The Spanish Tragedy*', *Studies in English Literature, 1500–1900* 14 (1974): 204.

CHAPTER 2

FIXING MODERATION: *TITUS ANDRONICUS* AND THE ARISTOTELIAN DETERMINATION OF VALUE

Titus Andronicus has long been recognised as indebted to Kyd's *The Spanish Tragedy*, but in thinking about the ways in which revenge tragedies make use of classical thought to shape their worlds, we would be misguided to expect Shakespeare to merely import the Aristotelian faculty psychology, unique to Kyd's own peculiar concerns, which animates that earlier work. To be sure, as Tzachi Zamir has eloquently argued, Shakespeare's earliest revenge tragedy *does* share with Kyd's play an abiding interest in arboreal imagery, one that powerfully serves to guide the play's mix of tragic pleasure and ethical instruction.[1] But while the linkages between *Titus Andronicus* and *The Spanish Tragedy* are many and varied, the amorphous Roman world of Shakespeare's play is decidedly not the world of Kyd's Spanish court, and the ontological frameworks constructed by each author remain markedly geared toward the particular dramaturgical needs dictated by the central conflicts staged within each play. Indeed, although *Titus Andronicus* concerns the travails of competing families, each jockeying for position and power within their reconfigured polities, Shakespeare remains less concerned than Kyd with how households may grow, prosper and preserve themselves, as even a cursory glance at Titus' pride in his sons' tomb would well attest. In terms of the underlying philosophical frameworks that work to shape reception of revenge on the early modern stage, the affinities between these two early revenge plays lie, then, not in a shared interest in a particular doctrine but rather in a shared dramaturgical strategy of marshalling familiar ideas – current in contemporary culture but with roots in classical thought – in order to anchor each play's revenge narrative into common assumptions about how the playworld as depicted operates on its most fundamental levels. If in Kyd's tragedy, this process takes shape in such a way as to align retribution with the most ubiquitous and essential of natural impulses, Shakespeare's tragedy, as we will see, figures revenge as a kind of return to a more balanced condition within a larger natural order. Distinct in his thematic, theatrical interests and thus in the specific philosophical ideas with which he will imbue his play, Shakespeare nonetheless shares with Kyd an allied method of invoking and, when needed, refashioning his era's philosophical assumptions in order to create a fully-realised, immersive world that, in its very construction, will help condition reception of the revenge enacted on stage.

For reasons ranging from Kyd's ostensibly limited classicism and the genre's popular appeal and reliance on bloody spectacle, *The Spanish Tragedy*, as we have seen, has seemed an unlikely place to find the shaping influence of classical philosophy, particularly its more subtle theories about what underwrites embodied action. How much more so has Shakespeare's *Titus Andronicus*. For even if most critics grant Shakespeare a wider philosophical range than that conventionally afforded Kyd, the play has consistently stood apart as one of exceptional brutality and intensely violent extremes. Declared 'a tissue of horrors', 'a heap of Rubbish', and 'one of the stupidest and most uninspired plays ever written',[2] *Titus* has elicited criticism from many quarters for being too much and not enough, excessive in its sensationalism yet lacking in its substance and stylistic organisation. Undoubtedly, Shakespeare's earliest revenge tragedy has also enjoyed favourable reappraisal among more modern critics, garnering like *The Spanish Tragedy* greater appreciation for its undeniable theatrical force, but even among such sympathetic readers the play's protagonist has nonetheless continued to seem both immoderate and erratic, unhinged by his own inclination toward extreme behaviour, his conduct neither rationally nor consistently governed. Whether among dismissive or receptive critics, *Titus* still stands as a play unlikely to be understood as especially invested in classical philosophy, let alone for the immediate relevance of such philosophy to a nightmarish world of persistent physical violence and trauma. But why has it seemed so obvious to read *Titus*' excesses as indicative of its purportedly chaotic form and philosophical crudeness? Why has its protagonist, as if embodying the flaws of the play as a whole, so clearly seemed an intemperate figure, deficient in both rhetorical and moral moderation? As we have seen with *The Spanish Tragedy*, outrageous stage violence – and even histrionic protagonists – can be informed by rather nuanced, refined philosophical doctrines. What's more, such doctrines, by constructing a subtle yet comprehensive ontological framework for a play, can, in turn, condition reception of the revenge narrative itself. Might a similar strategy be found at work in Shakespeare's *Titus Andronicus*, the play's excesses themselves part of a more finely-wrought engagement with classical thought?

    Rather than being merely the product of a muddled aesthetic, *Titus*' excesses signal, in much the same way the reduplicated tropes of the vegetative did for *The Spanish Tragedy*, the underlying ontological predicates which condition the atmosphere of Shakespeare's play, giving form to the revenge narrative as it unfolds. Throughout this early tragedy, Shakespeare consistently uses extremity as a means to frame and define the ethical, a representational strategy that exhibits sophistication and nuance amid, even through, sensational display and one that taps into a pressing set of cultural concerns prominent in the late sixteenth century. For excess and moderation, taken up throughout *Titus Andronicus*, stand as established conceptual categories in early modern England, shaped by continual explication and revision. As such, they represent a key instance in early modern culture where thinkers had to trace the ways in which ontological assumptions translate into embodied ethical action. As Shakespeare's first Roman play, where allusions to a turbulent Roman history and culture abound, *Titus Andronicus*, with all its horrors, seems far removed from the deliberative measures of Greek philosophy. Yet when situated within the predominant Aristotelian ethical theory of the early 1590s, *Titus Andronicus* reveals a remarkably coherent underlying structure and – perhaps even more surprising – a deeply moderate protagonist, who exhibits a strain of noble equanimity and a sense of reasoned temperance. By embedding within this turbulent, savage play a set of prevailing ontological assumptions about the nature of genuine moderation, Shakespeare creates a narrative of retribution that – even as it horrifies – resonates as appropriate, as fitting with the very essence of the world as figured forth throughout the play.

At stake in this chapter, then, is a rereading of *Titus Andronicus* that intends to alter our understanding of the play's excesses by defining moderation in ways that may at first seem counter-intuitive, even bizarre. For Aristotelian ethics – deeply ingrained in late sixteenth-century England and central to *Titus* – understands the ethical mean as the point of moral equilibrium between two diametrically opposed extremes, an immaterial ontological ground for ethics that only comes into full physical realisation when bodily enacted. Absolute yet also culturally intuited, the ethical mean admits a theoretical range of action as 'moderate', depending upon the circumstance. Moreover, as a site of social stability yet hermeneutic uncertainty, the mean requires perpetual fixing – in the sense of not only locating but also repairing. Contingent upon context, it requires continual identification and, when dislocated by rampant immoderation, restoration. In *Titus Andronicus*, Shakespeare treats the contextual determination of moderation and the mean's ontological fixity as compatible. This paradox of flexible rigidity helps position Titus as horrible yet just, noble while savage, as he negotiates the shifting terms of Rome's civic contract. As Rome becomes increasingly chaotic in its flouting of gratitude (the social mean discarded by the feckless Saturninus), Titus must refashion moderation within his newly altered context. His corrective revenge reintroduces two traits implicit in the city's initial contract based on gratitude (and absent in the crimes against his family) – namely, proportionality and a calculation of equivalent exchange. Shakespeare creates a remarkable series of ethical relocations throughout the play, recontextualising Titus, surnamed Pius, in extreme circumstances in a world grown immoderate. Within this context and informed by an ethical system attuned to the role of contingent circumstances in the translation of abstract ontological values into embodied acts, Titus' horrific violence functions not, as we might initially intuit, as excessive but rather as quite the opposite, as a type of radically adaptive moderation-in-extremity.

Between the Intrinsic and Contextual: Aristotelianism and the Early Modern Formulation of Value

As Charles B. Schmitt and David A. Lines have shown, the decline of Aristotelianism in early modern England has been significantly misunderstood. Indeed, as we have seen in the previous chapter, even the finer points of Aristotelian faculty psychology persisted well into the seventeenth century, and if Aristotle's natural philosophy proved tenacious even when subjected to intense interrogation from sceptical quarters, the philosopher's ethical theories, under considerably less strain, remained notably dominant throughout the age. While not 'considered an *auctoritas* in some infallible sense', Aristotle was 'the main authority in moral philosophy far into the sixteenth century', his ethics informing university systems and published materials throughout Europe.[3] In particular, *The Nicomachean Ethics* 'perhaps as much as any other work from antiquity, emerged from the Reformation struggles as a keystone of both Catholic and Protestant education'[4] and was the standard text for curricula in moral philosophy.[5] However, Aristotle's influence extended beyond the university system, since 'there was a general revival of interest in philosophy, particularly of the Aristotelian tradition, in England during the last quarter of the sixteenth century'.[6] The philosopher's works were frequently republished, a testament to Aristotle's widespread appeal beyond the university.[7] Printed more than any of Aristotle's other texts, the *Ethics* went through numerous translations.[8] At the time Shakespeare wrote *Titus*, Aristotelian moral philosophy informed literary texts engaging with myriad political and ethical issues, helping to shape their representations of moderation and excess.

The conflicted hermeneutics of fixing value in late Elizabethan England appeared across a wide array of discourses, including economic, racial, religious and legal ones, some of which have received ample attention in *Titus* criticism. In its most directly material expression, the notion of value arose with the currency devaluation crisis of the 1590s, which raised the question of whether value existed intrinsically or emerged from a seemingly arbitrary cultural consensus (or, for that matter, from royal fiat). According to Jesse M. Lander, 'The crisis of value that roiled the world of late sixteenth-century England' derived partly from Elizabeth's '"calling down" [of] the base coinage to its "true" value', an act that, in conjunction with rapid inflation, had 'a corrosive effect on the coin's ability to function as a standard of value' and 'put enormous strain on the language of value in its various forms'.[9] As Jonathan Gil Harris has recently shown, 'not only the debasement of England's currency but also unprecedented volatility in international exchange rates' exacerbated this crisis and prompted attempts to fix the coin as a 'common measure of value'.[10] The 'movement of bullion across national borders' called further attention to 'the mutability of financial value in the course of foreign currency exchange' and provided avenues for 'imagin[ing] rival models of value as inherent or extrinsic'.[11] Indeed, as Harris has convincingly argued, early modern inquiries into the relationship between 'intrinsic telos' and 'socially imposed nomos' – notably, the very sort of tension we saw at work in Kyd's translation of Tasso – extended beyond economic discourses to theories of language and even disease as well.[12] Moreover, the discourses of religious belief also participated in the crisis of fixing value in the late sixteenth century. The hermeneutics behind Protestant and Catholic disagreements pointed to a transcendent absolute, at once knowable yet stubbornly elusive, across differing cultural traditions. And in legal matters, 'by the late 1580s, the location of equity had become a political issue, as a result of the growing antagonism between common law and prerogative jurisdictions'.[13] Consistent across varying perspectives and concerns, the contested discourses of value shared a governing presupposition, however, that true value not only existed but required deciphering. In the midst of social flux, fixing a median point of consensus, particularly regarding ethical value, proved essential for developing a just society: the variability of context necessitated, not obviated, fixing an ethical mean.

The contested semiotics of value figured in the myriad discourses briefly surveyed here exemplifies the central quandary posed by the age's prevailing Aristotelianism: determining if the ethical mean is absolute and transcendent, situational and contextual, or (as Aristotle intimates) some tenuous fusion of the two.[14] Academic yet pragmatic, the question fundamentally shapes how one construes the 'ethical'. Since the mean, by its very nature, exists in contradistinction to two extremes, Aristotle often defines it relationally, by expressing it through opposition, articulating what it is *not*. One may find the mean of bravery, for example, by avoiding both cowardice and foolhardiness, two deviations from the mean that exhibit, respectively, too much or too little regard for one's safety.[15] Thus, ascertaining the mean relies in some measure upon context, for the point of recklessness or cowardice may shift, depending upon circumstance. This reliance on context at once creates moderation and allows for extremity, for it prompts the ethical person to '"save extreme reactions for extreme situations"'.[16] Such a formulation promotes patient endurance yet opens the possibility of justifiably extreme reactions, provided they are proportional to extreme circumstances. Therefore, when Aristotle speaks of the ethical mean, he points not simply to an appropriate, ontologically-grounded action but to an appropriate *range* of such action, adaptable as the occasion warrants. Recognising that locating the mean remains inherently fraught but nonetheless indispensable, Aristotle often advocates approximating virtue as closely as possible.

The influence of context on finding the mean likewise shapes Aristotle's taxonomy of distributive and rectificatory justice, two formulations particularly alert to the complexities of ascertaining transcendent value within socially fraught conditions and ones, as we will see, that figure centrally in the imperial election and the sacrifice of Alarbus. Here, as in personal ethics, just exchange exists on a potentially variable (and, therefore, disputable) point of equilibrium; consequently, ethical behaviour admits a range of possibility. In Book 5 of the *Ethics*, Aristotle distinguishes between distributive justice, or the proper distribution of goods, and rectificatory justice, the legal justice rendered for physical injury.[17] Governing the 'distributions of honour or money or the other things that fall to be divided among those who have a share in the constitution',[18] distributive justice ultimately leaves imprecise just how such division should occur. Aristotle predicates distributive justice on merit, but, as he readily admits, merit proves a notoriously slippery concept to fix in place, 'for all men agree that what is just in distribution must be according to merit in some sense, though they do not all specify the same sort of merit'.[19] While the indeterminate designation of 'merit' precedes the enactment (or, perhaps, approximation) of distributive justice, rectificatory justice remains contextually shaped by its reactive nature. Describing physical suffering (not just material dispossession) as a type of disequilibrium between a gainer and loser, Aristotle explains that

> this kind of injustice being an inequality, the judge tries to equalize it; for in the case also in which one has received and the other inflicted a wound, or one has slain and the other been slain, the suffering and the action have been unequally distributed; but the judge tries to equalize things by means of the penalty, taking away from the gain of the assailant.[20]

Recognising that 'the term "gain" is applied generally to such cases – even if it be not a term appropriate to certain cases, e.g. to the person who inflicts a wound – and "loss" to the sufferer', Aristotle argues that 'at all events when the suffering has been estimated, the one is called loss and the other gain'.[21] Rectificatory justice, as 'the intermediate between loss and gain', must, therefore, attend to context, for the judge resets the fulcrum in order to 'equalize things by means of [a] penalty', but does so only *after* 'the suffering has been estimated'.[22] The impulse to establish the ethical mean remains not simply a matter of personal hermeneutics but the particular concern of a just society seeking to maintain civic order, as the process of ascertaining such ontologically-grounded value within complex, heavily contested situations becomes multiplied across all the overlapping transactions within a given polity.

Within his taxonomy of justice, Aristotle articulates a third category known as 'justice in exchange',[23] a formulation especially attuned to the importance of gratitude or grace for ensuring equitable transactions, ones which appropriately translate the value of the ethical mean into the social commerce of daily life. While justice in exchange has often been read as a precursor to modern economic theory, recent scholarship has persuasively recuperated its broader purview – current well into the seventeenth century – as a category that encompasses the determination of value in *any* type of exchange.[24] Justice in exchange, according to Aristotle, is the 'sort of justice [that] hold[s] men together – reciprocity in accordance with a proportion and not on the basis of precisely equal return', since 'it is by proportionate requital that the city holds together'.[25] Immediately after observing that 'it is by proportionate requital that the city holds together', Aristotle states that 'men seek to return either evil for evil – and if they cannot do so, think their position mere slavery – or good for good – and if they cannot do so there is no exchange, but it is by exchange that they hold together'.[26] After Aristotle discusses the exchange of 'evil for evil [. . .] good for good', he contemplates graciousness: 'This is why they give a prominent place to the temple of the Graces – to promote the requital of services; for this is characteristic of grace – we should serve in return one who has shown grace to us, and should another time take the initiative in showing it. Now proportionate return is secured by cross-conjunction.'[27] As Aristotle moves from revenge ('men seek to return evil for evil') to his exposition on 'cross-conjunction', or the geometric proportion used to secure proportionate return, his emphasis on grace takes central place. Grace, necessary 'to promote the requital of services', facilitates Aristotle's ethical economy of justice in exchange: the absence of grace signals the breakdown of fair requital, a marked deviation, in social terms, from the ontological ground represented by the ethical mean.

Fixing the Mean in Early Modern England

Drawing on Aristotle's taxonomy of justice and understanding such absolute values as dependent, in practical terms, upon a process of estimation, early modern authors frequently emphasised the importance of correctly establishing proportionality for ensuring a healthy polity.[28] While *Aristotles politiques, or discourses of government* (1598) provided in the vernacular the philosopher's detailed explication of the 'two kindes of Justice, the one commutative, the other distributive', such concepts already permeated the era's writing.[29] Detailing the various modes of '*Justice, or Righteousnes*', William Burton, for example, explains how justice 'is either distributive or corrective' and observes how the very word signifies 'truth it selfe, and faithfulnes in words and promises'.[30] At the same time, early modern thinkers mediated such appeals to this theoretical absolute by noting the contingencies of one's situational context. As Matthieu Coignet observes after explicitly invoking Aristotle's *Ethics*, wise laws 'regardeth things in particular, as they change, and attaineth to experience by exercise & time'.[31] Gabriel Harvey, likewise, notes how equity depends upon 'a respective valuation of persons' and requires the ruler 'to estimate and preferre his subjectes accordingly'.[32] Proportionality, at once an absolute value yet also dependent upon estimation, serves to protect and sustain the country as a whole.[33] As Richard Becon avers, 'a common-weale mightily corrupted [...] is squared and reformed onely by the rule and line of Justice which wee call distributive', a value essential for reforming 'the enormities and mischiefes' of the land.[34] Indeed, as Jacques Hurault explains while discussing equitable exchange, 'the body of a common-weale could not endure if every man should not succour one another by such interchange'.³⁵ Following Aristotle, early modern authors understood that finding the proper proportion, an absolute value intuited within specific contexts, remained essential for the very survival of the polity.

Deeply invested in Aristotle's detailed taxonomy of justice as a means for maintaining civic order, Shakespeare's contemporaries considered the ethical mean both an ontological reality, an absolute value to which one should aspire, and a value one must approximate, its precise point difficult to fully ascertain. When Samuel Brandon invokes 'The golden meane, which doth not swarve', his formulation carries a double meaning: the mean appears as a straight path (in contrast with, say, the erratic nature of wantonness) but also as one fixed in place.³⁶ The mean's fixity, its role as an absolute value central to good order, appears likewise in Thomas Gainford's claim that King James is 'Unto the golden Meane [. . .] *linked* fast', a connection with the '*constant* Truth' that provides such grounding for England that it appears among other nations as itself 'the golden meane twixt two extreames'.³⁷ Richard Brathwaite shares this notion of the mean's constancy, declaring he seeks for himself 'that *grounding* on a golden meane' that will help him 'attaine a glorious end'.³⁸ For all the ways the golden mean appears as a fixed point providing ontological ground for one's ethics, however, it also was understood as something of an approximation. Gervase Markham expresses just this notion of latitude, of the mean as something that admits a range of action, when he declares 'Thrice happie [are] they that *in* a meane do *move*, / That golden meane which makes all creatures blest.'³⁹ Indeed, as Thomas Morton notes while discussing 'the mediocrity [by which] the extreames may be knowen', even defining the 'extreames' with precision can prove challenging. 'It is hard to give any real example of it,' concedes Morton, 'because the nature of man being in continuall motion, is alwaies either under or above, this state of sinfulnesse.'[40] As a point between extremes at which one could aim, the mean frequently seemed an intuitive concept, a range of theoretically appropriate behaviour, known when seen but only seen within a given context.

Taking Aristotle's formulation of virtue seriously, then, many early modern authors expressed deep concern at the prospect rampant immoderation could entirely eclipse – in essence, abolish – the very marker by which such behaviour could even register as 'immoderate' in the first place. Richard Brathwaite conveys something of this sense when he complains about those who 'exceed or come short of [the] meane' and then 'square and hammer it till it be reduced to a proposed meane' only.[41] For most, though, the threat to the ethical mean as a useful marker of virtue derived from persistent and intense wantonness. For what if such debasement were to become widespread? Always under siege, the mean seemed perpetually vulnerable to encroaching extremes. Josuah Sylvester observes, for example, how the 'Golden Mean can hardly stand / Betwixt these Two Extreames, vpright',[42] while John Phillips, amid a litany of his countrymen's vices in *A sommon to repentance* (1584), likewise declares that the 'golden meane is utterlie vanquished'.[43] Such pervasive immoderation, however, does more than simply make the mean illegible; it also threatens to install evil in its very place. Lamenting 'the filthy factions' who live 'without either meane or measure', for instance, Austin Saker argues that not only is 'the goulden meane [. . .] quite rejected' but also the ethical space reserved between two extremes is wholly lost, so that 'belike the Divell daunced just in the middle'.[44] As the era's commonplaces had it, '*Temperance* alone is the sustainer of civill quietnesse',[45] and such discourses invited consideration, then, of what would happen should immoderation become ubiquitous, overwhelming not just individuals but countries as well. What would happen to the ethical mean, that is, if, to use the language of *Titus Andronicus* itself, the polity became a 'wilderness of tigers?'

From Gratitude to Ingratitude: (Un)Settling the Mean in *Titus'* Rome

Shakespeare frames *Titus'* representation of civic piety – in language notably evocative of the *Ethics* – by raising the issue of the ethical life as distinguished by consistent virtue yet also shaped by the vicissitudes of circumstance. In doing so, he suggests that context influences ethical value. Shakespeare introduces the plight of the Andronici family by picturing Titus as a type of Priam, having lost his sons in battle on behalf of the state. 'Romans,' Titus intones, 'of five and twenty valiant sons, / Half of the number that King Priam had, / Behold the poor remains, alive and dead' (1.1.82–4).[46] Marcus assures his brother that these dead sons have 'aspired to Solon's happiness' (l.1.180), a reference to Solon's dictum that no man may be called happy until he is dead and finally beyond fortune's caprice. In the *Ethics*, Aristotle himself invokes Priam and Solon to frame his inquiry into what constitutes the virtuous life. Asking if happiness derives from being good or having good fortune, Aristotle emphasises the former but admits the possibility of the latter. He argues that

> there is required, as we said, not only complete virtue but also a complete life, since many changes occur in life, and all manner of chances, and the most prosperous may fall into great misfortunes in old age, as is told of Priam in the Trojan Cycle; and one who has experienced such chances and has ended wretchedly no one calls happy. Must no one at all, then, be called happy while he lives; must we, as Solon says, see the end?[47]

This tension between 'complete virtue' and a 'complete life' recurs in *Titus*, suggesting that context may indeed influence ethical value, that the measure of a person's life may derive from not only action but also situation and circumstance.

Shakespeare most saliently establishes the instability of the ethical mean endemic to Rome through the disputed election, an instance of distributive justice where political ideology defines merit, and where self-interest – except in the notable case of Titus himself – defines political ideology.[48] In the clamorous contest for 'rule and empery' (1.1.19), each rival presumes a discernible point of equilibrium, locating that point, however, in his own understanding of merit. Thus, when Marcus entreats Bassianus and Saturninus to 'Plead your deserts in peace and humbleness' (l.1.48), each brother accepts the proposition, perceiving the election as a matter of equitable valuation. Bassianus, for example, agrees to 'Commit my cause in balance to be weighed' (l.1.58), while Saturninus, even in the syntax of his request, invites his auditors to weigh his merit as on a balance: 'Rome, be as just and gracious unto me / As I am confident and kind to thee' (1.1.63–4). The rivals employ rhetoric here that will be echoed in the play's repeated iterations of *suum cuique*. This rhetoric belies a fraught endeavour, however, for as Aristotle had observed, each individual defines merit differently and according to his own political ideology: 'democrats identify it with the status of freeman, supporters of oligarchy with wealth (or with noble birth), and supporters of aristocracy with excellence'.[49] Such formulations for designating merit may remain tenable within each political philosophy. Across ideological divides, however, merit becomes even more contested, since the political consensus needed to establish it breaks down.

Shakespeare's play reveals the indeterminacy of median value even further by receding yet another level, by blurring the political ideologies of the rival claimants. Saturninus, who will rule as absolute tyrant, employs language reminiscent of Aristotle's description of the 'supporters of oligarchy'; his is the argument of noble birth, more specifically, of primogeniture. Saturninus also emphasises whom he addresses. He first entreats the 'Noble patricians, patrons of my right' to 'Defend the justice of my cause in arms' (1.1.1–2) and then calls his 'followers' to 'plead my successive title' because 'I am his first-born son', urging them not to 'wrong mine age' (1.1.3–5, 8). Bassianus' counterargument, at first glance, suggests the Aristotelian 'supporters of aristocracy' who identify merit with 'excellence', for he bases his appeal on 'virtue', as well as 'justice, continence, and nobility' (1.1.14, 15). However, he concludes his speech by striking a distinctly democratic note. Bassianus, like those who 'identify [merit] with the status of freeman', blends the rhetoric of virtue and excellence into a democratic appeal, for he does not address the patricians specifically but tells the people, 'But let desert in pure election shine, / And, Romans, fight for freedom in your choice' (1.1.16–17). As the rivals adopt different ideologies in order to arrogate power, the variability within concepts of merit becomes amplified by the variability both of ostensibly homogeneous political ideology and, more broadly, of context.

Titus stands notably apart from this display of unrestrained self-aggrandisement, adapting instead to a radically altered political landscape – an open throne, immense popular support, weak rival candidates – by neither arrogating absolute power to himself nor shifting his political fealties for personal advantage. Bassianus had appealed to the Romans' 'freedom' and desire for 'pure election', invoking 'justice, continence, and nobility' as desirable attributes. In contrast, Marcus enters to announce that the people 'have by common voice' already 'in election for the Roman empery / Chosen Andronicus surnamèd Pius' (1.1.21–3), because 'a nobler man, a braver warrior, / Lives not this day within the city walls' (1.1.25–6). The reason for Titus' popular appeal quickly becomes clear in Marcus' first address to his brother:

> Titus Andronicus, the people of Rome,
> Whose friend in justice thou hast ever been,
> Send thee by me, their tribune and their trust,
> This palliament of white and spotless hue,
> And name thee in election for the empire. (1.1.182–6)

Positioning Titus as not only a friend to the people of Rome but also a friend *in justice*, Marcus describes Titus' popular support as deriving from two manifestations of the ethical mean in social action. Both justice and friendship, at their core, focus on equity and the mean; both require equanimity, a balance wrought by fair and mutual exchange. And here, it is justice – the quest for the equitable mean – that becomes the means for Titus' intimate affiliation with the people. Shakespeare underscores the sense of equivalence wrought here between soldier and populace by joining the two in a single verse line: 'Titus Andronicus, the people of Rome' (l.1.182). Paradoxically, this fundamental sense of equanimity leads to Titus receiving, yet rejecting, power. Having served for forty years as a soldier (l.1.196), he perceives political duty as beyond his capacity; he demurs and instead expresses loyalty to the emperor he has served by electing 'our emperor's eldest son' (l.1.227).

In the sacrifice of Alarbus, Titus also appears noble – although not entirely blameless – within the context of Aristotelian rectificatory justice, on account of his relative degree of mercy and, more particularly, by his privileging self-denial over full equanimity in a matter that concerns him personally. For in rectificatory justice, it will be recalled, 'the judge tries to equalize' the disproportion wrought when 'one has slain and the other been slain' and 'the suffering and action have been unequally distributed'.[50] Since Aristotle defined rectificatory justice as 'intermediate between loss and gain', one may reasonably wonder if Titus' wrongs, when weighed by an impartial judge, would warrant greater recompense than he himself exacts given that he kills only one of Tamora's sons rather than all. Titus has Alarbus killed for the Andronici '*brethren* slain', noting that 'religiously *they* ask a sacrifice', and Alarbus must die 'T' appease *their* groaning shadows that are gone'. Upon the sacrifice, Lucius remarks, 'Remaineth naught but to inter our *brethren*', and Titus makes his 'latest farewell to *their* souls' (1.1.126, 127, 129, 149, 152 [emphasis added]). If one pillar of Aristotelian rectificatory justice resides in the equalizing of injuries, one might plausibly find in Titus' sacrifice of Alarbus a measure of restraint, a notable refusal to demand even more when placed in the adjudicating role over a matter that touches him personally. With twenty-one sons killed in battle and the whole array of captured enemies before him – not just Alarbus, but Tamora, Demetrius, Chiron, and Aaron – Titus calculates his loss in a context that might very well allow a space between gain and loss that admits the taking of multiple lives.[51] Yet here, Titus denies his right and eschews full equity for a sacrifice of one. Such a reading of Titus' act as restrained, as a variation of mercy, makes Lavinia's unfortunate reference to her father while pleading with Tamora (Lavinia says, 'O, let me teach thee for my father's sake, / That gave thee life when well he might have slain thee' [2.3.158–9]) more understandable and, indeed, reasonable. Within the context of the animating ethos which seems to shape Titus' actions, she assumes him merciful and the piety of gratitude ordering Rome's earlier interaction as still potentially redeemable.[52]

While Titus' sense of equity and his gratitude to the state do not completely exonerate his moral failings, they do mitigate them, for he nobly – even if sometimes foolishly and myopically – seeks public order before self-gratification. Indeed, Titus is 'Pius' precisely because his civic selflessness, paradoxically, constitutes his identity. In killing Alarbus, as in killing Mutius and Lavinia, Titus evinces an often-overlooked selflessness. Although he remains personally involved in Alarbus' sacrifice, Titus identifies his dead sons by their civic roles – as 'brethren' rather than 'sons'. The distinction reminds us that Titus functions here not simply as a father but rather in a doubly official capacity – as returning general and potential emperor-elect.[53] This scene occurs between the people's selection of Titus and his final refusal of power, a placement that seems designed to highlight Titus' civic role. His slaying of Mutius, likewise, occurs only after his son draws his sword in the streets of Rome and publicly threatens his father, an affront to civic order and the filial gratitude that supports it. Even when Titus kills Lavinia, he recognises the deed as both an 'outrage' (5.3.52) that parallels Lavinia's '*stuprum*' (4.1.78) (the Latin means not simply 'rape' but 'outrage', as well) and as needing 'A reason mighty, strong, and effectual; / A pattern, precedent, and lively warrant / For me, most wretched, to perform the like' (5.3.43–5). Whatever the degree of Titus' moral failings, he tends to respond to disruption rather than to simply cause it; he errs on the side of keeping communal order and remains noticeably less inclined towards the self-gratifying, community-fracturing excesses exhibited by his enemies. Titus' piety, however imperfect, nonetheless notably privileges the ethos of gratitude over unrestrained self-interest.

The exchanges that accompany Titus' refusal of the empery and his transfer of power to Saturninus reveal that gratitude functions – although in a markedly variable, uncertain way – as a type of currency in *Titus Andronicus*.[54] Bassianus, for example, attempts to forestall Titus' selection of Saturninus by playing to gratitude, claiming that 'thanks to men / Of noble minds is honorable meed' (1.1.218–19). Although Titus chooses to reject Bassianus' claim, the fundamental premise that gratitude functions as mediating currency appears again just a moment later. The tribunes consent to Titus' impending choice 'To gratify the good Andronicus / And gratulate his safe return to Rome' (ll. 223–4). The repetition of 'gratify' and 'gratulate' identifies Titus' political capital as originating in a mutually understood ethos of reciprocity. The converse, of course, occurs throughout Saturninus' rule, as equitable exchange dissolves into ingratitude. As a result, Titus will send his arrows into Rome, declaring himself 'old Andronicus, / Shaken with sorrows in ungrateful Rome' (4.3.16–17), a sentiment Marcus echoes in 'Tak[ing] wreak on Rome for this ingratitude' (4.3.34). Likewise, when the First Goth bemoans Titus, 'Whose high exploits and honorable deeds / *Ingrateful* Rome *requites* with foul contempt' (5.1.11–12 [emphasis added]), he explicitly conflates unjust exchange (the requital of contempt for honor) with the abrogation of gratitude. If, as Aristotle had argued, 'it is by proportionate requital that the city holds together' and that grace 'promote[s] the requital of services', Rome disregards both the proportionate return found in justice in exchange and the gratitude needed for maintaining a priori terms for fair trade.

Saturninus' ascension to the throne brings the greatest test yet to Roman social cohesion. By dissolving the 'unit [. . .] fixed by agreement' (to use Aristotle's rhetoric of material and social currency) in favor of dissimulation,[55] the new emperor single-handedly resets the definition of the normative in Rome. Saturninus had used the rhetoric of gratitude when he requested that the people be 'just and gracious' to his claim (1.1.63), but a later invocation of gratitude suggests his faulty understanding of its importance. After receiving the crown, Saturninus directs his first words as emperor to Titus:

> Titus Andronicus, for thy favors done
> To us in our election this day,
> I give thee thanks in part of thy deserts,
> And will with deeds requite thy gentleness. (1.1.237–40)

Shakespeare has the emperor counterpoise 'I give thee thanks' against 'of thy deserts'. By doing so, Shakespeare underscores the limitations inherent in *how* the emperor perceives the deed of requital. In response to Titus' 'favors done', Saturninus will offer thanks 'in part' and then 'deeds' that will 'requite [. . .] gentleness'. Rather than the natural outgrowth of gratitude, Saturninus' promised deeds become an *addition* to his verbal display. He seems to conceptualise thanks and deeds as distinct entities, a rhetorical move suggesting that gratitude functions for Saturninus *only* on the level of language. Although he acknowledges the social function and centrality of gratitude, the new emperor's words here reflect a rejection of the economy of gratitude, which will become brutally apparent in successive scenes.

At first, Saturninus seems to participate in the ethos of gratitude by making Lavinia the second half of his promised requital to Titus ('And for an onset, Titus, to advance / Thy name and honorable family, / Lavinia will I make my empress' [1.1.241–3]), staking the people's fidelity to him upon this display of gratitude:

> Thanks, noble Titus, father of my life.
> How proud I am of thee and of thy gifts
> Rome shall record, and when I do forget
> The least of these unspeakable deserts,
> Romans, forget your fealty to me. (1.1.256–60)

Yet when Titus relinquishes Tamora, and Saturninus appropriates Tamora for himself, he unravels the bonds created by exchange among the Romans. For at the very moment Titus formally declares Tamora to be Saturninus' charge ('Now, madam, are you prisoner to an emperor' [l.1.261]), Saturninus voices interest in his new possession: 'A goodly lady, trust me, of the hue / That I would choose, were I to choose anew' (1.1.264–5). This exchange of Lavinia for Tamora not only breaks faith with Titus – if faith there ever was – but also leads to a public, material eschewing of traditionally ordered exchange itself when Saturninus declares 'Ransomless here we set our prisoners free' (l.1.277). Here, Saturninus' caprice (eschewing gratitude for disproportionate exchange), more than Titus' slaying of Alarbus (showing grace by disavowing full personal satisfaction), initiates chaos.

As the focus of Saturninus' whim, Tamora becomes emblematic of a new social order in which dissimulation, rather than common adherence to a fixed ethical value, mediates social commerce. Notably, the new empress immediately recognises the importance of masking disproportionate exchange by a false show of equivalency. For while Tamora affects a disinterest that would have equity for all, maintain the social mean, and continue the commerce of gratitude, she employs the rhetoric of Rome's civic piety – specifically, the language of gracious equity – simply to ensure her own tenuous hold on power. Claiming she must 'speak indifferently for all' (1.1.433), Tamora thus postures neutrality but also signals her method for navigating the court, for it is by 'speak[ing] indifferently' that Tamora survives: her apparent impartiality conceals and enacts the substitution of proportionate exchange for the disproportionate. Indeed, she explicitly articulates her strategy in these very terms, advising Saturninus to:

> Dissemble all your griefs and discontents [. . .]
> Lest, then, the people [. . .]
> Upon a just survey take Titus' part,
> And so supplant you for ingratitude. (1.1.446, 448–50)

Behind Tamora's rhetoric of moderation and impartial speech exists a systematic attempt to forestall and subvert a just appraisal via dissimulation. Eclipsed by the play's more graphic crimes, the emphasis here on dissembling in conjunction with ingratitude signals a fundamental shift away from communal grounding in the ethical mean and toward the introduction of inequality and disproportionate return within Rome.

If, as Aristotle noted, 'ready-wit' signals the constitution of one's fundamental ethos while dishonesty marks one as inequitable by nature,[56] Shakespeare heightens the villainy of 'high-witted Tamora' (4.4.35) by emphasising – of all things – lying. Tamora's ready-wit for lying reveals her character as fundamentally (not simply strategically) dishonest, a trait that undermines the idea of her complicity in Lavinia's rape and mutilation as a revenge, enacting proportion in her own right. At the beginning of the scene, Tamora is preoccupied not with thoughts of revenge for Alarbus but with desire for Aaron, until he informs her of the impending assault. Tamora's role in the prearranged plot consequently seems less like revenge and more like an occasion to employ her ready-wit. Tamora's elaborate fiction that Bassianus and Lavinia 'have ticed me hither to this place' in order to leave her to a 'miserable death' (2.3.92, 108) proves superfluous, a fabrication that aligns Tamora with Aristotle's blameworthy liar who deceives even 'where nothing is at stake'.[57] For neither expediency nor strategic calculation renders a fictitious reason necessary. At the very least, the idea that Lavinia's rape and Bassianus' murder occur as revenge for Alarbus begs the question of causality. Reading revenge here requires one to believe that Aaron, Demetrius and Chiron would have acted differently had Alarbus lived. Moreover, Tamora complies not only with Lavinia's rape but also with Bassianus' murder, although he played no part in Alarbus' slaying. Tamora's temporary claim to sympathy in the Alarbus scene derives from her (convincing) adoption of the language of equity, yet that claim is undercut by her subsequent villainies and her dubious connection to any consistent ethos of equity. Tamora's unbounded power in Rome, it seems, frees her not to revenge a son she hardly mentions but to practise her deceptive, self-gratifying ways without restraint.

Redefining Moderation in Extremity: Titus, Marcus and Consuming Sorrow

This relocation of moderation and extremity recontextualises Titus in a 'wilderness of tigers' (3.1.54), a new culture of extremes at once disorienting and devouring. Accordingly, Titus acclimates to his overwhelming sorrow and threatening environment by figuring both in terms of consumption. While Titus changes referents – at times grief threatens to swallow him, at others he absorbs sorrow to the point of overflowing – his metaphors always centre on consumption. Titus understands the extreme immoderation that surrounds him as consuming the innocent and recognises his radical recontextualisation as creating a dissolution of boundaries, between him and his grief and between him and the culture of extremes that caused it. Titus assumes that the world *must* consume something. He describes the earth as having a 'dry appetite' (3.1.14), pleads that his tears may 'staunch' it (3.1.14), begs the earth 'refuse to drink my dear sons' blood' (3.1.22), and describes Saturninus, Aaron and the Goths as devourers: 'How happy art thou then,' he wryly declares to Lucius, 'From these devourers to be banishèd!' (3.1.56–7). Fearlessly confronting his family's suffering, Titus responds to Marcus' warning 'I bring consuming sorrow to thine age' (3.1.61) with 'Will it consume me? let me see it then' (3.1.62). Unlike Hieronimo in *The Spanish Tragedy*, who seeks oblivion, Titus adapts by immersing himself in his grief.

Through their shifting use of vehicle and tenor, Titus' metaphors of consumption metonymically enact the tumbling inversion of fixed point and context characteristic of Saturninus' Rome. Shakespeare counterbalances Titus' express desire to be (further) consumed by Marcus' news with imagery of being filled to capacity. Thus, Titus flips the metaphor of consumption when he asks upon seeing his daughter:

> What fool hath added water to the sea
> Or brought a faggot to bright-burning Troy?
> My grief was at the height before thou cam'st
> And now like Nilus it disdaineth bounds. (3.1.68–71)

While here Titus' grief 'like Nilus [. . .] disdaineth bounds', a moment later he will be 'as one upon a rock' (3.1.93) and will act as one

> Environed with a wilderness of sea,
> Who marks the waxing tide grow wave by wave,
> Expecting ever when some envious surge
> Will in his brinish bowels swallow him. (3.1.94–7)

Titus' grief, like Nilus', absorbs to overflowing, yet Titus, isolated on a rock, confronts the raging sea *external* to him, the sea that threatens to take *him* into *it*. Throughout the third act, the rhetoric of excess as a flood continually changes so that, when comforting Lavinia, Titus imagines their cheeks likewise as both flooded and flooding: with 'miry slime left on them by the flood' yet also making 'a brine pit with our bitter tears' of the fountain below (3.1.126, 129). Titus, engulfed by his family's grief, perceives his experience as a personal dissolution into sorrow and the surrounding context, a context where meaningful ethical referents have themselves likewise dissolved.

As Titus merges with his grief, he acclimates wholly to his environment, and from the outset his reaction to the crimes against his family – for all its intensity – presents an almost organic sense of proportionality and an Aristotelian temperance of anger, preparing for his revenge to appear as a redefined moderation within extreme circumstances. Aristotle delineates two failings in respect to temper, two deviations from the mean: on one side, an excessive passivity that never rises to anger and, on the other, a rash disposition to seek revenge. Aristotle dismisses the former as a culpable 'unirascibility' and likens the latter to 'hasty servants who run out before they have heard the whole of what one says and then muddle the order', concluding that a rash disposition 'by reason of the warmth and hastiness of its nature [. . .] springs to take revenge'.[58] By contrast, 'the man who is angry at the right things and with the right people, and, further, as he ought, when he ought, and as long as he ought, is praised'.[59] While a 'good-tempered man' is 'thought to err rather in the direction of deficiency', and is 'not revengeful, but rather tends to make allowances', making too many such allowances is also morally culpable. For 'the deficiency, whether it is a sort of "unirascibility" or whatever it is, is blamed'.[60] Such people 'are thought to be fools' or 'thought not to feel things nor to be pained by them'.[61] Moreover, since such a man 'does not get angry, he is thought unlikely to defend himself', and he is inclined to being 'slavish'.[62] Thus, good temper neither hastens to revenge nor unthinkingly forbears. Indeed, Aristotle qualifies his earlier repudiation of revenge by appealing to circumstance and perception:

> the man who strays a little from the path, either towards the more or towards the less, is not blamed; since sometimes we praise those who exhibit the deficiency, and call them good-tempered, and sometimes we call angry people manly, as capable of ruling. How far, therefore, and how a man must stray before he becomes blameworthy, it is not easy to state in words; for the decision depends on the particular facts and on perception.[63]

Since 'it is not easy to define' this ethical mean or 'at what point right action ceases and wrong begins',[64] Aristotle opens a space for expressing anger under particular circumstances, speculating 'how far [. . .] and how a man must stray' before he is deemed immoderate.

Given Titus' emphasis on excess as a flood and his view of himself as a container that cannot contain, his deep sense of proportion is both remarkable and easy to overlook. Titus neither lacks irascibility nor rushes to revenge. Given his circumstances, Titus falls within the Aristotelian mean, for he eschews a 'slavish' passivity but also stands in stark contrast to the hasty servants who rashly run off. Instead, Titus deliberately and unflinchingly confronts his family's pain, slowing the dramatic pace and signalling his temperate anger. In fact, no movement towards revenge occurs until after Titus' lengthy ruminations. By the same token, Titus clearly remains affected by his family's woes, proves himself (if proof was needed) as capable of defending himself, and thereby avoids Aristotle's 'unirascibility'. By markedly slowing the dramatic action in the third act as Titus anguishes over his family's trauma, Shakespeare uses Titus' effusions of flooding and consumptive imagery, paradoxically, to signal the Roman's containment, preparing us to encounter his subsequent revenge as a type of moderation fashioned to meet extreme circumstances.[65]

Within this Aristotelian context of anger, Titus and Marcus contrast rather sharply, with Marcus – contrary to most critical valuations of him – appearing to be actually further from the mean than the intensely distraught Titus.[66] At first glance, this judgement may seem counterintuitive. Marcus, after all, fashions himself as Titus' moderator. When, for example, Titus tells Lavinia that 'with our sighs we'll breathe the welkin dim / And stain the sun with fog' (3.1.211–12), Marcus checks what he perceives as hyperbole, remonstrating, 'O brother, speak with possibility, / And do not break into these deep extremes' (3.1.214–15). Portraying Titus' speech as doubly excessive (as 'deep extremes') and unnatural (one that Titus must 'break into'), Marcus invites his brother to infuse his speech with realism, entreating Titus to 'let reason govern thy lament' (3.1.218). After Titus receives the heads of his two sons, Marcus yet again poses as moderating force, promising

> now no more will I control thy griefs:
> Rend off thy silver hair, thy other hand
> Gnawing with thy teeth; and be this dismal sight
> The closing up of our most wretched eyes. (3.1.259–62)

Even when he invites rage, Marcus remains a foil to Titus, who falls silent: 'Now is a time to storm; why art thou still?' (3.1.263). When Marcus regards outbursts as inappropriate, Titus rages; when he deems it 'time to storm', Titus subsides. Marcus understands Titus' subsequent laughter as impropriety, asking 'Why dost thou laugh? It fits not with this hour' (3.1.265). This contrast between the brothers functions as the one constant throughout the scene's many reversals, with Marcus always supposing himself the moderating influence.

But if, as I have suggested, Titus acts in accordance with the mean in respect to anger (even in his apparent extremes), then Marcus becomes something altogether different. And the moderation offered by Marcus is no moderation at all but rather the 'unirascibility' noted by Aristotle. For we may think of Titus and Marcus as polarities framing an indistinct mean. Marcus tries to dissuade Titus from emotional extremes, but Titus explicitly challenges his ostensibly moderate responses to the aggressions against them. Titus depicts his 'extremes' as the compassionate, reasonable response to his suffering child. He reasons as he rages:

> When heaven doth weep, doth not the earth o'erflow?
> If the winds rage, doth not the sea wax mad,
> Threatening the welkin with his big-swollen face?
> And wilt thou have a reason for this coil?
> I am the sea; hark how her sighs doth blow!
> She is the weeping welkin, I the earth:
> Then must my sea be movèd with her sighs,

> Then must my earth with her continual tears
> Become a deluge, overflowed and drowned,
> For why my bowels cannot hide her woes,
> But like a drunkard must I vomit them.
> Then give me leave; for losers will have leave
> To ease their stomachs with their bitter tongues.
>   (3.1.221–33)

Returning Marcus' appeal to 'reason' back onto itself, Titus points to Lavinia as 'reason for this coil', as she 'becomes an icon that justifies and excuses vengeance, a reminder of the Andronici's just title to their acts of retribution'.[67] Moreover, Titus claims that Lavinia makes his 'extremes' not only reasonable but necessary: 'Then *must* my sea be movèd with her sighs, / Then *must* my earth [. . .] / Become a deluge, overflowed and drowned.' Merging with his own grief, Titus has merged with his daughter's pain – her sighs, her tears, her woes. As Titus both consumes and is consumed by Lavinia's pain, he calls attention to his suffering daughter and suggests that Marcus' appeal to reason is a tepid response to present suffering. Marcus' initial response to Lavinia was to desire the identity of her attacker so that he might 'rail at him to ease my mind' (2.4.35). Titus, in contrast, renders a more appropriately intense response and moves towards something more reciprocal than a mere verbal thrashing conjoined with personal relief. Under the circumstances, Titus' response seems both proportionate and reasonable, especially compared to that of Marcus. Shakespeare does not offset a reasoning brother with a frenzied one. Rather, he gives us a father both reasoning and frenzied, an uncle rational yet soft-tempered.

Shakespeare has Marcus step aside to let his brother 'storm' only to have a clear-eyed, calm Titus then adopt the language of equilibrium, proportion and moderation even in his resolve to revenge. Immediately after receiving the heads of his two sons, Titus depicts revenge as a reinstitution of equilibrium, a direct response to the complete collapse of proportionate exchange in Rome.⁶⁸ His language distinctly invokes proportionality:

> For these two heads do seem to speak to me,
> And threat me I shall never come to bliss
> Till all these mischiefs be returned again
> Even in their throats that hath committed them. (3.1.271–4)

While the heads 'seem to speak', the move to return mischiefs 'even in their throats' represents, as Gillian Murray Kendall has shown, a shift 'back into the literal: we find later that it is literally in their throats that Titus finds his revenge – by slitting them'.⁶⁹ This shift into literalness occurs precisely because proportionate exchange requires a material, equivalent return. Visually enacting the emphasis on proportionality inherent in this language of reciprocity, Titus invites his family to adopt a physical stance mirroring his vow to revenge each injustice: 'You heavy people circle me about, / That I may turn me to each one of you / And swear unto my soul to right your wrongs' (3.1.276–8). Titus' rhetoric of righting the wrongs of his family channels his vengeful energies – just as he had directed his previous martial exploits – not simply into the service of his own interests but also of others.

Marcus' unirascibility in the context of such extreme brutality reveals a misguided understanding of balance that makes Titus keep his brother at a remove from his plans: ''Tis sure enough, an you knew how [. . .] / You are a young huntsman, Marcus; let alone' (4.1.95, 101). Marcus misreads this statement as acquiescence to fate, forgetting that Titus earlier vowed vengeance, and thinks Titus 'so just that he will not revenge' (4.1.128). Yet Titus may remain alert to Marcus' limitations as a revenger. For although Marcus vows to 'prosecute by good advice / Mortal revenge upon these traitorous Goths, / And see their blood or die with this reproach' (4.1.92–4), Shakespeare has subtly challenged Marcus' ability to muster the anger that it takes to do so. Upon finding

Lavinia wandering in the woods, Marcus had imagined producing only a verbal assault ('O that I knew thy heart, and knew the beast, / That I might rail at him to ease my mind!' [2.4.34–5]). Even here, Marcus' first response to knowing 'the beast[s]' is to exclaim that this knowledge is enough 'To stir a mutiny in the mildest thoughts / And arm the minds of infants to exclaims' (4.1.85–6). The chasm is wide and deep, however, between a mutiny of thoughts and exclamations and grinding a mother's sons into pudding. When Titus tells Marcus, the 'young huntsman' to 'let alone', he repudiates his brother's direct help but not, however, the hunt itself, as his move to revenge, imbued throughout with the sensibility of restoring a mean, takes shape as an explicit effort to restore equanimity and balance within the Roman polity.

Re-establishing Proportionate Return in Rome: Titus' Revenge as Moderation-in-Excess

Although Titus speaks of his hunt as righting others' wrongs, his revenge develops within this altered ethical economy as a type of justice in exchange rather than rectificatory justice – not as the equalisation of injuries mediated through law but as the extra-legal enactment of equivalent return. Rendering like for gruesome like, Titus not only now acts outside any official capacity, but he also seeks (can *only* seek) equivalent return. Aristotle notes that justice in exchange, or reciprocity, 'fits neither distributive nor rectificatory justice – yet people *want* even the justice of Rhadamanthus to mean this'.[70] 'In many cases', he continues, 'reciprocity and rectificatory justice are not in accord' such as when 'an official has inflicted a wound, he should not be wounded in return'.[71] Rectificatory justice, implemented by someone in a judicial capacity, may apply when Titus is the returning conqueror but clearly does not when he seeks to injure the royal family in return for his family's suffering. Moreover, while rectificatory justice functions on a mathematical proportion of *equal* return, justice in exchange relies on *equivalent* return. Since precisely equal return is quite impossible here,[72] Titus seeks equivalency, his revenge consequently adopting an aesthetic parallelism with the crimes against his family.

It may, indeed, seem radical to think that Titus' revenge, rather than functioning as mere lunacy wrought by extreme duress, is structured instead by the rational principles of Aristotelian exchange theory. But the correlation in both ancient and early modern discourse between justice in exchange and retribution – as well as Titus' own obvious investment in social contracts – prompts such a reading. As John Kerrigan notes, Aristotle recognised the affinities between justice in exchange and vengeance: 'The author of the *Metaphysics* was impressed by the teleology of revenge plots, by their eye-for-eye attentiveness to lucid causal relations, while the social analyst of the *Nicomachean Ethics* found in their mutual violence an instructive obverse to that principle of benign reciprocity which he recommends in his writings about friendship.'[73] Not merely a classical preoccupation, the notion that 'commutative justice also comprises and transcends the principle of revenge or simple reciprocity' appears in early modern representations of vengeance as well.[74] Since early modern revenge narratives 'transmitted *structurally* notions of justice that are to be found in the "theoretical" material of the time' – even in instances lacking 'conscious collusion between the literary and the moral'[75] – we have good cause, indeed, for thinking of justice in exchange as shaping the various forms of equivalent trade throughout the play. Moreover, since 'revenge tragedy [. . .] deals in a conventionalized way with basic issues which everyday experience, socio-legal practice, and ethical speculation have made relevant',[76] it makes sense that *Titus Andronicus*, as a play that 'repeatedly integrates contractual language with brutalized bodies',[77] would apply the prevailing constructs of Aristotelian exchange theory to its most violent acts. If Titus' brutal revenge – structured by a rational principle of social contract and functioning, thereby, as an altered form of justice in exchange – strikes us as intensely dissonant, the strangeness of the notion derives from the very distance between ourselves and a culture deeply rooted in Aristotelian ethical epistemology. The rather surprising substructure of moderation beneath the grotesque appearance of Titus' revenge, however, emerges throughout each stage of the play's denouement as Titus systematically repays, in kind, the pain inflicted upon the Andronici.

Notably, Titus exhibits his sense of equitability by creating proportionate exchange, an equivalent return, even in his method of vengeance, for since the crimes against his family take shape as, and during, a hunt, he likewise figures his revenge as hunting. This is a remarkably clever turn, for, as A. C. Hamilton has noted, the hunting of Lavinia itself occurs as an inversion. 'In the second act,' Hamilton explains, 'the formal hunt of the panther and the deer which celebrates the marriages is inverted: the black panther is Aaron who hunts the deer, Lavinia, and the marriage celebration ends with the death of the bridegroom and the rape and savage mutilation of the bride'.[78] When Titus tells Marcus to 'let alone', he employs the hunting trope to emphasise the importance of isolating Demetrius and Chiron:

> But if you hunt these bear whelps, then beware:
> The dam will wake, an if she wind ye once.
> She's with the lion deeply still in league,
> And lulls him whilst she playeth on her back,
> And when he sleeps will she do what she list. (4.1.96–100)

As Titus plans to isolate 'these bear whelps' from their 'dam', he inverts the mechanics of the play's most heinous crimes in order to create equivalency where he cannot obtain precise equality. Aaron had advised Tamora's sons to separate Lavinia from the other women in the woods, to 'single you thither then this dainty doe' (2.1.117), something Demetrius echoes to Chiron later: 'We hunt not, we, with horse nor hound, / But hope to pluck a dainty doe to ground' (2.2.25–6). Tamora, as yet unaware of the plot, also foreshadows 'a double hunt' (2.3.19), and Marcus relates his tragic discovery by explaining that he 'found her straying in the park, / Seeking to hide herself, as doth the deer / That hath received some unrecuring wound' (3.1.88–90). Creating an aesthetic proportion between shocking *scelus* and final retribution by transposing the roles of hunter and hunted in his revenge, Titus reveals again his characteristic sense of equity while also seeking to return his city to a space ordered by fair exchange.

Not only does Titus' revenge invert the strategic mechanism of dividing and conquering figured in the *scelus*, but it also reacts to the Goth family crimes by precisely inverting them. Where Demetrius and Chiron single out Lavinia from other Roman women and divide her (in multiple ways), Titus divides the two sons from their mother and, in a single paste, returns them to her. Titus, having the heads of his two sons, grinds the heads of Tamora's sons for her food. Titus confronts Demetrius and Chiron:

> Hark, villains, I will grind your bones to dust,
> And with your blood and it I'll make a paste,
> And of the paste a coffin I will rear,
> And make two pasties of your shameful heads,
> And bid that strumpet, your unhallowed dam,
> Like to the earth, swallow her own increase. (5.2.186–91)

By 'rear[ing]' a 'coffin' and entombing the sons in their 'unhallowed dam', Titus creates a sharp counterpoint to the interment of his own sons in the 'sacred receptacle' (1.1.95) of his 'father's reverend tomb' (2.3.296). Imagining his revenge as a pious rite, Titus inters Demetrius and Chiron in a manner befitting their lives, something Lucius also does to the bodies of Tamora and Aaron at the play's end. Moreover, where the tomb will close Titus' sons off to him forever, Tamora will forever have her sons too much with her.[79] Titus had planned to return 'these mischiefs [. . .] even in their throats that hath committed them', and he ensures that she swallows their remains. In this grotesque reshaping of Titus' piety, Shakespeare creates a type of proportion, an enactment of equivalent exchange, that retains the sense of equilibrium figured in the earlier Roman civic contract. In an ungrateful city, Titus reinstitutes proportionate return through revenge.

As Titus inverts the crimes against his family, the punishment of Aaron likewise takes on a sense of equivalent exchange, revealing the thoroughness of the Andronici's translated ethic of moderation and proportionate return. Aaron represents the most extreme inversion of traditional piety, but he also functions structurally to foreshadow (fittingly, in reverse) the justice about to be enacted by Titus. Before Titus' revenge, Publius commands of Tamora's sons, 'stop close their mouths, let them not speak a word' (5.2.164), a sentiment which Titus reiterates not once but twice ('sirs, stop their mouths, let them not speak to me' [5.2.167] and 'What would you say if I should let you speak? / Villains, for shame you could not beg for grace' [5.2.178–9]). This silencing of the victims mimics Tamora's 'I will not hear her speak, away with her!' (2.3.137) and forces the sons into the mute pleaders they themselves had made of Lavinia. But it also recalls the scene immediately prior where Lucius *invites* exposition from Aaron: 'say on, and if it please me which thou speak'st, / Thy child shall live', says Lucius (5.1.59–60), and he anticipates, again in relief, Tamora's demise. Whereas Tamora eats to the point of surfeit and Demetrius and Chiron speak no further words, Aaron, in his punishment, will consume nothing and yet speak fully. Shakespeare describes Aaron, like Tamora, as a 'ravenous tiger' (5.3.5), but he also depicts the Moor as a *producer* of evil, in addition to being a devourer of good. Thus, 'this execrable wretch' and 'breeder of these dire events' (5.3.177, 178) who loosed misery on the Andronici must himself waste in an earthy pit: 'set him breast-deep in earth, and famish him. / There let him stand and rave and cry for food' (5.3.179–80). Aaron, who operates largely uninhibited after Tamora's incorporation into Rome, must be 'fastened in the earth' (5.3.183). In contrast to Tamora, Aaron must consume nothing and instead be swallowed himself. At once ravenous and execrable, Aaron will starve even as he feeds the earth.

As the social order of Rome disintegrates with the dissolution of the equivalent exchange to be found in gratitude, the proportionate return figured in Titus' revenge, while gruesomely enacted, serves as a type of moderation in extreme circumstances and restores graciousness and equity to Rome.[80] The restoration of order, imbued with the language of proportionality and the mean, concludes with the contrast between Aaron's extreme impiety and Lucius' moderate – if to some problematic – valuation of events. Lucius' installation replaces the ingratitude that marred the play with a new antithesis, namely, 'Rome's gracious governor' (5.3.146). With the restoration of graciousness – a condition where, to recall Aristotle, people repay 'good for good [. . .] evil for evil' – Marcus invokes the rhetoric of proportion rendering 'tear for tear, and loving kiss for kiss' and even shapes the image of infinite grief into something mathematically reasonable, a ratio meet and proper to his debt: 'O, were the sum of these that I should pay / Countless and infinite, yet would I pay them' (5.3.156, 158–9). The return of an equitable society makes Marcus' speech appropriate to the circumstance. Lucius, proving himself the 'gracious governor', honours the dead emperor's status, orders him interred 'in his father's grave' by 'loving friends', but commands Tamora's body to be thrown 'forth to beasts and birds to prey' (5.3.191–2, 198). Recreating consumption of like by like, the new emperor enacts a just exchange by returning the brute-like to the brutes: 'her life was beastly and devoid of pity, / And being dead, let birds on her take pity!' (5.3.199–200). Interestingly, Lucius leaves this 'ravenous tiger' (5.3.195) to the beasts and birds of prey but only imagines the birds – not the beasts – as showing pity, underscoring that even the beastly consume their own in a type of fitting justice. With the return of a state characterised by gratitude, the traditional piety that dispatches Romans to family tombs and foreign barbarians to the wilds and the disinterested earth also returns.

Titus Andronicus prompts us to contemplate the moral ambiguities and the culpabilities distributed between Roman and Goth that permeate its central narrative. But the play's underlying Aristotelian framework also invites us to consider ethical value as not only variable but also discernible, if only faintly so, through its persistent appeal to equity. Shakespeare's play creates an enduring sense that equity does, in fact, exist – even if its precise location may be contested. For even during the cataclysmic shifts that unsettle Rome, gratitude consistently functions, whether positively in its application or negatively in its neglect, as the final standard for action, something which Romans and Goths alike acknowledge. The unethical extremes of Saturninus' Rome radically recontextualise Titus and create a milieu that requires a corrective response proportionate to the surrounding immoderation. Within its context and given its preoccupation with equity, Titus' revenge appears grotesque yet within the range of measured behaviour. Indeed, Titus' just response to Rome's excesses reveals that the ethical person must simultaneously identify and resist extremes in order to find the mean, even if following such behaviour might resonate as extreme under ordinary circumstances. The mean – as a site at once absolute and intuited, threatened yet defined by extremity – continually requires identification and revision. It requires, in short, a perpetual process of fixing moderation.

By establishing the ethical mean as central to his play, Shakespeare constructs an underlying framework that shapes the way his characters think and the terms upon which their exchanges take place. Since the mean represents an absolute value, it functions as an ontological ground for ethics; at the same time, the mean must also find expression in embodied action. As such, this classical doctrine traverses – in a manner not wholly dissimilar to that of the vegetative soul as seen in *The Spanish Tragedy* – the boundaries between immaterial concept and the materiality of lived experience. Understood variably as immaterial theory and material action, that is, the mean serves as the philosophical mechanism linking embodied experience to the conceptual structures undergirding the play. As Shakespeare invokes various manifestations of the ethical mean, he proceeds to depict Titus' revenge in those very terms, making the final retribution seem fitting, thereby, in yet another way, as consonant with how the very world, as understood by the characters themselves, should operate on its most rudimentary levels. For whether affirmed or circumvented, the ethical mean permeates the play, functioning as the standard in relation to which the characters must, by necessity, situate themselves. Through such a clever manipulation of Aristotelian ethical philosophy, Shakespeare's earliest revenge tragedy reveals once more not only the capacity of theatre, even at its most violent, to appropriate classical philosophy for radical, innovative ends but also the dramatist's ability to condition audience reception of retribution itself by constructing a subtle ontological framework within the fictive world of the theatre.

In *The Spanish Tragedy*, as we have seen, Thomas Kyd created an ontological framework for his play that served to situate Hieronimo's revenging action within the era's shared understanding of what the vegetative soul meant for embodied action. In this way, Kyd helped naturalise Hieronimo's revenge by tethering it into the most basic of organic impulses governing his playworld. Even though in *Titus Andronicus* Shakespeare likewise creates a comprehensive set of ontological assumptions in order to anchor his revenger's actions, Shakespeare does not so much depict Titus' retribution as an organic outgrowth, an instinctive expression, of one's natural disposition, a traversal between immaterial concept to embodied action rooted in the era's faculty psychology. Instead, he figures Titus' violent deeds as a kind of civic restoration that, rather than merely arbitrary or dependent upon pragmatic desires for a social contract, aligns with an ontologically-grounded value recognised by both Romans and Goths – even if, at key moments, in their abrogation of it – as indeed integral to the very mechanics governing their world. Where *The Spanish Tragedy* returns us to the indistinct dividing line between immaterial and material by repeatedly invoking the faculty of the immaterial soul responsible for all material reproduction and increase, *Titus Andronicus* does so by recalling the traversal between theoretical absolute value and embodied acts. Where the first adopts this strategy in order to figure revenge as an instinctive outgrowth, emerging, as it were, from the very building blocks of organic life, the second does so to depict retribution as a return to a sense of civic balance that begins in the abstract and notional, the intelligible, that is, but not, in its first order, materially sensible. Drawing on philosophies that especially concern their particular dramatic interests at the time – the preservation of households for *The Spanish Tragedy*, unifying civic order in *Titus Andronicus* – each writer appropriates ideas rooted in classical philosophy yet prominent across a wide array of popular discourses in their own day as well. In doing so, both Kyd and Shakespeare tellingly create atmospheres for their plays which, rather than remaining simply ornamental or evocative of indistinct moods, instead construct comprehensive philosophical systems which themselves work, in scenes both central and marginal, to condition reception of retribution as somehow apposite – on a deeply fundamental level – within the worlds created for the early modern popular stage.

Notes

1. 'Wooden Subjects', *New Literary History* 39.2 (2008): 277–300.
2. Frederick S. Boas, *Shakspere and His Predecessors* (London: John Murray, 1896), 138; Edward Ravenscroft, *Titus Andronicus, or The Rape of Lavinia* ... (1687), sig. A2ʳ; and T. S. Eliot, 'Seneca in Elizabethan Translation', in *Selected Essays 1917–1932* (London: Faber and Faber, 1932), 82.
3. David A. Lines, *Aristotle's 'Ethics' in the Italian Renaissance (ca. 1300–1650): The Universities and the Problem of Moral Education* (Leiden: Brill, 2002), 79.
4. Charles B. Schmitt, 'Aristotle's Ethics in the Sixteenth Century: Some Preliminary Considerations', in *The Aristotelian Tradition and Renaissance Universities* (1979; rpt. London: Variorum Reprints, 1984), 87–112 (nonsequential pagination), esp. 94.
5. Lines, *Aristotle's 'Ethics'*, 78.
6. Charles B. Schmitt, *John Case and Aristotelianism in Renaissance England* (Montreal: McGill-Queen's University Press, 1983), 26–7.
7. Schmitt, 'Aristotle's Ethics', 89–90.
8. John Wilkinson's 1549 edition, the first in English, was followed by several commentaries, including Samuel Heiland's in 1581 and John Case's *Speculum quaestionum* in 1585; see Schmitt, *John Case*, 23, 24.
9. '"Crack'd Crowns" and Counterfeit Sovereigns: The Crisis of Value in *1 Henry IV*', *Shakespeare Studies* 30 (2002): 138, 143 and 146.
10. *Sick Economies: Drama, Mercantilism, and Disease in Shakespeare's England* (Philadelphia: University of Pennsylvania Press, 2004), 93.
11. Ibid. 84–5.
12. Ibid. 85.
13. A. N. McLaren, *Political Culture in the Reign of Elizabeth I: Queen and Commonwealth 1558–1585* (Cambridge: Cambridge University Press, 1999), 230.
14. See Joshua Scodel, *Excess and the Mean in Early Modern English Literature* (Princeton: Princeton University Press, 2002), 1–11.

15. See Aristotle, 37–43 (2.6.–2.7). I follow *Aristotle: The Nicomachean Ethics*, trans. Sir David Ross, rev. J. L. Ackrill and J. O. Urmson (Oxford: Oxford University Press, 1984), cited by page number(s) and book and chapter number(s).
16. Sarah Broadie, *Ethics with Aristotle* (New York: Oxford University Press, 1991), 99.
17. On Aristotle's taxonomy of justice, see D. D. Raphael, *Concepts of Justice* (Oxford: Clarendon Press, 2001), 43–55.
18. Aristotle, 111 (5.2).
19. Ibid. 112 (5.3).
20. Ibid. 115 (5.4).
21. Ibid. 115 (5.4).
22. Ibid. 115 (5.4).
23. Ibid. 117 (5.4).
24. See Gabriel Danzig, 'The Political Character of Aristotelian Reciprocity', *Classical Philology* 95 (2000): 401 and Lindsay Judson, 'Aristotle on Fair Exchange', *Oxford Studies in Ancient Philosophy* 15 (1997): 147–75. On justice in exchange and early modern social contract, see Lynn Johnson, 'Friendship, Coercion, and Interest: Debating the Foundations of Justice in Early Modern England', *Journal of Early Modern History* 8 (2004): 46–64.
25. Aristotle, 117–18 (5.5).
26. Ibid. 118 (5.5).
27. Ibid. 118 (5.5).
28. On the era's concern with establishing proportional exchange, see Linda Woodbridge, *English Revenge Drama: Money, Resistance, Equality* (Cambridge: Cambridge University Press, 2010), 259–61.
29. London, 69, Iiijr.
30. William Burton, *Certaine questions and answeres, concerning the knowledge of God* (London: 1591), 56v.
31. *Politique discourses upon trueth and lying* (London, 1586), 34–5.
32. *Pierces supererogation or A new prayse of the old asse* (London, 1593), 94–5.

33. *Aristotles politiques* (1598) observes that 'Recompense, *or mutuall preferment equally bestowed, dooth preserue and defend Cities*' (69, Iiijr).
34. *Solon his follie, or a politique discourse* (London, 1594), 59, H2.
35. *Politicke, moral, and martial discourses* (London, 1595), 179.
36. *The tragicomoedi of the vertuous Octauia* (London, 1598), n.p.
37. *The vision and discourse of Henry the seuenth Concerning the vnitie of Great Brittaine* (London, 1610), 46.
38. *Essaies vpon the fiue senses with a pithie one vpon detraction* (London, 1620), 51.
39. *The famous whore, or noble curtizan conteining the lamentable complaint of Paulina, the famous Roman curtizan* (London, 1609), D2.
40. *A treatise of the threefolde state of man* (London, 1596), 358–9.
41. *The English gentleman* (London, 1630), 311.
42. *All the small vvorkes of that famous poet Iosuah Siluester gathered into one volume* (London, 1620), 276.
43. London, A.iii.,v.
44. *Narbonus The laberynth of libertie* (London, 1580), 23.
45. Brathwaite, *The English gentleman*, 313.
46. I follow the Pelican Shakespeare text of *Titus Andronicus*, ed. Russ McDonald (New York: Penguin, 2000).
47. Aristotle, 19 (1.9–1.10).
48. On the mixed ideologies and self-interest of the claimants compared to Titus' role as 'ethical icon', see Gail Kern Paster, *The Idea of the City in the Age of Shakespeare* (Athens: University of Georgia Press, 1985), 58–60.
49. Aristotle, 113 (5.3).
50. Ibid. 115 (5.4).
51. See Deborah Willis, '"The gnawing vulture": Revenge, Trauma Theory, and *Titus Andronicus*', *SQ* 53 (2002): 35–6. See also 'The Lamentable and Tragical History of *Titus Andronicus*' (ca. 1655–65) which alludes to 'the fall of his five and twenty Sons in the Wars of Goths' (reproduced in John Kerrigan, *Revenge Tragedy: Aeschylus to Armageddon* [Oxford: Clarendon Press, 1996], fig. 9).

52. On Alarbus' death as taking the place of 'a more bloody and wide-ranging retribution, expiating the debt owed by the Goths to the Roman dead while leaving Tamora's family injured but surviving', see Danielle A. St Hilaire, 'Allusion and Sacrifice in *Titus Andronicus*', *SEL Studies in English Literature 1500–1900* 49.2 (2009): 313.
53. Rectificatory justice 'can be manifested only by someone who is acting in a judicial or quasi-judicial capacity'; see J. O. Urmson, *Aristotle's Ethics* (Oxford: Basil Blackwell, 1988), 76.
54. On the breakdown of gratitude as 'integrating force' in *Titus*, see Euguene M. Waith, 'The Metamorphosis of Violence in *Titus Andronicus*', in *Titus Andronicus: Critical Essays*, ed. Philip C. Kolin (New York: Garland, 1995), 106.
55. Aristotle, 121 (5.5).
56. Ibid. 103 (4.8).
57. Ibid. 101 (4.7).
58. Ibid. 42 (2.7); 173 (7.6).
59. Ibid. 96 (4.5).
60. Ibid. 96–7 (4.5).
61. Ibid. 97 (4.5).
62. Ibid. 97 (4.5).
63. Ibid. 98 (4.5).
64. Ibid. 98 (4.5).
65. Urmson observes that 'the doctrine of the mean does not require the doctrine of moderation' (J. O. Urmson, 'Aristotle's Doctrine of the Mean',' in *Essays on Aristotle's Ethics*, ed. Amélie Rorty (Berkeley: University of California Press, 1980), 157–70.
66. On Marcus as a moderating force to Titus, see Francesca T. Royster, 'White-limed Walls: Whiteness and Gothic Extremism in Shakespeare's *Titus Andronicus*', *SQ* 51 (2000): 440.
67. Katherine A. Rowe, 'Dismembering and Forgetting in *Titus Andronicus*', *SQ* 45 (1994): 296.
68. On the breakdown of gift-exchange and political contract here, see Ibid. 293.
69. Gillian Murray Kendall, '"Lend Me Thy Hand": Metaphor and Mayhem in *Titus Andronicus*', *SQ* 40 (1989): 302.

70. Aristotle, 117 (5.5).
71. Ibid. 117 (5.5).
72. In addition to the other crimes against the Andronici, Lavinia's wound is 'unrecuring' (3.1.90): that is, both incurable and unique.
73. Kerrigan, *Revenge Tragedy*, 5.
74. Ullrich Langer, 'The Renaissance Novella as Justice', *Renaissance Quarterly* 52 (1999): 317.
75. Ibid. 339–40.
76. Ronald Broude, 'Revenge and Revenge Tragedy in Renaissance England', *Renaissance Quarterly* 28 (1975): 47.
77. Thomas P. Anderson, '"What is Written Shall Be Executed": "Nude Contracts" and "Lively Warrants" in *Titus Andronicus*', *Criticism* 45.3 (2003): 310.
78. '*Titus Andronicus*: The Form of Shakespearian Tragedy', *Shakespeare Quarterly* 14 (1963): 207.
79. On the affiliation of Lavinia's womb with the tomb and Tamora's stomach with Lavinia's womb, see Coppélia Kahn, *Roman Shakespeare: Warriors, Wounds, and Women* (London: Routledge, 1997), 52, 70.
80. See also Harry Keyishian, *The Shapes of Revenge: Victimization, Vengeance, and Vindictiveness in Shakespeare* (Atlantic Highlands, NJ: Humanities Press, 1995), 48.

CHAPTER 3

'A FINE PATE FULL OF FINE DIRT': HAMLET AMONG THE ATOMISTS

If the presence of comprehensive philosophical systems undergirding the brutal revenges of both *The Spanish Tragedy* and *Titus Andronicus* seems surprising, the idea that Shakespeare's *Hamlet* likewise constructs a cohesive ontological framework that serves to shape its narrative may, at first glance, seem so commonplace as to not warrant much notice at all. *The Spanish Tragedy* and *Titus Andronicus* have garnered praise for their undeniable theatrical appeal, but they have not been considered – beyond perhaps a general appreciation of their broad Senecanism – as especially invested in classical philosophy. *Hamlet*, by contrast, a play as much concerned with metaphysics as with 'carnal, bloody, and unnatural acts' (5.2.364), has enjoyed unique praise among revenge tragedies for both its performative force and its wide range of philosophical interests. In ways charted out in my introduction, however, Shakespeare's play has frequently been understood as treating the components of philosophising and revenging as largely in tension with each other, with the protagonist's ruminations appearing, more often than not, as an impediment to revenge or, at the very least, as an exceptionally consuming prelude to it. But if Hieronimo's revenge is of a piece with his earlier desires to grow and preserve his household and Titus' vengeance, a form of moderation-in-extremity, emerges from his pre-existing notions of a grounded ethical mean, might Hamlet's varied concerns likewise cohere more fully? Might his extended ruminations and sudden revenge appear similarly connected, that is, to a deeper network of ontological predicates, ones which subtly serve to align his deeds, as they did for Hieronimo and Titus, with the most rudimentary elements comprising the world he inhabits? In *The Spanish Tragedy* and *Titus Andronicus*, Kyd and Shakespeare situated their protagonists within worlds informed by philosophies particularly attentive to the imperceptible, immaterial realities undergirding embodied action, conditioning, in the process, perception of the retribution enacted on stage. Might we find such a clever and potent dramaturgical strategy at work in *Hamlet* as well, and, if so, what might that look like in a play where the chasm between immaterial and material – between, say, thought and action, spirit and embodied existence – has seemed rather pronounced indeed?

It's not especially startling to think of *Hamlet* as philosophical *per se*, but recalling the ways other revenge drama tends to anchor retribution into ontological ground which reaches back even to the imperceptible and immaterial invites us to reconsider many of our default perceptions regarding the composition of the world – and the brooding protagonist's disposition toward it – in Shakespeare's most famous play. For a protagonist concerned with the advancement of his household, Kyd drew on the Aristotelian faculty psychology underwriting the era's discourses of *oeconomia*. For the eponymous hero of his earliest revenge tragedy, preoccupied with balance and civic order, Shakespeare tapped into his culture's shared understandings of the ethical mean. In each of these instances, the playwright marshalled philosophical concepts, rooted in classical culture yet current in myriad ways within his own, which evoked, each in its distinct way, the traversal between imperceptible ontological concept and embodied social action. Just as importantly, the concepts appropriated for these plays suited the dramaturgical needs of each author, coinciding with the plays' central concerns while also exerting their own force, giving form and nuance to the process of retribution in its unfolding. In *Hamlet*, Shakespeare gives us a protagonist beset with apparently conflicted impulses as he yearns to escape his own painful memories even as he obsessively holds on to the dead – for him as much a question of tracing the decaying body as mourning the departed spirit – while he, moreover, plots a revenge designed to set right the legacy of his recently departed father. Preoccupied with a unique constellation of concerns that centres on what happens when the impressions made by the living start to fade into oblivion – when, that is, the material immediacy of one's lived presence as registered in bodily form, memory and history starts to disappear – *Hamlet* employs a dramaturgical strategy akin to that found in its predecessors yet one that distinctly begins, remarkably enough, with the material itself, however attenuated it may be, in its drift toward apparent oblivion. In *Hamlet*, as we will see, Shakespeare gives shape to the prince's conflicted impulses and final revenge by infusing his world with a kind of materialist ontology, evident at every turn by the protagonist's frequently overlooked *delight* in a material world which retains for him, whatever its limitations, a measure of promise nonetheless.

Although Hamlet repeatedly returns to contemplating the physical composition of his surroundings with marked alacrity, the play's disposition toward materiality has persistently registered within literary criticism as rather monolithic, purportedly setting an intrinsically debased material world against a more desirable immaterial one. Whether pointing to the undiscovered country of the afterlife or to an imperceptible interiority within one's body, the play has seemed to depict a protagonist ill at ease with, even repulsed by, the physical world he inhabits. If our critical heritage has estranged philosophy and retribution in *Hamlet* in the ways outlined in the introductory chapter, critics have also perceived in the play, that is, a philosophical disposition towards materiality that has appeared overwhelmingly negative. In fact, Hamlet's ostensible disgust with matter and his distrust of external forms have become somewhat axiomatic, taken up throughout some of the finest contemporary readings of the play. Janet Adelman, for instance, argues that Hamlet's first 'soliloquy establishes the initial *premise of the play*' by depicting Hamlet as finding 'his own flesh as sullied and wish[ing] to free himself from its contamination by death'.[1] Hamlet, Adelman argues, perceives that 'in its grossness flesh was *always* rank, its solidness *always* sullied'.[2] What's more, if Hamlet has seemed inordinately preoccupied with matter as contaminated, so too has such matter seemed a source of epistemological confusion. Patricia Parker, for example, cites Hamlet's disgust with his mother's sexuality, noting that 'the matter of woman' functions 'as *lapsus*, error, detour, frailty',[3] while Margaret Ferguson likewise avers that 'matter [operates] as an obstacle to unity of opinion'.[4] In a similar fashion, Don Parry Norford asserts the play stages 'a breakdown of communication between the inner and outer worlds' and that 'the *very point of the play* seems to be that the phenomenal world lacks that stability that would make it "real"'.[5] Matter in *Hamlet* has often appeared, therefore, as *inevitably* and *invariably* debased, a corrupted substance both repulsive and deceptive by its very nature.

But is Hamlet's disgust with the material world so absolute? While Hamlet inveighs against the 'unweeded garden / That grows to seed' (1.2.135–6), for example, he depicts not matter but its employment as corrupted, complaining 'How weary, stale, flat, and unprofitable / Seem to me all the *uses* of this world' (1.2.133–4).[6] Hamlet's discontent with 'the uses of this world' suggests his disgust derives not from the garden itself but from how it is managed, from, that is, its very 'unweededness'. Moreover, he notably does not call nature, or the world, 'rank and gross' but rather observes that 'Things rank and gross in nature / Possess it merely' (1.2.136–7), a figure that expresses dissatisfaction with *those that are themselves* rank and gross in nature (that is, corrupt in their own right) that take over the world. Even if we take Hamlet's famous lament over his 'too too sallied flesh' (1.2.129) to mean 'sullied', as some editors have it (following neither the two quartos nor the Folio's 'solid'),[7] the prince's desire for his flesh to remain a type of definable materiality (to 'resolve itself into a dew') and his subsequent emphasis on the uses of the world suggests that he may think of 'sullied' as less a property of flesh and more a type of accretion, something obtained by one's commerce within an already-debased milieu. And, if the famous 'vicious mole of nature' (1.4.24) indeed indicates a corrupted materiality, a besetting original sin, Hamlet frames this image with marked qualification, stating that this 'chances in particular men' and even crafting the simile 'As in their birth, wherein they are not guilty, / Since nature cannot choose his origin' (1.4.23–6). 'The dram of evil' may well 'all the noble substance dout / To his own scandal', but this significantly depicts the 'dram of evil' simply as more *potent*, the 'substance' as 'noble', and this phenomenon – when it occurs – as occurring only in 'these men' (1.4.36–8). To the extent that *Hamlet* portrays a debased materiality, then, the emphasis remains that matter *can* be corrupted, not that it inherently is so.

In fact, *Hamlet* registers an abiding interest in not only matter but, more specifically, its smallest particulates, signalling thereby its subtle – and unexpected – investment in atomist thought, a materialist philosophy notably sanguine toward the physical world that posits indivisible motes compose everything in existence. Traditionally affiliated with atheism yet increasingly synthesised with theism by early modern authors, atomism provided novel ways of reimagining the composition of bodies and minds. Since atoms never disintegrate entirely, they offer the posthumous body a kind of continuing identity: constituent particles – like 'the noble dust of Alexander' (5.1.193–4) – remain inviolable and thus capable, at least in theory, of later reconstitution. Moreover, atomism figures perception, memory and even time itself as material phenomena, the effect of thin layers of atoms impressing the matter of the mind, a process that, quite literally, gives 'the very age and body of the time his form and pressure' (3.2.23–4). Both these aspects of atomist theory – the body as comprised of faint particulates, perception, memory and time as generated by a form of material imprinting – inform the course of Hamlet's revenge. If Hamlet's desire for dissolution and release from memory characterises his seeming delay, it also reveals his notable *un*willingness to dissociate fully from the material world, seeking as he does an ontological stability amid the dust. Likewise, since Hamlet understands time as material, collective memory as an accretion – as 'out of joint' (1.5.191) and able to 'soil our addition' (1.4.20) – he confronts a unique dilemma: how can he avenge the crimes against his father (something that necessitates recalling old Hamlet's vulnerability) yet preserve him in memory as integral? By invoking the 'incestuous, murd'rous' uncle (5.2.308) explicitly and the father thus only obliquely at the moment of revenge, Hamlet attempts to remould the court's collective memory, the most proximate record of historical time. In doing so, Hamlet's revenge, of a piece with his prior ways of conceptualising embodied existence and aligned with the subtle ontological assumptions permeating the play, functions as a kind of material accretion to the past, substantially recasting both murder and incestuous marriage as principally characterised by the devastation which awaits the villainous. In his brooding and revenge, Hamlet seeks comfort, then, in the prospect of an unblemished materiality but a comfort that remains theoretical and contingent, and the most intense poignancy of his tragic demise emerges precisely from this persistent refusal, even until his dying breath, to abandon the tantalising if elusive consolations proffered by the material world itself.

On Things and Nothings: Matter, Mind and Mortality in Atomist Philosophy

Although atomism's philosophy of matter accords well with *Hamlet*'s representation of the body as dust and of perception and memory as material imprints, atomism's affiliation with atheism and Epicureanism makes it seem an unlikely influence on a character who rails against Claudius' 'heavy-headed revel[s]' (1.4.17) and trusts a 'divinity that shapes our ends' (5.2.10). Yet the philosophy's multivalence invites such uneasy engagements; its reception in early modern Europe signals just such eclectic possibilities. First postulated by Leucippus, taken up by Democritus and Epicurus, and most fully articulated in Lucretius' *De rerum natura*, atomism posits that indivisible, microscopic particles compose everything in existence.[8] A theory of prime matter that argues all form and motion emerge from the rearrangement of imperceptible motes, atomism concomitantly presupposes the existence of the void, or vacuum, amid which such fine particles circulate. For the atomist, the conceptual category of *nothing* remains as crucial as the indestructible atom itself: the two, co-existing, comprise the entirety of the universe. Corollary to this materialist philosophy as articulated in the Lucretian model is the repudiation of divine influence. Indeed, Lucretius predicates his theory on the functional absence of the supernatural, declaring that 'our starting-point will be this principle: Nothing can ever be created by divine power out of nothing'.[9] The atomist maxim that 'out of nothing came nothing' not only obviates theistic belief, then, but also, in its materialist emphasis, articulates a doctrine incompatible with the creation of the world *ex nihilo*. Moreover, atomism's privileging of the material further aligns the philosophy with an Epicurean emphasis on sensory perception and pleasure, an affiliation that would ensure its scandalous reputation in some quarters of early modern English thought. A philosophy of matter intriguing in its account of form and motion yet disturbing in its metaphysical and ethical implications, atomism would become a contested quantity for many early modern authors.

If the range of responses to atomism during the sixteenth and early seventeenth centuries, as we will see in a moment, reveals a considerably more favourable response to atomism than existing historiographies tend to allow, atomism's surprising purchase with early modern audiences derives, in part, from its compelling explanatory power and, what's more, its reassuring sense of matter's indestructibility and capacity for recomposition after dissolution. Indeed, the intangible, imperceptible atom promises a remarkable sense of permanence amid impermanence. Figuring a world where solid mass resolves itself into other forms, Lucretius states that he 'will reveal those *atoms* from which nature creates all things and increases and feeds them and into which, when they perish, nature again resolves them' (28). While disavowing the supernatural in favor of a wholly materialist philosophy, Lucretius retains a type of eternal existence through matter that will never 'perish utterly'. Recognising that a reader might become 'mistrustful of my words because these atoms of mine are not visible to the eye' (35), Lucretius adduces wind and erosion as phenomena that signal the movement of imperceptible particles. Just as the observable world suggests the existence of atoms, for Lucretius, the *continuation* of this world points to their indivisibility. He reasons that 'the particles of matter in the course of ages would have been ground so small that nothing could be generated from them so as to attain in the fullness of time to the summit of its growth' (43). This prime matter, intuited by close parsing of the observable yet nonetheless ultimately indivisible in itself, consistently remains. Theorising a solid and resolvable materiality capable of reconstitution, Lucretian atomism asserts the perpetual presence of undying matter as a source of ontological stability, a grounding as it were, amid fluctuations in form.

Within atomist philosophy, these mobile, microscopic atoms give rise to perception by materially impressing the sensory organs, and, while such impressions can prompt false visions, atomists treat the senses as epistemologically reliable, locating instead errors of judgement in the mind's higher faculties. Indeed, Lucretius begins his analysis of perception with an immediate turn to phantoms, a prelude to his defence of the ultimate reliability of the senses:

> Now I will embark on an explanation of a highly relevant fact, the existence of what we call 'images' of things, a sort of outer skin perpetually peeled off the surface of objects and flying about this way and that through the air. It is these whose impact scares our minds, whether waking or sleeping, on those occasions when we catch a glimpse of strange shapes and phantoms of the dead. Often, when we are sunk in slumber, they startle us with the notion that spirits may get loose from Hades and ghosts hover about among the living, and that some part of us may survive after death when body and mind alike have been disintegrated and dissolved into their component atoms. (35, 43, 131)

As Lucretius posits the senses as epistemologically reliable, the supernatural as non-existent, he confronts a dilemma: how does one account for visions of ghosts? To safeguard his claim for perception as generated by 'an outer skin or film' emanating from objects (131), Lucretius returns repeatedly to the question of phantoms in order to draw a distinction between sensory stimuli and the interpretations applied to them. Describing the 'great many flimsy films from the surface of objects flying about [. . .] in all directions', Lucretius argues that these fine motes 'penetrate [. . .] the body and set in motion the delicate substance of the mind and there provoke sensation' (152–3). '[S]o it is,' Lucretius reasons, 'that we see the [. . .] phantoms of the dead whose bones lie in the embrace of earth' (153). For Lucretius, though, the fault lies not with impressions made by microscopic matter but with the interpretations humans apply to them. 'Here, as always,' Lucretius avers, 'we do not admit that the eyes are in any way deluded' for things perceived must be 'discerned by the reasoning power of the mind' (142). If interpretation errs, perception itself always remains true. 'What then,' Lucretius concludes, 'are we to pronounce more trustworthy than the senses?' (145).

The movement of atoms that comprises perception, moreover, gives rise to a very real type of material history in Lucretius, for what we think of as 'having happened' is actually an accident of the motion of atoms, a residual impression made by changes occurring in a particular locale or space. For Lucretius, 'accidents' denote 'things whose advent or departure leaves the essence of a thing intact', a concept that stands in opposition to 'properties', or characteristics that 'cannot be detached or separated from a thing without destroying it', such as weight to rocks or heat to fire (40). Lucretius argues that 'Time by itself does not exist; but from things themselves there results a sense of what has already taken place, what is now going on, and what is to ensue. It must not be claimed that anyone can sense time by itself apart from the movement of things or their restful immobility' (40–1). A function of atomic movement, time emerges quite literally from place, 'for we could put it that whatever has taken place is an accident of a particular tract of earth or of the space it occupied' (41). Since history and time exist as accidents of matter's motion, such conceptual categories enter into being as by-products of the microscopic. Within the framework of atomist thought, memory, history and time take on, then, a material character, shaped by the pressures of atomic motion and possessing in their way a physical form.

Atomic motion generates perception and even time and history themselves, but it also accounts for the soul's – and, more narrowly, the memory's – dissipation at death, a mortalism that promises release from painful remembrance while also yielding a type of material continuance through the indestructible particles comprising the body. Akin to water that 'flows [. . .] from a broken vessel,' the spirit, argues Lucretius, 'is similarly dispelled and vanishes' upon death, since the air, 'far more tenuous than our bodily frame' (112), cannot contain the soul's atoms. 'Mind,' Lucretius concludes, 'cannot exist apart from the body and from the man himself who is, as it were, a vessel for it' (112). Notably, Lucretius cites memory as both evidence for and source of consolation within such mortalism. Noting the absence of memory at birth, Lucretius first inquires why, 'if the spirit is by nature immortal', do humans 'retain no memory of an earlier existence, no impress of antecedent events' (116). Indeed, 'if the mind's operation is so greatly changed that all record of former actions has been expunged', he argues, 'it is no long journey [. . .] from this experience to annihilation' (116). Lucretius concludes that 'it follows that death is nothing to us and no concern of ours, since our tenure of the mind is mortal' (121). In fact, he argues, 'even if the matter that composes us should be reassembled by time after our death and brought back to its present state', such reconstitution 'would still be no concern of ours once the chain of our identity had been snapped. We who are now are not concerned with ourselves in any previous existence: the sufferings of those selves do not touch us' (121). Imagining atoms re-forming 'into the self-same combinations as now' – a theoretical possibility that early modern authors gave serious consideration as well – Lucretius reassures his readers that the 'mind cannot recall this [prior existence] to remembrance' (122). If atoms endure, the spirit – and all its attendant memory and suffering – does not. Admitting a type of materialist afterlife, classical atomism displaces a cognitive, spiritual one.

A School that Most Demonstrates Religion: Rethinking the Reception of Atomism in Early Modern Europe

For a long while, literary scholars and intellectual historians tended to think of the tenets of atomism as prominent in ancient philosophy, hidden 'beneath a veil of almost total obscurity' in medieval thought,[10] and revived in *late* seventeenth-century scientific circles, garnering sporadic attention in late sixteenth- and early seventeenth-century England principally through oppositional discourses focused on its reputed atheism.[11] As the recent work of David A. Hedrich Hirsch, Jonathan Gil Harris and Gerard Passannante has shown, this narrative can overstate the dormancy of atomism in Shakespeare's age,[12] but it also, as we will see, likewise overestimates the extensiveness of theistic objections to the philosophy's ostensible atheism. To be sure, the affiliation of atomism with atheism – by no means inconsequential – did affect the philosophy's reception within England, and this affiliation frequently occasioned comment within the variegated discourses of the period, sometimes to near exclusion of other issues. But even while atomism evoked in some circles the scandal of atheism, many early modern authors exhibit marked, if at times guarded, interest in the philosophy around the turn of the century, a crucial stage in the gradual sanitisation of atomist thought that further underscores its allure in England during Shakespeare's time. While, for example, Thomas Harriot, cautious amid charges of impiety made against him, avoids openly aligning himself with 'politically or theologically unorthodox' modes of thought such as atomism, he nonetheless more privately espouses 'the atomic philosophy in mathematics and physics'.[13] Other proponents of atomism such as Daniel Sennert and Nicholas Hill, on the other hand, maintain more visible affiliation with the philosophy in their attempts to synthesise its central tenets with Aristotelianism.[14] Notably, some prominent critics of atomism such as Robert Greville, Edward Herbert and Sir Kenelm Digby express, even in their refutations, interest in various underlying assumptions of atomist thought itself.[15] While Giodorno Bruno and 'almost all subsequent atomists' take care 'in one way or another to criticize the implausibility, explanatory poverty, and impiety of Greek atomism',[16] they do so while pursuing its theory of matter, their criticisms partly an attempt to render atomic thought more amenable to their own culture. Indeed, 'in the last decade of the sixteenth century [. . .] we find Democritean atomism all of a sudden held up as a powerful scientific model',[17] perhaps most prominently by Francis Bacon, 'one of the earliest in England to attempt to "purify" the atomic doctrine and make it acceptable as a natural philosophy'.[18] If the works of Robert Boyle, Pierre Gassendi and others integrate atomist philosophy with theism later in the seventeenth century,[19] such synthesis has roots – not fully appreciated in historiographies of the philosophy's reception in England – in many earlier works by Shakespeare's contemporaries.

Although some early modern authors thus contend, in one way or another, with atomism's traditional affiliations with atheist thought, others relate the philosophy's central ideas with a notable absence of negative critique and even, on occasion, exhibit a studied interest in the philosophy's intriguing components, most saliently its emphasis on infinitesimally small, mobile particulates. As early as 1579, for instance, George Puttenham's 'Partheniades' considers various theories of the world's creation, observing that:

> Some weene it must
> Come by recourse of praty moates,
> Farr finer then the smallest groates
> Of sand or dust
> That swarme in sonne,
> Clinginge as faste as little clotes
> Or burres uppon young children's cotes
> That slise and runne.[20]

For Puttenham, the 'praty moates' of atomism,[21] mobile and capable of reconfiguration, become imaginable – in a manner not unlike *Hamlet*'s later iterations of 'fine dirt' (5.1.101) – only through recourse to metaphor, as 'farr finer' than 'the smallest groates / Of sand or dust' and as 'little clotes / Or burres'. While Spenser incorporates (without qualitative judgement) a hymn to Venus drawn from Lucretius for *The Faerie Queene*, Puttenham's other contemporaries likewise tend to emphasise the microscopic and multitudinous nature of motes when alluding to atomism as well. In 'Elegie 13. Julia.', Donne likens disturbances of the mind to 'those atoms swarming in the sun', while the poet will describe his disordered private correspondence as arriving 'as Atomes' that nonetheless cohere to form a full body.[22] Most famously, in 'An Anatomy of the World, the First Anniversarie', Donne will declare how the world 'Is crumbled out againe t'his Atomis. / 'Tis all in pieces, all cohaerence gone'.[23] Even Ben Jonson – who mocked 'all those atomi ridiculous / Whereof old Democrite and Hill Nicholas / One said, the other swore, the world consists'[24] – owned and heavily annotated an edition of Lucretius' *De rerum natura* with approving marginalia.[25] Moreover, Shakespeare, who 'had access to Lucretius through Montaigne',[26] seems especially allured by the image of the microscopic atom. Mercutio figures the minuscule Queen Mab as 'drawn with a team of little atomies'; Celia avers, 'It is as easy to count atomies as to resolve the propositions of a lover'; and Phebe describes eyes as so fragile that they 'shut their coward gates on atomies'.[27] What's more, scholars have long noted the affinities between the Duke's reminder to Claudio in *Measure for Measure* that he 'exists on many a thousand grains / That issue out of dust' (3.1.20–1) and the central tenets of Lucretian atomism.[28]

Perhaps most remarkably, though, even within works predominantly sceptical or outright hostile to atomist thought, some early modern authors, evincing an eclecticism we will likewise see at work in *Hamlet*, open the possibility that atomism's materialist mechanics could prove compatible with theistic metaphysics. Sir John Davies' 'Orchestra' (1596), for instance, invokes atomism within a largely sceptical frame but quietly shifts its critique from repudiating the theory of atoms itself to taking issue with the underlying metaphysics such a theory has traditionally presupposed:

> Or if this (All) which round about we see
> (As idle Morpheus some sicke braines hath taught)
> Of undevided Motes compacted bee,
> How was this goodly Architecture wrought?
> Or by what meanes were they together brought?
> They erre that say they did concur by chaunce,
> Love made them meet in a well-ordered daunce.[29]

At first, it seems as though Davies will take issue with atomism's theory that the universe is 'Of undevided Motes compacted' since he figures the philosophy as the product of 'sicke braines' susceptible to 'idle Morpheus'. But his complaint lies less with the materialist underpinnings of the theory and more with the larger metaphysical issue centred on questions of causation. 'They erre', Davies concludes, not for saying the world consists of motes but for saying 'they did concur by chaunce'. In fact, Davies subtly and without explanation shifts into *accepting* the image of motes that 'meet in a well-ordered daunce' to compose the world we see. Still later, he will reiterate his emphasis on a director to atomic formation, noting 'so Loves smooth tongue, the motes such measure taught / That they joyn'd hands, and so the world was wrought'.³⁰ His objection, it would seem, lies not with the existence of motes but the underlying account of who or what brings those motes together – whether the world is governed by mere chance or by a personified Love that ultimately serves as the source of all order.

In a similar fashion, Josuah Sylvester's translation of Du Bartas' *Divine Weeks and Works* (1605) assumes an adversarial posture towards atomism yet nonetheless shifts into an altogether different mode, adopting without censure – indeed, apparently approvingly – an extended passage detailing atomist thought. Early in the work, the author describes God's instantaneous creation of matter *ex nihilo* and then seems to reject Democritean atomism outright, declaring:

> Once All was made; not by the hand of Fortune
> (As fond Democritus did yerst importune)
> With jarring Concords making Motes to meete,
> Invisible, immortal, infinite.³¹

Since Du Bartas depicts creation occurring at 'once' and counters the notion of matter as 'immortal' and 'infinite', he may seem thereby to reject atomism *in toto*. Yet elsewhere, Du Bartas remains intrigued by, even approving of, such a mechanistic physics, and the emphasis at the outset of his poem centres primarily on repudiating an atheistic claim, the notion that matter came into existence merely 'by the hand of Fortune'. Indeed, Du Bartas' poem later takes a decided turn in favour of atomist thought, exhibiting a disposition at odds with the work's larger protestations against atomist philosophy and its affiliated metaphysic. The translation runs thus:

> For All that's made, is made of the *First Matter*
> Which in th'old *Nothing* made the All-Creator.
> All that dissolves, resolves into the same.
> Since first the Lord of Nothing made this Frame,

> Nought's made of nought; and nothing turns to nothing:
> Thinges birth or death, change but their formall clothing:
> Their Formes doo vanish, but their bodies bide;
> Now thick, now thin, now round, now short, now side.[32]

Synthesising competing claims of the universe's underlying order,[33] Du Bartas notably affirms the atomist dictum that 'Nought's made of nought; and nothing turns to nothing' but does so by grounding such materialist claims in an otherwise orthodox theism: 'Nought's made of nought', he claims '*Since* first the Lord of Nothing made this frame'. Thus, once he's secured a *theoretical* place for creation *ex nihilo*, the author seems comfortable allowing for the dicta of atomist materialism to hold sway over the mechanics of the universe. What's more, by imagining that 'Forms do vanish, but their bodies bide', Du Bartas here posits a continuity of matter that, as we will see, finds expression among other early seventeenth-century Christian authors intrigued by the extended implications of Lucretius' theory of matter. The architecture of Du Bartas' claims reveals just how thinkable a theistic atomism became well before the late seventeenth century. For all their apprehension towards atomism, writers such as Davies and Du Bartas nonetheless tantalisingly hold out the possibility that objection to the philosophy should lie with the ideological uses to which it has been put rather than with the theory of motes itself.

While in the years immediately preceding Shakespeare's *Hamlet* Davis and Du Bartas incorporate atomist concepts impartially (perhaps even approvingly) within larger works ultimately arguing against the philosophy, other early modern authors position atomist materialism as consonant with a theistic metaphysic in more pronounced, definitive ways. Where Denis Lambin merely claims he can read 'good [. . .] Latin like Lucretius' without detriment to his piety,[34] Francis Bacon goes further still, arguing that, in fact, the divide between atomism and theism is really no divide at all:

> Nay, even that school, which is most accused of atheism, doth most demonstrate religion; that is, the school of Leucippus and Democritus and Epicurus. For it is a thousand times more credible, that four mutable elements, and one immutable fifth essence, duly and eternally placed, need no God, than that an army of infinite small portions or seeds unplaced, should have produced this order and beauty without a divine marshal.[35]

By arguing atomic complexity more requires a 'divine marshal' than mere elementalism would, Bacon valorises atomism by recourse to theism, a line of reasoning to which he regularly returns. In 'Coelum', for example, he asserts Democritus 'came somewhat nearer to the truth as declared in the divine narrative; for that represents matter without form as existing before the six days' works',[36] and, when contemplating 'the natural motion of the atom' in *De sapientia veterum*, argues atoms cohere because of the 'impulse of desire impressed by God upon the primary particles of matter'.[37] For Bacon, even the apparent randomness of atomic arrangements signals the presence of God and 'makes the supreme divine Providence all the more to be admired, as that which contrives out of subjects peculiarly empty and destitute of providence, and as it were blind, to educe by a fatal and necessary law all the order and beauty of the universe'.[38] When Thomas Browne argues in *Religio Medici* (1642) that the 'doctrine of *Epicurus*, that denied the providence of God, was no Atheism, but a magnificent and high-strained conceit of his Majesty',[39] he was participating in a project of recuperation and transformation of the classical atomists well under way as early as the late sixteenth and early seventeenth centuries. For well before Browne himself creates something out of nothing, spinning theism out of atheism, Bacon's recurrent claims about atomism reveal the era's capacity for reimagining such materialist mechanics as potentially compatible with theistic thought.

Early Modern Atomism, Theism and the Body's Reconstitution

Perceiving in the dust of the grave the microscopic atom, Shakespeare's contemporaries, in fact, frequently interpreted such fine particles as signifying divine providence, the indestructible mote as facilitating rather than obstructing religious meditation. In his elegy for Henry Frederick, for instance, John Taylor declares that the grave may momentarily 'keep [. . .] his dust' but 'must restore each Atom backe againe / When that day comes, that stands beyond all night'.[40] Robert Boyd's *A spirituall hymne or The sacrifice of a sinner* (1628) likewise finds the mote amid the body's dust and finds consolation that 'No Atome of thy scattered dust' will miss the final resurrection.[41] William Drummond's *Flowers of Sion* (1623), an extended meditation on death, depicts the body's atoms, reconstitutable in various forms, as specifically pointing to divine omniscience and care for the created order:

> This World is as a Cabinet to GOD, in which the small things (how ever to vs hidde and secret) are nothing lesse keeped, than the great [. . .] Not any Atome of the scattered Dust of mankind though daylie flowing under new Formes, is to Him unknown: and His Knowledge doth distinguish and discerne, what once His power shall waken and raise up. Why may not the Arts-master of the World, like a Molder, what he hath framed in diverse shapes, confound in one masse, and then severally fashion them out of the same?[. . .] And can not the Almightie raise and refine the bodie of Man, after never so many alterations on the Earth?[42]

While Drummond finds religious consolation in the indestructible, traceable and reconstitutable atom, this theoretical move represents neither a late development in Christian thought nor a heterodox divergence from it. For even Juan Luis Vives' translation of St Augustine's *City of God* (1610), asserts in a chapter on the 'buryall of the dead' that God 'knowes how to restore every *Atome* of his worke' and, later, argues for God's capacity 'to recollect and unite every *atome* of the bodie'.[43] For each of these authors, the fine particles of the grave's dust point to the atom; for each, the atom signifies the promise of divine providence and eventual restoration.

As atomism became more thinkable within a theistic frame, it also thus provoked closer scrutiny of the body's decomposition and resurrection, a line of inquiry most fully explored in the years surrounding *Hamlet* by John Donne whose work, alternating between disgust and exhilaration, frequently depicts dust as signifying the even smaller, imperceptible particles which comprise the body. Throughout his writings, Donne exhibits keen interest in the immutable atom. 'The First Anniversary of the World' speaks of the world as 'crumbled [. . .] againe t'his Atomis' (ll. 212); 'The Exstasie' makes mention of 'th'Atomies of which we grow' (ll. 45–8); and the 'Second Meditation' imagines that 'Man, who is the noblest part of the Earth, melts so away' that various forces 'not only melt him, but Calcine him, reduce him to Atomes, and to ashes'.[44] For Donne, the body that melts, thaws and resolves itself into atoms and ash, however, invites even closer inquiry, a prospect at once disturbing yet exciting. Donne more fully takes up this dialectic in a sermon preached at Lincoln's Inn:

> Painters have presented to us with some horror, the sceleton, the frame of the bones of a mans body; but the state of a body, in the dissoluation of the grave, no pencil can present to us. Between that excrementall jelly that thy body is made of at first, and that jelly which thy body dissolves to at last; there is not so noysome, so putrid a thing in nature [. . .] Thy skinne, and thy body shall be ground away, trod away upon the ground. Aske where that iron is

> that is ground off of a knife, or axe; Aske that marble that is worn off of the threshold [. . .] and with that iron, and with that marble, thou mayst finde thy Fathers skinne, and body [. . .] The knife, the marble, the skinne, the body are ground away, trod away, they are destroy'd, who knows the revolutions of dust? Dust upon the Kings high-way, and dust upon the Kings grave, are both, or neither, Dust Royall, and may change places; who knows the revolutions of dust?[45]

If the 'dissoluation of the grave' that returns us to 'excrementall jelly' may horrify Donne, he contemplates at length the gradual wearing away of the body's constituent parts with no small amount of alacrity. Like iron 'ground off of a knife or axe' or 'marble that is worn off the threshold', so too 'thou mayst finde thy Fathers skinne, and body', Donne argues, trying to trace the segmented, particularised body in death to its imperceptible motes and noting the epistemological quandary they pose: 'who knows the revolutions of dust?' For Donne, and, as we will see, for Hamlet in the graveyard, horror gives way to fascinated speculation, and the decomposing body becomes not simply a site of revulsion but excited inquiry as well, a site that invites the speculator to consider what lay beyond the visible, palpable dust. Donne's excremental jelly and revolutions of dust, like the 'fine dirt' that fills a 'fine pate' (5.1.101), represent not the end of human dissolution but rather the last sensible state apprehensible to the human observer before passing into more microscopic decay.

If, as the body's finest particulates transition into a form unrecognisable as corporeal, the atom's *imperceptibility* frustrates Donne's desire to trace and know, its *immutability* enables him to maintain belief in the retention of a type of identity grounded in the material, a theoretical concept that renders atomist philosophy a surprising source of comfort when contemplating death.⁴⁶ For at what point does a particle cease to be a component piece of an individual? If never quite fully, as atomism might suggest, does a person perpetually remain on some level materially identifiable, even if only to God? The unchanging atoms of a person's body will resist detection by the human observer, but they will nonetheless always remain, in some measure, of that person. Contemplating the body worn down by trauma, time or disease, for instance, Donne inquires elsewhere:

> Where be all the splinters of that Bone, which a shot hath shivered and scattered in the Ayre? Where be *all the Atoms of that flesh*, which a Corrasive hath eat away, or a Consumption hath breath'd, and exhal'd away from our arms, and other Limbs? In what wrinkle, in what furrow, in what bowel of the earth, ly *all the graines of the ashes of a body* burnt a thousand years since? [...] What cohaerence, what sympathy, what dependence maintaines any relation, any correspondence, between that arm that was lost in Europe, and that legge that was lost in Afrique or Asia, scores of years between? One humour of our dead body produces worms, and those worms suck and exhaust all other humour, and then all dies, and all dries, and molders into dust, and that dust is blowen into the River, and that puddled water tumbled into the sea, and that ebs and flows in infinite revolutions, and still, still God knows in what Cabinet every seed-Pearle lies, in what part of the world *every graine of every mans dust lies* [...]⁴⁷

Splinters of bone, atoms of flesh, grains of the ashes of a body, limbs severed on different continents years apart – all become reduced to particles smaller than dust.⁴⁸ Yet all remain identifiable to God as nonetheless belonging to the original individual: for God still knows the location of 'every seed-Pearle', knows where 'every graine of every mans dust lies'. If the revolutions of dust lie beyond human comprehension, the circulation of atoms – and the identity of each – remains known to God. Indeed, in 'Obsequies to the Lord Harrington, Brother to the Countesse of Bedford' (1633), Donne imagines that even in cannibalism, an ultimate mingling of bodies, a perfect recomposition or resurrection remains possible because 'God knowes where every Atome lyes'.[49] For Donne, such atomisation poses emotional, theological and cognitive challenges, but it also becomes a site of intense interest and, rather surprisingly, even a strange and paradoxical form of comfort as well. For the dissolved body retains even in its smallest constituent parts some marker of original human identity, capable therefore of resurrection on the last day.[50]

The idea that the body's immutable atoms might retain some ontological connection to the identity of the deceased even provoked speculation whether a second self could emerge from the rearrangement of motes over time, a line of inquiry that reveals how thoroughly even sixteenth-century writers considered the implications of atomism for the posthumous body. In his commentary for his 1564 edition of *De rerum natura*, for instance, Denis Lambin considers the possibility, broached by Lucretius himself, of a second self born of reconstituted atoms:

> Anyone might ask, 'Can it be that another Me, made out of the same matter, existed many centuries ago, or may be born many centuries later?' Lucretius therefore replies that if we look back over the immense expanse of time past, and if we consider the many and multifarious movements of matter, it is not unbelievable that the basic elements of which any one man is made today were, long ago, placed in the same order as that in which they are assembled now, and will be assembled hereafter. However – even if you grant that – he denies below that the man who now is, the one that was, and the one that will be are the same, because there has been a rupture of life by death.[51]

Positing a concomitant retention and loss of identity, Lambin's gloss maintains the notion that matter may prove theoretically traceable while reconstituted into new forms but also affirms the difference between such forms caused through the 'rupture of life by death'. Notably, after all the requisite atomic perambulations, what ultimately drops away, what in the end disintegrates, however, are not the material markers of the original man but rather the troubles he encountered in his own time. For Lambin observes that 'the calamities to befall that man made out of the same matter in the future would be nothing to the man who had lived before; neither would the misfortunes of him who had lived before pertain to him who, compounded of the same matter, was to live in the future'.[52] In his own copious marginalia in his edition of *De rerum natura*, Montaigne, in a similar fashion, remarks that 'since the movements of the atoms are varied, it is not unbelievable that atoms once came together – or will come together again in the future – so that another Montaigne be born'.[53] If not the atomic reconfiguration of Donne's resurrection, such ruminations nonetheless trace the revolutions of dust *forward*, finding in the rearrangements of atoms a comforting duality: namely, a release from temporary calamity and a type of continued identity, even if only at the level of the microscopic. Whatever the precise form of emotional comfort or intellectual excitement drawn from atomist philosophy, thinkers such as Donne, Lambin and Montaigne, among others, found the theory worthy of sustained consideration, frequently contemplating in the process the implications immutable motes have for both the mind and posthumous identity.

Hamlet among the Atomists

The gradual separation of atomism's materialist predicates from Epicurean ethics and atheist metaphysics makes more plausible the philosophy's connection to *Hamlet*, but the play's repeated focus on fine dust, posthumous bodies capable of re-formation, conceptual nothings and the materiality of senses and even memory all bring to the fore atomist thought as a crucial context for understanding Shakespeare's Denmark. To be sure, atomism appears as neither prevailing nor unalloyed framework for the play. Yet the particular constellation of concerns shared by play and philosophy remain striking. Hamlet famously broods on his 'noble father in the dust' (1.2.71), desires his own dissolution 'into a dew' (1.2.130), considers the body as mere 'quintessence of dust' (2.2.278), as 'compounded [. . .] with dust, whereto "tis kin' (4.2.4), and, contemplating skulls in the graveyard, marvels at a 'fine pate full of fine dirt' (5.1.101). Imaginatively tracing 'the noble dust' of Alexander and Caesar (5.1.193), Hamlet also theorises an ultimately irreducible material identity, capable of reconstitution into new forms. Moreover, amid the many fine particulates of Hamlet's rhetoric, Shakespeare brings repeated iterations of nothingness. Insisting on a dialectic between 'thing' and 'nothing', virtually everything in *Hamlet* offers itself as an admixture of what is and what is not, of materiality and immateriality. As Amy Cook succinctly notes, 'In *Hamlet*, few things are as powerful as nothing [. . .] Nothing comes up thirty times in *Hamlet*. The presence of nothing in the text calls attention to the absence that nothing is supposed to stand for.'[54] As the fine dust of *Hamlet* circulates in a world acutely alert to conceptual nothings, Shakespeare likewise constructs a highly palpable world, one where even the failure of sight becomes indicative of 'eyes without feeling' (3.4.78). Shakespeare signals, in short, an investment in atomism that he invokes more explicitly in other contemporaneous drama: in Mercutio's ruminations on Queen Mab's team of 'atomies', Celia and Phebe's two references to 'atomies' in *As You Like It*, and the Duke's (likely) Lucretian allusions in *Measure for Measure*. All written near the time of *Hamlet*, such plays join the constellation of tropes within Shakespeare's most famous tragedy to suggest atomism as probable, even compelling, influence.

Indeed, despite its status as the era's most dominant mode of conceptualising physical materiality, Aristotelian hylomorphism would seem to hold less purchase on many of the ways *Hamlet* figures matter, particularly corporeal matter, than what we find in the period's theistically inflected atomism. Although modern scholarship has contested whether Aristotle himself actually subscribed to a notion of prime matter,[55] Shakespeare's contemporaries inherited an Aristotelian tradition that posited a substratum of durable matter, capable of changing into different forms. The play's representation of materiality frequently sits uneasily with the era's received Aristotelianism, however. For Aristotle, physical matter breaks down to the four elements, with prime matter subtending these, but this indeterminate matter frequently receives less pride of place than the elements themselves, remains infinitely divisible, and, in the case of substantial change, transforms from one instantiation to another only with a marked 'exchange of contraries'.[56] These features, not prevalent in *Hamlet* itself, may invite us to look elsewhere for understanding the play's materiality, but Aristotelianism's sense of material identity should give us even further pause. Aristotelian hylomorphism, as its name indicates, places considerable emphasis on form, the essence which defines a given entity, and, as 'things are defined by their functions',[57] in the case of substantial change, it would be curious to insist on describing a new entity (with its new form) by recourse to its previous instantiation. Indeed, even if one were so inclined, doing so would predominantly serve to reveal discontinuities, rather than a sense of persistent identity, between instantiations. What's more, Aristotle, inclined to figuring bodies as breaking down into elements, differentiates homogeneous and heterogeneous parts – the latter conveying function and identified with the body, the former, though composing the latter, strikingly not – and tends to separate the substratum of corporeal parts from individual identity itself.[58] The Renaissance was highly syncretic, the theatre inveterately eclectic, and to recuperate atomist influence on *Hamlet* is not to affirm the wholesale absence of Aristotelian resonances. But close inspection suggests the revived atomism of Shakespeare's day as markedly more consonant with the particularised material world as represented throughout the play than the indeterminate prime matter proffered by the era's Aristotelian tradition.

Informed by early modern adaptations of atomist thought, *Hamlet*, as we will see, depicts the world as composed of fine particles, perception and memory as generated by material force or the pressure of physical events upon the mind, and this mode of thinking infuses the play with a species of materialist ontology that will subtly, though unmistakably, shape the course of Hamlet's revenge. Indeed, Hamlet approaches the task of revenge in ways that have registered as contradictory yet that emerge, in fact, from shared assumptions about the nature of matter and the mind's operations. Seeking release from his own pain yet immediately called upon to remember and avenge his father, Hamlet will both desire his own corporeal dissolution and elaborately plan his retribution. While these two endeavours have seemed inherently incompatible – ostensibly alternating between dithering rumination and active vengeance – both reveal Hamlet's remarkably deep connection to and investment in the material world. Yearning for death, Hamlet will express his desire for release from painful memory by imagining dissolution into an imperturbable substance, safe from the vicissitudes of life; in doing so, he will notably figure the body as particularised and memory as materially contingent, as palpably shaped by the physical force of lived experience. In his revenge, Hamlet will likewise seek to undo – and, in this case, recast – the material contours that give rise to memory and even history in order to secure the identities, and thus legacies, of his father and uncle. In both rumination and revenge, that is, Hamlet will imagine manipulating the material foundations of memory, the pressures of received events that imprint the mind, in order to remedy distressing or errant remembrances. Hamlet's brooding and his revenge, each in its own way, then, will prove deeply materialist. However fraught in their application, the materialist assumptions animating Hamlet's dual desires emerge from a set of atomist predicates unbound from their Epicurean and atheist affiliations, and, what's more, contribute to the play's broader representation of materiality as central to even the most ephemeral of phenomena.

But what of the ghost that opens the play, a ghost classical atomism would disallow except as mere hallucination yet Shakespeare figures as, potentially, a true supernatural phenomenon? If Hamlet's investment in theism and aversion to Epicureanism has tended to mask the play's atomist influences, the presence of the ghost, arguably a real supernatural visitation, would seem to establish a world wholly at odds with atomist thought. Yet the very eclecticism endemic to early modern engagements with atomist philosophy admits – indeed, as we have seen, insists upon – space for a spiritual world as real as the material one. Perhaps most remarkably, though, even the ghost that frames the play and sets the prevailing conditions within which Hamlet will seek his dual objectives signals, in multiple ways, the play's preoccupation with a type of materialist ontology attuned to the presence of fine particulates. For through the ghost – itself the most unlikely of vehicles for introducing a materialist strain informed by atomism – Shakespeare will establish a world where even the phantasmic becomes understood as wielding material force, perception and memory as emerging from the impress of fine matter on the mind. The ghost that will destabilise comfortable, perhaps rigid, schemes for conceptualising the world will direct attention, through its very ephemerality, to the faintest particles of matter and, through its inscrutability, the materiality and (paradoxically) reliability of the senses. Both the ghost's calls to 'remember' and Hamlet's fevered response, moreover, will figure remembrance, capable of erasure and reinscription, as quite literally grounded in the material. The ghost, that is, will help establish strains of materialist ontology especially invested in a particularised view of matter as central to the play.

Whether hallucination or true supernatural visitation – as classical atomists and their more eclectic early modern appropriators would, respectively, claim and allow – the ghost poses an epistemological quandary that gets worked out by its observers, especially Horatio, in strikingly materialist terms. Indeed, the ghost, much like the atom itself, stands on the extreme verge between material and immaterial, provoking and disturbing the imagination. 'A mote it is,' Horatio tells us, 'to trouble the mind's eye' (1.1.112). When Shakespeare's scholar figures the ghost as 'mote' – the preferred term for 'atom', as we have seen, in Davies, Sylvester, Puttenham and others – the play may not exactly instantiate atomism on stage, but neither does the phrase gesture towards the inscrutable or perplexing in a merely generalised way. 'Mote' nicely captures the ambiguous ontological status of a ghost that appears in 'variously real and unreal forms'.[59] The ghost's function as disruptive to the imagination has been taken as metaphor, but the very same linkage of sight with imagination via the materiality of a mote appears centrally in atomist thought. Lucretius, recall, accounts for what 'stimulates the imagination' by theorising a 'great many flimsy films' of atoms that 'penetrate [. . .] the body and set in motion the delicate substance of the mind and there provoke sensation' leading people to see 'phantoms of the dead whose bones lie in the embrace of earth'.⁶⁰ Even the imaginative functions of the mind remain susceptible here to the pressures or imprints of material force. The mote that troubles the mind's eye, whether in seemingly hallucinogenic events or externally real ones, quite literally impresses and disturbs the mind. If Horatio – unlike Lucretius yet akin to early modern commentators on atomism – allows for supernatural possibility, he notably shares with atomists of all stripes a mode of thinking about such visions in materialist terms. The ghost, existing on the cusp of materiality and immateriality, even with all its ethereal qualities, becomes understood in one way or the other as nonetheless phenomenologically real.

By depicting the ghost as admixture of corporeality and incorporeality, Shakespeare also locates in the apparition that opens the play the very duality of thing and nothing at the core of atomist thought and signals, in the process, that the point of contact (as it were) between material and immaterial will function centrally to the ontology of the play.⁶¹ Arriving on the ramparts, Horatio asks 'has this thing appeared again tonight', and when Barnardo responds, 'I have seen nothing' (1.1.21–2), the two foreshadow a crucial epistemological challenge posed by the ghost: how to account, in any meaningful way, for a 'thing' which is also 'nothing' or, conversely, a 'nothing' which assumes the properties of a 'thing'. As an 'apparition' (1.1.28), 'illusion' (1.1. 127), and 'spirit' (1.1.171), the ghost inexplicably phases from place to place (''Tis here. / 'Tis here. / 'Tis gone' (1.1.142–4)) and remains 'as the air invulnerable' (1.1.145). Yet it also exhibits a marked materiality. Visible, audible, able to hear and (apparently) smell (1.5.58), the ghost registers as 'something more than fantasy' (1.5.54), as a 'mote' (1.5.112), as 'truepenny' (1.5.153), as an 'old Mole' (1.5.165), and 'a worthy pioner' (1.5.166). It also palpably affects those on the ramparts. Horatio declares the ghost 'harrows' him (1.1.44), alluding to the 'harrow' used to 'stir the soil [. . .] or cover in the seed', an image itself of the forceful admittance of a fine particulate and literally meaning (*OED*) to 'lacerate or wound the feelings of; to vex, pain or distress greatly'. Concomitantly figured as material and immaterial, the mote-like ghost challenges the adequacy of existing taxonomies: 'In what particular thought to work,' Horatio confesses, 'I know not' (1.5.67). As Christopher Warley has argued, the fact that 'there is something more to this ghost than "air invulnerable"' destabilises 'Horatio's initial skepticism' as well as 'the religious awe of Marcellus'.[62] The indeterminate status of the ghost necessitates a new mode for synthesising otherwise incompatible philosophies. What's more, such persistent juxtaposition of thing and nothing as constitutive of a specific entity invites audiences to consider when the former ends and the latter begins, subtly drawing attention, that is, to the smallest particulate, the farthest most point of the material increasingly attenuated in its drift towards apparent nothingness.

Despite such inscrutability, however, the ghost's visitation likewise reveals a strand of materialist ontology operant in the play that emphasises the substantive nature and surprising reliability of the perceptive faculties.[63] The guards initially invite Horatio to observe 'this dreaded sight twice seen of us' that he 'may approve our eyes' (1.5.25, 29), and the scholar soon substantiates their visual witness, affirming, as well, the value of his own: 'Before my God, I might not this believe / Without the *sensible and true* avouch / Of mine own eyes' (1.5.56–8). The hendiadys 'sensible and true', as George T. Wright notes, affirms 'the sensorily accurate testimony of his eyes', but where Wright sees 'the two elements of the hendiadys' as 'grammatically [. . .] [but] not semantically parallel', they may, in fact, share a deeper link still. Since 'sensible' also signifies 'capable of feeling',[64] Horatio here signals an element of materiality to his sight: it is Horatio's sight, materially grounded, that registers as true. In this regard, the play's portrayal of vision shares affinities with atomist epistemology which figures the sensible as tantamount to true.⁶⁵ For Lucretius, remember, denies 'that the eyes are in any way deluded', proclaims nothing 'more trustworthy than the senses', and ascribes all errors instead to 'the reasoning power of the mind' (145). Notably lacking the post-visitation incredulity of, say, Banquo, who (with arguably less cause) wonders 'Were such things here as we do speak about' (1.3.83), Horatio confirms the guards' account, declaring 'each word made true and good' (1.2.210). The visitation on the ramparts will invite doubt regarding its import or significance but not, it would seem, its very presence or reality as a thing actually perceived. The ghost that palpably affects its witnesses reveals not only their investment in a type of materialist ontology but also how even the faintest instantiations of the physical carry a material force to them, influencing the senses and even the mind. For all that the ghost unsettles and disrupts, this troubling mote leaves intact a mode of thinking about substantial form that draws attention to the finest, most subtle expressions of materiality and figures the operations of the mind as susceptible to the imprints of material force.

Through the ghost's visitation, Shakespeare also signals how memory, figured as a type of material imprint on the mind, can be reinscribed with new signification by subsequent events, a process that can mitigate painful memory and alter the first register of recorded history. Immediately after the ghost's departure, Hamlet responds:

>   Remember thee?
> Yea, from the table of my memory
> I'll wipe away all trivial fond records,
> All saws of books, all forms, all pressures past,
> That youth and observation copied there,
> And thy commandment all alone shall live
> Within the book and volume of my brain,
> Unmixed with baser matter. (1.5.97–104)

While Hamlet articulates his vow to remember through tropes centred on early modern compositional practices, he also depicts remembrance, even more fundamentally, as material, its formation as a kind of physical impression, a manipulation even of matter's finest particles. By describing memory as recording 'all pressures past' – and, later, 'the very age and body of the time' as having 'form and pressure' (3.2.23–4) – Hamlet depicts the impress of material force as central to the formation of personal and collective history, something that emerges here in his tropes of erasure and reinscription. Whether reshaping the furrows of a wax tablet or clearing dust from a hornbook, Hamlet's image for forgetting entails manipulation of the finest gradations, contours, or granules that stand for memory.[66] Whether in forgetting or remembering, then, Hamlet conceives of memory's functions in evocatively materialist ways, and his desire to preserve his father's words as 'unmixed with baser matter' remains suggestive not only of writing kept apart, pristine, but also of the raw materials of lived history that impress the mind and generate memory in the first place. Hamlet's attempt to erase past memory and to perfectly preserve new ones will fail – at least in the absolutist terms he envisions here – but, however fraught his project, his preoccupation with the material contours of memory signals his interest in re-forming the very matter of thought, remembrance and history as a means of easing the pain of pressures past.

Hamlet and the (Fine) Matter of Remembrance: Reshaping the Material Contours of Memory

While the murder of his father and the ghost's visitation force Hamlet to re-evaluate his standing amid a corrupt court as well as his disposition towards the supernatural, Hamlet responds to trauma by focusing rather closely on the material afterlives of the dead: the continuation of the physical remains themselves and of the lost personality now materially inscribed in the memory of the living. For all the profound social, political and theological upheaval he faces, Hamlet confronts the radically reconfigured or destabilised networks of family, court and cosmos with a notable turn to the material and minute. Critics, of course, have long noted Hamlet's inward turn, his penchant for parsing thought and obsessively telling over of his own interiority, of 'that within which passes show' (1.2.85). But the disruptions caused by his personal circumstances also prompt Hamlet to meditate frequently on the nature of the material world and not simply with the sense of disgust that criticism has tended to amplify. Rather, Hamlet will find in the minutest structures and movements of the material a way of making sense of – in some cases, of remedying – the chaos surrounding him. For as he desires release from painful memory, he will find solace in the thought of dissolution into insentient particles, safe from the buffets of fortune; as he addresses the intemperate, untimely forgetfulness of others, Hamlet will focus on reminding those at court of his father's nobility and Claudius' inadequacy, acts he perceives as freshening the material inscriptions of memory from either unnatural erosions or deadening accretions. In all of this, Hamlet will exhibit a remarkable attachment to the physical world, finding both emotional comfort and intellectual stimulation in an ultimately durable though imperceptible materiality. While he will increasingly confront the inherent limitations of trying to maintain control over the matter of memory, Hamlet, throughout his travails, will process his perplexing milieu by reading it through the lens of a materialism consonant with his more religious sensibilities, finding in his various contemplations of the physical world a measure of solace.

Despite all the ghost's enjoinders to remember, Hamlet famously yearns for death to free him from memory and its attendant pains, but by repeatedly imagining such release in terms of corporeal dissolution into insentient parts, he displays an often overlooked *un*willingness to disassociate from a materiality in which he remains intellectually – and, to a striking degree, emotionally – invested. In his first soliloquy prior to the ghost's visitation, for instance, Hamlet broods:

> O that this too too sullied flesh would melt,
> Thaw, and resolve itself into a dew,
> Or that the Everlasting had not fixed
> His canon 'gainst self-slaughter. (1.2.129–32)

After articulating this desire to dissolve into a more rudimentary state of being, Hamlet details his woes, specifically his mother's remarriage, and plaintively asks, 'Must I remember?' (1.2.143), the desire to dissolve proving of a piece with his desire to forget. Most notably, however, Hamlet's fantasy of corporeal disintegration – not unlike Montaigne's or Lambin's – imagines escape not from materiality but rather a particular instantiation of it. For here, Hamlet tellingly *doesn't* posit an immaterial, interior self leaving the degradations of a tangible, material form; rather, he contemplates his current material form disintegrating, transmuting and recohering into a new and different one, the component parts still theoretically identifiable as ontologically linked with the original body. Hamlet desires to dissolve, that is, not into a purely spiritual state or simply into nothingness but rather into another state of material being, 'into a dew', *sans* memory. In this daydream, the insensibility of matter renders it more appealing, the material world becoming for Hamlet a site, therefore, of *desire*, a place which he doesn't so much wish to escape from as *return to*, unencumbered by the pangs of troubled memory.

Even after the ghost indicates sentience may well survive the body's death, Hamlet still longs to escape consciousness by returning to a merely material state, persisting throughout in setting the ostensible virtues of cognition against the insensibility of matter itself. While recounting his discontent with life to Rosencrantz and Guildenstern, for example, Hamlet muses:

> What a piece of work is a man, how noble in reason, how infinite in faculties, in form and moving how express and admirable, in action how like an angel, in apprehension how like a god: the beauty of the world, the paragon of animals! And yet to me what is this quintessence of dust? Man delights not me [. . .] (2.2.273–8)

By articulating his disillusionment with humanity by declaring it no better than dust, Hamlet may seem to depreciate the former by setting it against the insignificance of the latter. But Hamlet here simply critiques those qualities which arguably should render humanity as superior to insentient matter but fail to do so, providing no negative valuation of dust itself, a dust Hamlet elsewhere revisits with considerable alacrity. Indeed, in looking past humanity's ostensibly higher functions to instead contemplate the body's manifold components, Hamlet here directs his attention, in the end, towards insentient particles rather than the powers of cognition, something he will shortly echo in his most famous soliloquy contemplating suicide. Considering his own death and what it would mean to not 'be', Hamlet yearns for an 'end' to 'the heartache, and the thousand natural shocks that flesh is heir to', a transformation into insentience he describes as 'a consummation devoutly to be wished' (3.1.56, 62–4). Desiring, then, his own 'quietus' (3.1.75), Hamlet notably seeks divorce not from the material world but from consciousness. For amid these thoughts of release from suffering and a return to unfeeling matter, Hamlet remains unnerved only by the possibility of continued cognition, the thought of 'what dreams may come' (3.1.66), the 'dread of something after death'. (3.1.78). Hamlet's disgust with the uses of this world may well drive him towards imagining the end of self-consciousness, but it also prompts him to more closely consider insentient materiality as a source of intriguing possibility and even emotional comfort.

While the thought of such material transformations provides Hamlet a measure of comfort by promising freedom from painful recollection, the prince's understanding of a world comprised of fine particles also shapes how he makes sense of – and, as we will see, tries to remedy – the untimely forgetfulness of others. In the same opening soliloquy where Hamlet imagines his own dissolution into a dew as escape from his travails, he considers as well Gertrude's perplexing forgetfulness. Distraught, his syntax fractured, Hamlet considers his mother's hasty remarriage, complaining:

> and yet within a month –
> Let me not think on't; frailty thy name is woman –
> A little month, or ere those shoes were old
> With which she followed my poor father's body
> Like Niobe all tears, why she –
> O God, a beast that wants discourse of reason
> Would have mourned longer – married my uncle
> [. . .]
> Within a month,
> Ere yet the salt of most unrighteous tears
> Had left the flushing in her galled eyes,
> She married. O, most wicked speed [. . .]
>   (1.2.145–51, 153–6)

As Hamlet attempts here to process Gertrude's failure to remember her first husband, he marks the brevity of elapsed time between funeral and remarriage by returning to curious, seemingly disjointed images – Gertrude's shoes, her tears – from the funeral procession itself. Yet, in a world where minute particles circulate, their movement generating a sense of memory and even time, Hamlet calls attention through these tropes to both the short temporal span and his mother's untimely amnesia by specifically noting how little material movement has occurred. Gertrude's footwear, unlike Donne's axe or threshold, exhibits no sign of wear, no sloughing off of fine particulates; the grains of salt, in similar fashion, still reside in her once-tearful eyes. Since Hamlet reads memory as material, oblivion as the distant promise of bodily decay, Gertrude's forgetfulness registers as all the more unnatural, outpacing as it does the natural erosions wrought by time.[67] For in so short a span what could possibly have displaced Hamlet's father from her mind with such celerity? 'Let me not think on it,' demurs the son. Seeking to understand Gertrude's failure to remember her first husband, Hamlet perceives such entrenched and seemingly purposeful forgetfulness in materialist terms and, called himself to remember and revenge, determines to freshen the memories of his lost father as part of his larger project of retribution.

Perceiving memory as a type of material impression, Hamlet will in short order design *The Mousetrap*, integral to his revenge, not only to confirm the ghost's word and Claudius' guilt but also to reinscribe the court's memory of his father and imprint Claudius' villainy – otherwise characterised by the bounty it enabled – with the narrative of its own future demise. If time, for Hamlet, can be 'out of joint', something he must 'set [. . .] right' (1.5.191–2), the players offer a means for reshaping the contours of memory and history. As artisans finer than 'Nature's journeymen' reconstituting bodies on stage (3.2.32–4), they hold a 'mirror up to nature' and show 'the very age and body of the time his form and pressure' (3.2.22–4). In doing so, they also palpably affect the mind, striking some 'so to the soul' (2.2.530), making 'the galled jade wince' (3.2.238), even rendering the king a 'stricken deer' (3.2.266). Through such force, theatre can recreate past and present time, freshen the inscriptions of malformed or overwritten memory.[68] When even Hamlet fears himself misled, the victim of errant perception, he worries his imagination might be 'as foul / As Vulcan's stithy' (3.2.82–3), an image of sooty accretion, something he imagines theatre cleansing away. Theatre, however, can reshape as well as refresh. Framed with Hamlet's desire to sustain 'a great man's memory' (3.2.125–7), *The Mousetrap* will recall his father to those at court. Yet it will also refashion him as more prescient than the recent history of Denmark seems to warrant. For the Player King anticipates his queen's remarriage upon his death, positioning him as in command of his own narrative, of events otherwise beyond his control. As Hamlet recounts yet adjusts the history of his father, he, likewise, reveals Claudius' crimes and, by making Lucianus 'nephew to the king' (3.2.240), superimposes upon them his uncle's own impending punishment. *The Mousetrap* revives otherwise neglected memories, then, but also, through the interpolation of new material, subtly introduces new meaning as well, invigorating Hamlet through its success, however short-lived, in reshaping the material contours of memory and history to his desired ends.

In the aftermath of *The Mousetrap*, Shakespeare signals the futility of Hamlet's efforts to maintain the memory of his father in its proper contours, however, since new events and wilful resistance – both beyond Hamlet's control – perpetually reinscribe the past with variant meaning and, what's more, reveal his own claim to a pristinely preserved memory as itself contingent, open to challenge. Hamlet's play successfully forces Claudius to remember 'a brother's murder', but the king purposely overwrites such memories, focusing instead on 'those effects for which [he] did the murder', ensuring his 'thoughts remain below' (3.3.38, 54, 97). When Hamlet confronts Gertrude, he anticipates a similar resistance, fearing the 'penetrable stuff' of her heart has been deadened by accretion, that 'damned custom' has 'brazed it so / That it be proof and bulwark against sense' (3.4.36–8). Gertrude, however, presents a different, more deeply troubling problem than simply overwritten memory. For when the ghost confronts Hamlet to 'whet [his] almost blunted purpose' (3.4.111) – to file and reshape, that is, Hamlet's own malformed or distorted thoughts[69] – Gertrude uses her son's singular behaviour to also figure *his* mind as the one wrongly imprinted: 'This,' she tells him, 'is the very coinage of your brain' (3.4.137). If Gertrude's charge reveals the tenuousness of claims made upon another's mind, Hamlet simply casts her assertion as yet another accretion, a 'flattering unction' that will 'skin and film' the soul, allowing infection underneath (3.4.145, 147). Amid such redoubled emphasis on thought as material imprint susceptible to malformation, Hamlet's desire to manipulate the contours of memory becomes increasingly exposed as vulnerable to the vagaries of will, circumstance and even the counter charges of others.

The coincident death of Polonius and the anticipated decay of his corpse likewise reveal Hamlet's own memory as limited, as unable to maintain purchase on increasingly attenuated matter as it drifts into imperceptibility, a condition that prompts Hamlet's reliance on fictive contemplation – itself easily mistaken for true recollection – in order to make sense of corporeal dissolution. In this, ironically, the particularised body itself confounds the prince's reliance on the matter of memory as means for preserving, in its way, the deceased. Hamlet imagined his own decay as welcome escape from memory; the disintegration of another into dust, however, noticeably vexes the memory, perception and, indeed, epistemology of the prince. For when Hamlet leaves his mother's closet, his memory of Polonius remains fresh, the body increasingly less so. Hamlet initially marks this disconnect between the inert matter of Polonius' remains and the living person now only recorded in memory, morbidly jesting that 'this counselor / Is now most still, most secret, and most grave, / Who was in life a foolish prating knave' (3.4.213–15). But even while trying to contrast the living and dead manifestations of Polonius, Hamlet betrays a mode of comprehending the deceased in which lifeless matter becomes understood by a social function it no longer properly possesses. Indeed, having 'compounded' Polonius' body 'with dust whereto 'tis kin' (4.2.4), Hamlet even projects the defining features of Polonius, counsellor to the great, onto the catalyst for his own disintegration, rendering the worms consuming the corpse as 'politic' and joined about the body in 'convocation' (4.3.20). While recalling the grave's capacity to strip the dead of all markers of social distinction, this jest also makes more visible the tendency (latent but less obvious) in Hamlet's earlier depiction of the corpse as a still, secret and grave counsellor: namely, to read matter through a personality that no longer inheres, to *use*, that is, the materials of memory while engaging, in fact, in an act of imagination. However comforting when considered in relation to his own death, the gradual progression from animated person to increasingly sallow corpse, skeleton, dust and, presumably, beyond, poses an epistemic quandary, then, that the powers of neither memory nor perception can adequately address and that necessitate a turn to speculative rumination instead.

So why does Hamlet, his prevailing assumptions towards both memory and matter so potently challenged, persist in his desire to imprint other's memories, secure release from his own, and imaginatively trace the revolutions of corporeal matter in the dust? At the outset, such objectives seemed largely unproblematic. Positing a world comprised of fine particles in which memory and perception develop through material impression, Hamlet acts in a manner relatively straightforward. For in order to make others remember as part of his revenge, he must, through the sheer force of lived experience, imprint the minds of others with the narratives he wishes them to recall; conversely, if he himself were to dissolve into his constituent parts, he would forget, gaining thereby release from his present travails. In both revenge and rumination, then, Hamlet's particular materialist ontology governs his actions. But the resistance of memory towards permanent reinscription on the one hand and the decay of bodies into imperceptible, ultimately untraceable particulates on the other reveal how, respectively, the matter of memory and memory's detachability from matter complicate (even as they motivate) Hamlet's objectives. If Hamlet cannot fully secure the imprints of memory in others, neither can he definitively remember the body's particles. The selectivity and mutability of remembrance and the inevitable reliance on imagination in following corporeal decay to its end (Hamlet's main focus for the rest of the play) present Hamlet with a potentially impossible epistemological quandary, necessitating a distinct, undeniable turn to fiction, an *aporia* that would suggest the collapse of materialist ontology as a site for obtaining direction for one's actions and certainly for drawing comfort or meaning at all. What, therefore, keeps Hamlet so heavily invested in contemplating the role, effects and status of matter, however attenuated it may become?

Modest Speculation: Indestructibility, Ataraxia *and the Reconstitution of Indistinguishable Matter*

Hamlet's remarkably fideistic commitment to drawing meaning from the material world emerges, in part, from his figuration of matter's finest particulates as ultimately indestructible, a theory that allows for a type of perpetual material identity and that provides thereby a measure of comforting stability. The indestructible particulate, after all, provides the prince with something permanent and inviolable, an irreducible something that always remains capable of being remembered, even if not by his own mind and thus only theoretically.[70] After noting how 'the king is not with the body' but rather 'the king is a thing [. . .] of nothing' (4.2.24–7), Hamlet avers that, in death, both the 'fat king' and 'lean beggar' prove 'but variable service – two dishes, but to one table' (4.3.22–4), the grave consuming both status and flesh. But amid staples of *memento mori* convention – the body as dust, death as social leveller – Hamlet subtly theorises vestiges of identity as remaining, on some level, with the body's constituent parts themselves. For when Hamlet reasons that 'a man may fish with the worm that hath eat of a king, and eat of the fish that hath fed of that worm', and concludes, therefore, that 'a king may go a progress through the guts of a beggar' (4.3.26–30), he retains a fantasy of corporeal *in*destructibility, a *terminus ad quem* where disintegration stops and identity somehow remains. Sharing the Lucretian assumption that 'there is evidently a limit set to breaking' (43), Hamlet traces the dissolution of flesh, that is, to a discernible endpoint. Notably, then, king and beggar prove for Hamlet epistemologically but not ontologically indistinguishable. However decayed, even debased, however emblematic of death's capacity to obliterate, the particles consumed by the beggar still remain marked, in Hamlet's mind, as those of the king. Vexed yet ultimately undeterred by the epistemological frustrations posed by bodies crumbled again into their particulates, Hamlet confronts death's undeniable capacity to strip all accoutrements of rank yet concomitantly persists in ascribing continued identity to the grains of dust comprising the posthumous body. For all his morbidity and grim rumination, Hamlet exhibits an often overlooked desire to find comfort in the material world he so minutely, even caringly, observes and contemplates.

Hamlet's speculation that material identity may in fact remain within the ultimately irreducible particles of the body recurs in the graveyard, and as he constructs fictitious histories for the multiple disinterred skulls encountered there, he signals once more how corporeal decay facilitates, even as it would otherwise seem to undermine, his adherence to a type of materialist ontology comforting in its proffered stability. As skulls emerge from the grave, Hamlet imagines personal histories for each. 'This might be the pate of a politician' or perhaps 'a courtier', 'Lord Such-a-one', Hamlet muses about the first, while a second, he reflects, might 'be the skull of a lawyer' (5.1.73–9, 92–3). Hamlet wonders:

> Where be his quiddities now, his quillities, his cases, his tenures, and his tricks? [. . .] This fellow might be in's time a great buyer of land, with his statutes, his recognizances, his fines, his double vouchers, his recoveries. [Is this the fine of his fines, and the recovery of his recoveries,] to have his fine pate full of fine dirt? (5.1.92–101)

Most immediately, the scene recalls the oblivion of the grave, the stripping of all markers of social status. But if the skulls' capacity to serve as general signifiers, applicable to all, renders them efficacious for *memento mori* rumination, this also, paradoxically, underscores the *limits* of memory. For these skulls might belong to politicians, courtiers, or lawyers, but they, equally, might not. Hamlet persistently assumes, however, that a material identity remains amid the dust, even if tracing such identity becomes increasingly difficult, even impossible. Noting how one skull 'had a tongue in it and could sing once', describing another as 'chopless', Yorick as 'chopfallen' and 'grinning', Hamlet charts the gradual wearing away of the body to ever-attenuated forms (5.1.71–2, 83–4, 182). For death disintegrates the body over time, commingling the smallest instantiations of the corporeal with the dust of the grave, frustrating the mind's capacity to differentiate. 'Here's fine revolution, an we had the trick to see't' (5.1.85–6), Hamlet declares as the sexton's spade turns, drawn not only to death's social levelling once more but also the circulation of the body's matter amid the dust, an interest in the minute emblematised in the 'fine pate full of fine dirt'. In all of these ruminations, Hamlet sounds remarkably like Donne, who, as we have seen, considers 'the dissoluation of the grave', how 'the skinne, the body are ground away, trod away', wonders 'who knows the revolutions of dust', and, seeking to follow 'all the Atoms of that flesh' dissolved by death, reaffirms a material identity theoretically traceable, even if only by God. If Hamlet shares with Donne moments of revulsion and horror amid such ruminations, he likewise bristles with intellectual excitement and finds a measure of comfort in contemplating the ultimate durability of the body's smallest particulates.[71]

Part of the appeal of an indestructible materiality for Hamlet derives from the prospect that one's matter, if nothing else, may experience in dissolution the *ataraxia*, or freedom from suffering, so elusive in other registers. Throughout the graveyard scene, Hamlet repeatedly draws attention to instances of imperturbability, evincing a yearning, exhibited elsewhere as well, for a sense of tranquillity amid the macabre, chaotic, or disheartening. Upon encountering the sexton, Hamlet marvels, 'Has this fellow no feeling of his business? A sings in gravemaking' (5.1.61–2), a comment plausibly tinged with as much envy as distaste. In similar fashion, Hamlet perceives in the bones littering the stage an insensitivity, an imperviousness, that arguably appeals as much as the body's decay disturbs. 'How the knave jowls it to the ground,' Hamlet observes about one skull, noting how another is 'knocked about the mazard with a sexton's spade' (5.1.72, 84–5) and inquiring why a third, 'does [. . .] suffer this mad knave now to knock him about the sconce with a dirty shovel' (5.1.94–6). For all the debasement figured forth here, Hamlet finds in this battered, insentient matter the very feature he, elsewhere, most envies in Horatio, whom he describes as 'one, in suffering all, that suffers nothing, / A man that fortune's buffets and rewards / Hast ta'en with equal thanks [. . .]' (3.2.65–7). As shovel strikes bone, Hamlet marvels anew at imperturbability amid affronts to one's personhood. Earlier, as he desired release from 'the heartache and the thousand natural shocks that flesh is heir to' (3.1.62–3), Hamlet had wondered who would endure the 'proud man's contumely', the 'law's delay', and 'the spurns / That patient merit of th' unworthy takes', when he could effect his own 'quietus' (3.1.71–5); here, the skulls, indifferent to the gravedigger's blows, have no need to report 'his action of battery' (5.1.96–7). If death brings a decay distressing in its grotesqueness, it also renders the remaining corporeal matter immune to the insults and natural shocks registered by the living, an immunity that draws Hamlet towards, rather than simply repels him from, the putrefied body.

Consider, too, Hamlet's ruminations on Alexander and Caesar. Here, Hamlet not only gestures once more to the *ataraxia* inherent in and symbolised by insentient matter but also theorises more explicitly – in a manner not unlike that of Lambin, Montaigne and Donne, all following Lucretius – about the possible reconstitution of one's corporeal matter, still ontologically marked as such, into another form over time. 'Dost thou think Alexander looked o' this fashion i' th' earth?' (5.1.187–8), Hamlet, holding Yorick's skull, inquires of Horatio. Horatio's response, 'E'en so' (5.1.189), prompts an extended ratiocination on what becomes of the body's finest particulates amid the dissolution of the grave:

> *Hamlet*: To what base uses we may return, Horatio! Why may not imagination trace the noble dust of Alexander till a find it stopping a bunghole?
> *Horatio*: 'Twere to consider too curiously, to consider so.
> *Hamlet*: No, faith, not a jot, but to follow him thither with modesty enough, and likelihood to lead it. Alexander died,

> Alexander was buried, Alexander returneth to dust; the dust is earth; of earth we make loam; and why of that loam whereto he was converted might they not stop a beer barrel?
> Imperious Caesar, dead and turned to clay,
> Might stop a hole to keep the wind away.
> O, that that earth which kept the world in awe
> Should patch a wall t' expel the winter's flaw!
> (5.1.192–206)

As Hamlet imaginatively traces the dust of Alexander and Caesar, he once more presupposes a core unit of indestructible, unalterable materiality, figuring the finest particulates as *of* the original bodies still, whatever permutations they experience over time.[72] What's more, Hamlet figures such inviolable particles as both stolid amid flux and impervious to suffering; blocking draughts of fluid and cold air, they resist moisture ('a sore decayer of your whoreson dead body' [5.1.162]) and the ravages of 'wind' and 'winter's flaw' (5.1.204, 206). In noting how 'noble dust' can return to such 'base uses' Hamlet, to be sure, registers the ignominy of death, but as a man whose nobility constrains as much as liberates – 'his greatness weighed, his will is not his own' (1.3.17) – Hamlet may well find 'base uses' appealing in their own way. By imagining Alexander and Caesar as insensible objects, Hamlet draws a measure of comfort from – as Lambin has it drawing on Lucretius – the 'rupture of life by death' and the ensuing liberation such instantiations 'compounded of the same matter' experience from 'the calamities' and 'misfortunes' of their temporal counterparts.[73] More importantly, however, Hamlet also allows here the very possibility articulated by Lucretius and his early modern commentators, namely, that a reconstituted material identity, a second (or even restored, original) self may exist due to the fact that corporeal matter remains ontologically identifiable, as retaining in some measure, that is, its original identity.

While Hamlet has principally registered as disconsolate in the graveyard, resigned or fatalistic in his subsequent evocations of divine providence, the prince's atomist mode of conceptualising matter not only admits space for the divine but also seems to enable the fideism he signals by the play's end. For if Hamlet finds in matter a continued existence, freedom from pain, and an ontological stability not structurally dissimilar to those promised by conventional belief, neither do these obviate more orthodox theism. Hamlet, moreover, assumes a sense of teleological direction for even the most lowly things: the dust of kings and beggars will provide 'variable *service*' (4.3.23), while Alexander and Caesar, stopping barrels or patching walls, likewise retain purpose, however inconsequential. Just as Hamlet imagines a teleological end governing the circulation of fine dust amid the grave, his materialist assumptions, interestingly enough, also inform his understanding of divine providence itself. For even Hamlet's clearest articulation of theistic belief imagines God as manipulating the finest bits of matter. 'There's a divinity that shapes our ends / Rough-hew them how we will' (5.2.10–11), Hamlet asserts, depicting the divine as more precisely filing, shaving, or carving that which Hamlet can only crudely fashion. Supernatural intervention or administration appears here – as with Donne's sharpened axe or worn threshold or, for that matter, the ghost's desire to 'whet' Hamlet's 'almost blunted purpose' (3.4.111) – as a form of direction towards a desired end expressed as control over the finest shavings or layers of matter. If, in Hamlet's world, the smallest particles retain purpose, divine intervention itself also becomes understood, then, through tropes of material wearing away. Indeed, Hamlet's most direct scriptural allusion, 'There is special providence in the fall of a sparrow' (5.2.197–8), tellingly points to death and entropy in order to assert a divinely-ordered teleology.[74] (The first quarto notably reads 'a *predestinate* providence' [17.45].)

Rather than standing as an alternative to religious sentiment, Hamlet's form of a materialist ontology remains compatible with, and even seems to facilitate, his sense of teleology and acceptance of providential order.

If, when confronted with the grave's silence and matter's most extreme attenuation, Hamlet still retains faith in divine providence and the perpetual durance of materiality itself, he likewise persists – despite earlier exposure of his efforts as contingent, open to undoing – in seeking to reinscribe the memories of those at court in his final assault on Claudius. When Hamlet, unobserved, had encountered his uncle after *The Mousetrap*, he mused:

> Now might I do it pat, now a is a-praying,
> And now I'll do't. And so a goes to heaven,
> And so am I revenged. That would be scanned.
> A villain kills my father, and for that
> I, his sole son, do this same villain send
> To heaven. (3.3.73–8)

In saying that his revenge 'would be scanned', Hamlet either indicates he must more closely scrutinise his own plan or, as many have noted, signals concern with how those at court, audience to his retribution, would interpret his act. (Q2's lack of punctuation between 'scanned' and the subsequent line commends the latter reading.) Indeed, throughout the play, Hamlet reiterates concern over how others remember his deed, even exhorting Horatio, while dying, to 'report me and my cause aright' (5.2.322–3) and to 'tell my story' (5.2.332). But what, precisely, does Hamlet wish others to see? At the moment he kills Claudius, the prince declares:

> Here, thou incestuous, murd'rous, damnèd Dane,
> Drink off this potion. Is thy union here?
> Follow my mother. (5.2.308–10)

Hamlet's omission of direct reference to his father may seem a neglect of his earlier vow to remember, his explicit reference to his 'mother' and to 'thy union' a possible delimiting of 'murd'rous' as signifying (especially for those still unaware of the regicide itself) only the queen's death rather than the previous king's. But Hamlet also figures Claudius as 'incestuous', a designation only sensible if one recalls old Hamlet. By invoking the father obliquely, Hamlet attempts here to rhetorically separate his father from the crimes that he must, as part of his vengeance, enumerate: he attempts, that is, to fulfil his vow of remembrance while also preserving his father as integral to those at court. Hamlet, at the same time, remoulds Claudius' kingship and legacy by exchanging the grandeur of royalty for the horror awaiting the murderous and incestuous. For if Claudius' villainy once allowed him to appear regal and powerful – even capable of casually bestowing 'an union [. . .] / Richer than that which four successive kings / In Denmark's crown have worn' (5.2.250–2) – Hamlet's revenge renders his uncle lowly and vulnerable, his 'union' openly mocked, as he dies unaided even amid his own court. Hamlet's vengeance, that is, strips away the grandeur of a kingship attained by villainy, transposing in its place the true fate of a 'damnèd Dane', struck down for his crimes of incest and murder. In thus setting right a time out of joint, in affecting the very form and pressure for the age and body of his own time, Hamlet palpably reshapes the memories of those at court, the first register of recorded history, in order to define Claudius as suffering the punishment (rather than as enjoying the pleasures) wrought by the crimes of the villainous.

Since Hamlet ultimately remains unable to either fix the contours of memory into permanent place or enjoy the *ataraxia* and continued existence the material world promises only in theory, the poignancy of his tragic demise emerges, in part, from his abiding emotional and intellectual attachment to a materiality that can only, in the end, frustrate his desires. The dying Hamlet entrusts his narrative to Horatio, yet his erstwhile reliable friend obscures as much as illuminates the past. His summation of events, whether born of genuine ignorance or wilful misdirection, consists exclusively of generalisations: 'So shall you hear', he declares:

> Of carnal, bloody, and unnatural acts,
> Of accidental judgments, casual slaughters,
> Of deaths put on by cunning and forced cause
> And, in this upshot, purposes mistook
> Fall'n on th' inventors' heads. (5.2.363–8)

What Horatio promises to 'truly deliver' (5.2.369) here, as others have noted, provides no specifics, extends no further than phrases equally applicable to other tragic tales. What's more, the scholar notably omits any reference to old Hamlet, the prince's studied obliqueness failing to provoke in him – or, for that matter, in the rest of the court – any recollection of the previous king that manifests itself in speech. The futility of Hamlet's endeavours to reshape memory, something he might well sense in his final moments, renders the tragic scene even more poignant; so, too, does his unwillingness or inability to fully disengage emotionally – despite all previous protests to the contrary – from the material world he must, perforce, forget. 'Things standing thus unknown, shall I leave behind me' (5.2.328), Hamlet mourns, his mind directed not towards his spiritual fate, the undiscovered country to which he now inexorably heads, but rather towards the physical world in which he, evidently, remains intellectually and emotionally invested.

While Hamlet's attachment to the material world may seem surprising in light of critical emphasis on the prince's expressions of disgust, the atomist influence on the play appears even more remarkable given traditional historiography of the philosophy's reception in England as principally concerned with its purported atheism. Yet, as we have seen, if some indeed condemn atomism for impiety, still others – with notable frequency and well before the thinkers of the *late* seventeenth century – recuperate its materialist mechanics while dismissing its atheistic metaphysics and Epicurean ethics. Such eclecticism makes available new ways of thinking about *Hamlet*'s interest in the body's finest particles as well as in the material nature of perception and memory. By synthesising rival philosophies in yet another way than previously appreciated, Shakespeare's play presents a world informed by a type of materialist ontology that, rather paradoxically, still allows for and even insists upon providential design. Within this context of late sixteenth-century selective appropriations of atomist thought, Shakespeare's protagonist governs his ruminations and final revenge – often seemingly at odds with each other – from a shared assumption about the composition of material form and the matter of memory. For Hamlet desires bodily dissolution in order to forget while simultaneously retaining a perpetual identity grounded in matter; he also seeks to reshape the material memories of others as means for securing the identities of his father and uncle. In doing so, Hamlet exhibits a profound *un*willingness to detach from the physical world and even conducts his revenge as a refashioning of the materials of memory and history. In both responses, however, Hamlet imagines tantalising possibilities unable to be realised with any precise certainty. Desiring to escape yet utilise the imprints of memory, Hamlet confronts, in his ruminations, an *ataraxia* and continued identity that remains only theoretical and, in his revenge, an identity preserved only in the contingent, unreliable memory he would otherwise recognise as inescapably transient. Remaining deeply invested in a material world that, ultimately, will only disappoint, Hamlet persists, even to his dying breath, in seeking in materiality a measure of comfort that, ironically enough, only ever exists in his own particular mind.

Notes

1. *Suffocating Mothers: Fantasies of Maternal Origin in Shakespeare's Plays,* Hamlet *to* The Tempest (New York: Routledge, 1992), 16–17, emphasis added.
2. Ibid. 17, emphasis added.
3. *Shakespeare from the Margins: Language, Culture, Context* (Chicago: University of Chicago Press, 1996), 263.
4. Margaret W. Ferguson, '*Hamlet*: Letters and Spirits', *Shakespeare and the Question of Theory,* ed. Patricia Parker and Geoffrey Hartman (New York: Methuen, 1985), 295.
5. '"Very Like a Whale": The Problem of Knowledge in *Hamlet*', *ELH* 46 (1979): 561, 563, emphasis added.
6. All citations come from *Hamlet*, ed. A. R. Braunmuller (New York: Penguin, 2001), emphasis added.
7. On 'sullied' as 'the frequently remembered text, though it nowhere appears', see Patricia Parker, 'Black Hamlet: Battening on the Moor', *Shakespeare Studies* 31 (2003): 135.
8. For the origins and doctrines of atomism, see C. C. W. Taylor, *The Atomists: Leucippus and Democritus: Fragments, a Text and Translation with a Commentary* (Toronto: University of Toronto Press, 1999), 157–88.
9. 31. All quotations come from Lucretius, *The Nature of the Universe*, trans. R. E. Latham (Baltimore: Penguin, 1961).
10. Jonathan Gil Harris, 'Atomic Shakespeare', *Shakespeare Studies* 30 (2002): 48.
11. On Renaissance engagement with, and resistance to, atomism, see Charles Trawick Harrison, 'The Ancient Atomists and English Literature of the Seventeenth Century', *Harvard Studies in Classical Philology* 45 (1934): 1–79; on critical neglect of early seventeenth-century atomists, see Christoph Lüthy, 'What to Do with Seventeenth-Century

Natural Philosophy? A Taxonomic Problem', *Perspectives on Science* 8.2 (2000): 169, 182.
12. See David A. Hedrich Hirsch, 'Donne's Atomies and Anatomies: Deconstructed Bodies and the Resurrection of Atomic Theory', *Studies in English Literature, 1500–1900* 31.1 (1991): 69–94; Harris, 'Atomic Shakespeare', 47–54; and Gerard Passannante, *The Lucretian Renaissance: Philology and the Afterlife of Tradition* (Chicago: University of Chicago Press, 2011).
13. Robert Hugh Kargon, 'Thomas Hariot, The Northumberland Circle, and Early Atomism in England', *Journal of the History of Ideas* 27 (1966): 129, 133.
14. See Robert Hugh Kargon, *Atomism in England from Harriot to Newton* (Oxford: Clarendon Press, 1966), 14–15 and Harrison, 'The Ancient Atomists', 5–8.
15. See Harrison, 'The Ancient Atomists', 5–8.
16. Christoph Lüthy, 'The Fourfold Democritus on the Stage of Early Modern Science', *Isis* 91 (2000): 453.
17. Ibid. 451.
18. Kargon, *Atomism*, 45.
19. On late seventeenth-century synthesising of atomism with theism, see Kargon, *Atomism*, 96 and Matthew R. Goodrum, 'Atomism, Atheism, and the Spontaneous Generation of Human Beings: The Debate over a Natural Origin of the First Humans in Seventeenth-Century Britain', *Journal of the History of Ideas* 63.2 (2002): 210–13.
20. *Ballads from Manuscripts*, ed. W. R. Morfill, vol. 2 (London: Ballad Society, 1873), 82, ll. 268–76.
21. On Puttenham's indebtedness to atomism here, see Harrison, 'The Ancient Atomists', 2 and W. R. Morfill, *Ballads from Manuscripts*, 82, n. 2.
22. 'Elegy 13. Julia', in *John Donne: The Complete English Poems*, ed. A. J. Smith (New York: Penguin, 1986), 113–14, ll. 29 and John Donne, 'To Sir G. F.', in *Letters to Severall Persons of Honour (1651): A Facsimile Reproduction*, ed. M. Thomas Hester (New York: Scholars' Facsimiles & Reprints, 1977): 73–4.

23. 'An Anatomy of the World, the First Anniversarie', in *John Donne: The Complete English Poems*, 276, ll. 212–13.
24. 'CXXXIII. On the Famous Voyage', in *Ben Jonson: The Complete Poems*, ed. George Parfitt (New York: Penguin, 1996), 86–92.
25. See Harris, 'Atomic Shakespeare', 48.
26. Ibid. 48.
27. *Romeo and Juliet* 1.4.57; *As You Like It* 3.2.227 and 3.5.13, in William Shakespeare, *The Complete Pelican Shakespeare* (New York: Penguin, 2002).
28. See L. C. Martin, 'Shakespeare, Lucretius, and the Commonplaces', *The Review of English Studies* 21.83 (1945): 177–9 and Katherine Duncan-Jones, 'Stoicism in *Measure for Measure*: A New Source', *The Review of English Studies* 28.112 (1977): 442.
29. In *The Poems of Sir John Davies*, ed. Robert Krueger (Oxford: Clarendon Press, 1975), 95, Stanza 20, ll. 1–7.
30. In Ibid. Stanza 21, ll. 6–7.
31. *The Divine Weeks and Works of Guillaume de Saluste Sieur Du Bartas Translated by Josuah Sylvester*, ed. Susan Snyder, vol. 1 (Oxford: The Clarendon Press, 1979), 112, ll. 30–4.
32. Ibid. 140, ll. 157–64. Snyder notes that 'side' signifies 'long or extensive' (vol. 2, 773, n. 164).
33. On Du Bartas' image of matter as 'more like Lucretius's cosmic whirl than anything in Aristotle', see Harrison, 'The Ancient Atomists', 15.
34. Qtd in Michael Andrew Screech, *Montaigne's Annotated Copy of Lucretius: A Transcription and Study of the Manuscript, Notes and Pen-marks* (Genève: Librairie Droz, 1998), 115.
35. 'XVI. Of Atheism', in *The Works of Francis Bacon*, ed. James Spedding, Robert Leslie Ellis and Douglas Denon Heath, vol. 6 (Cambridge: Cambridge University Press, 2011), 413.
36. 'XII. Coelum; Or The Origin of Things', in Ibid. 723.
37. *De sapientia*, in Ibid. 729–30.
38. Ibid. 731. On Bacon's abiding interest in atomism, see Robert M. Schuler, 'Francis Bacon and Scientific Poetry', *Transactions of the American Philosophical Society* 82.2 (1992):

34–45; Silvia Manzo, 'Francis Bacon and Atomism: A Reappraisal', in *Late Medieval and Early Modern Corpuscular Matter Theories*, ed. Christoph Lüthy, John E. Murdoch and William R. Newman (Leiden: Brill, 2001), 209–43; and Reid Barbour, 'Remarkable Ingratitude: Bacon, Prometheus, Democritus', *Studies in English Literature, 1500–1900* 32.1 (1992): 82–4.
39. *Religio Medici and Other Works*, ed. L. C. Martin (Oxford: Clarendon, 1964), 20.
40. *Great Britaine, all in blacke for the incomparable losse of Henry, our late worthy prince* (London, 1612), C4r.
41. London, 1628, C3v.
42. Edinburgh, 1623, 77.
43. Augustine, *Of the citie of God with the learned comments of Io. Lod. Viues.* (London, 1610), 901, Hhhh.
44. 'Second Meditation', in *John Donne, Devotions upon Emergent Occasions*, ed. Anthony Raspa (Montreal: McGill-Queen's University Press, 1975), 11.
45. 'A Sermon Preached at Lincoln's Inn', in *The Sermons of John Donne*, ed. Evelyn M. Simpson and George Potter, vol. 3 (Berkeley: University of California Press, 1956), 105–6.
46. On the atom as providing 'a stabilizing center and limit to [. . .] dissolution' and securing an 'immortal physicality', see Hirsch, 'Donne's Atomies and Anatomies', 69–70, 76. 'It is precisely this preoccupation with disintegration and re-integration, with finding both the limit to destruction and the germ of creation,' concludes Hirsch, 'which makes the atom so attractive to Donne' (78).
47. 'A Sermon Preached at the Earl of Bridgewaters house in London', in *The Sermons of John Donne*, ed. Simpson and Potter, vol. 8, 97–8, emphasis added.
48. On Donne's interest in 'atomic fluctuation' here, see Matthew Horn, 'John Donne, Godly Inscription, and Permanency of Self in *Devotions upon Emergent Occasions*', *Renaissance Studies* 24.3 (2010): 368–9.
49. *The Epithalamions, Anniversaries and Epicedes*, ed. W. Milgate (Oxford: Clarendon Press, 1978), 68, l. 62.

50. On 'the gradual atomization' of the body as a source of comfort for Donne, see Felecia Wright McDuffie, *To Our Bodies Turn We Then: Body as Word and Sacrament in the Works of John Donne* (New York: Continuum, 2005), 51–2.
51. Qtd in Screech, *Montaigne's Annotated Copy of Lucretius*, 135.
52. Ibid. 136.
53. Ibid. 134.
54. 'Staging Nothing: *Hamlet* and Cognitive Science', *SubStance* 35.2 (2006): 83. As John Hunt argues, 'The nonbeing lurking at the material center of being announces itself everywhere in the play's corporeal imagery' ('A Thing of Nothing: The Catastrophic Body in *Hamlet*', *Shakespeare Quarterly* 39.1 [1988]: 28).
55. See Daniel W. Graham, 'The Paradox of Prime Matter', *Journal of the History of Philosophy* 25.4 (2008): 475–90 and H. M. Robinson, 'Prime Matter in Aristotle', *Phronesis* 19.2 (1974): 168–88.
56. See Robert Sokolowski, 'Matter, Elements and Substance in Aristotle', *Journal of the History of Philosophy* 8.3 (2008): 268–9, 275–6.
57. Thomas Ainsworth, 'Form vs Matter', *The Stanford Encyclopedia of Philosophy*, ed. Edward N. Zalta (Spring 2016 edition), URL = <https://plato.stanford.edu/archives/spr2016/entries/form-matter/>
58. See Sheldon Cohen, 'Aristotle's Doctrine of the Material Substrate', *The Philosophical Review* 93.2 (1984): 190–3 and Graham, 'The Paradox of Prime Matter', 485.
59. Bruce Danner, 'Speaking Daggers', *Shakespeare Quarterly* 54.1 (2003): 46.
60. *The Nature of the Universe*, 152–3. See also 131.
61. On 'the possible kinds of interface between matter and spirit' as integral to the play, see Mary Thomas Crane, *Shakespeare's Brain: Reading with Cognitive Theory* (Princeton: Princeton University Press, 2010), 125.
62. 'Specters of Horatio', *ELH* 75.4 (2008): 1029.
63. On the 'considerable insistence on the reliability of sight' in the play, see Lisa Hopkins, *The Cultural Uses of the*

Caesars on the English Renaissance Stage (Farnham: Ashgate, 2008), 47.
64. See Edith Frances Claflin, 'The Latinisms in Shakespeare's Diction', *The Classical Journal* 16.6 (1921): 351–2.
65. Indeed, later Hamlet tellingly invokes 'eyes without feeling' as indicative of *ab*normality (3.4.78).
66. On Hamlet as 'raz[ing] his internal *loci*', see Leah Marcus, *Unediting the Renaissance: Shakespeare, Marlowe, Milton* (London: Routledge, 1996), 164.
67. On forgetting as a kind of 'erasure and erosion', see Garrett A. Sullivan, *Memory and Forgetting in English Renaissance Drama: Shakespeare, Marlowe, Webster* (Cambridge: Cambridge University Press, 2005), 14.
68. On Hamlet's 'strangely material sense of drama as a pliable substance that can take a kind of cast or impression of the surrounding culture' and the ways 'external actions leave an impression on the brain', see Crane, *Shakespeare's Brain*, 149–50.
69. The ghost enters to 'whet' Hamlet's 'purpose', but, as the Player King has just noted, 'purpose is but a slave to memory' (3.2.184).
70. In this, Hamlet shares marked affinities with Donne, who understands that 'the atom as the limit to the self's deconstruction might also serve as the origin of that self's reconstruction' and whose 'attraction to the concept of the atom' derives from 'the permanence of physicality that such a concept offers' (Hirsch, 'Donne's Atomies and Anatomies', 71, 78).
71. T. McAlindon notes without further comment that 'the graveyard scene [...] contributes to a Lucretian sense of the interdependence of life and death' (*Shakespeare's Tragic Cosmos* [Cambridge, Cambridge University Press, 1991], 110).
72. On Hamlet's figuration as based upon the notion of a 'radically transformed monistic substance', see Paul Cefalu, 'Damnéd Custom ... Habits Devil': Shakespeare's *Hamlet*, Anti-Dualism and the Early Modern Philosophy of Mind', *ELH* 67.2 (2000): 426.
73. Qtd in Screech, *Montaigne's Annotated Copy of Lucretius*, 135–6.

74. On the fall of the sparrow as exhibiting providential care even to the level of the atom, see George Abbot, who declares 'the smallest dust and Atomus is made and guided by God', a fact that recalls how 'not a sparrow lighteth on the ground [. . .] but by his leave'. *An exposition vpon the prophet Jonah* (London, 1600), 587.

CHAPTER 4

'VEIN BY VEIN': THE PNEUMATICS OF
RETRIBUTION IN JOHN MARSTON'S
ANTONIO'S REVENGE

Performed at St Paul's by the resident children's company the same time Shakespeare's *Hamlet* appeared at the Globe, John Marston's *Antonio's Revenge* has sat uneasily with its fellow revenge tragedies. Marston's play shares numerous distinctive features with *Hamlet* and, with the rival companies staging their plays within just months of each other, the trajectory of influence between the two has remained an open question.[1] For all its temporal and thematic proximity to Shakespeare's most famous work, however, *Antonio's Revenge* has never fully emerged from the shadows of theatrical history. Like *The Spanish Tragedy* and *Titus Andronicus* before it, Marston's play has been faulted for its crude sensationalism, but where its predecessors have enjoyed rewarding theatrical runs in their own right as well as broader critical appreciation for their manifest performative appeal, *Antonio's Revenge* has remained comparatively neglected in both performance and criticism. If not outright parodic as some have claimed, the play nonetheless retains a satiric edge that can make it seem difficult to pin down. Self-conscious in its manipulation of audience expectation, the play famously exculpates its revengers in its final scene, a denouement that, when taken alone, defuses right at the moment of combustion but, when considered in light of its predecessors, generates its theatrical force precisely *by* defusing, by resolutely defying expectation, that is, to give one final, subversive thrill. In addition to the happenstances of literary history where the play remains tethered to *Hamlet* yet overshadowed by it, akin to Kyd's and Shakespeare's early work yet enjoying fewer advocates on its behalf, Marston's *Antonio's Revenge* contributes as well to its own sense of distinctiveness, perhaps dislocation, then, by depending as it does upon the very conventions of theatrical retribution it so enthusiastically traduces.

As with theatrical fortunes, so with philosophical engagements: *Antonio's Revenge* has seemed a play of curious mixtures. Aligned less with *Hamlet*, its nearest contemporary, than with *The Spanish Tragedy* and *Titus Andronicus*, Marston's play has registered as less refined or expansive in its philosophical range, deliberative about even the afterlife only to a very limited degree and likewise not terribly troubled, on this mortal coil, about the potential complications of absolving its revengers in the end. At the same time, Marston's play has, in a manner, appeared markedly *anti*-philosophical, extensively and pointedly mocking the very notion of Stoic resolve. Kyd may have Hieronimo read a book of Seneca only to discard it, but Marston has his principal characters positively excoriate the philosophy. Hamlet may yearn for an ultimately elusive *ataraxia*, something he enviously perceives in Horatio himself, but Marston's Antonio shares no such obsession, while Pandulpho, the aspiring Stoic, hardly expresses fealty to the philosophy before ultimately abandoning it, with gusto. Even the play's exhaustive preoccupation with the explicitly corporeal carries with it less *Titus'* interest in the parallels between dismembered bodies and fractured political allegiances – the correspondence, that is, between the body and body politic – and more a grotesque revelling in somatic functions seemingly for their own sake. Few today would share T. S. Eliot's bewilderment over how 'anyone could write plays so bad and that plays so bad could be preserved and reprinted',[2] but neither has *Antonio's Revenge* benefited from the recuperative counter-discourses surrounding Kyd's and Shakespeare's earlier works, and one could well be left wondering what place, if at all, the philosophical might hold for this unusual play, particularly with its pronounced delight in disgust and in the most minute operations within the hidden recesses of the traumatised body. What, exactly, is Marston about here?

One reason *Antonio's Revenge* has been a difficult play to get a handle on lies in its peculiar constellation of seemingly disparate interests. At particular issue has been the play's curious preoccupation with valorising its revenging heroes, with ridiculing (often at length) Stoic figures, and with detailing, in equal measures of relish and disgust, the interior workings of the human body. Each of these ostensibly disconnected strands, prominent throughout the play, has seemed a distinctive quality that sets *Antonio's Revenge* apart in kind from other revenge drama. Unlike other revenge tragedies, for instance, 'we get no such warning against admiring the revengers too much' and it seems that 'Marston means to have Antonio emerge at the end not only alive but as a hero'.[3] At the same time, 'Marston's odd revenge play' seems uniquely focused on mocking 'the private sovereignties of stoicism', and 'Stoic *apatheia*', or freedom from emotion, reappears as a singular obsession of the author, 'a posture of ethical poise that sustains particular humiliation in *Antonio's Revenge*'.[4] While some critics investigate such parallel strands of the play's ethics, still others centre on the almost 'infantile repugnance to elementary biological facts' evinced in Marstonian drama, noting how Marston's revenge tragedy seems especially preoccupied with the 'various parts of anatomy', attending with great care 'to heart and stomach, to ribs and breasts, to veins and arteries'.[5] Closely depicting the body's functions, disparaging Stoic ethics, and extolling its revengers as heroes – Marston's play seems busy indeed. Yet while criticism almost invariably focuses on one of these three issues, literary scholars have yet to account for *why* Marston seems so concerned with such matters or how they relate, if in fact they do, to each other. How, after all, should we evaluate the contorted ethical and natural philosophies embedded within *Antonio's Revenge*?

Marston's ethical critique that valorises revenge and devalues Stoic *apatheia* depends, surprisingly enough, directly upon his understanding of the body's interrelated vascular and respiratory systems. If Marston's interest in revenge, Stoicism and the body has been well documented, his preoccupation with blood and its singular relation to respiration has been conspicuously overlooked, in part because of the tendency to read Marstonian blood as merely metonymic, as signifying by turns lineage, guilt, or propitiation, as it might well in another revenge play. Yet for Marston, blood and, just as importantly, highly-refined air, or *pneuma*, features centrally in the very philosophical substructure of his drama. In fact, at every stage of the revenge narrative, this interest in blood and its attendant air, smoke, or fume appears, repeatedly directing attention to the faintest instantiations of corporeal matter throughout the play. As Antonio contemplates stabbing Julio, for instance, he speculates that he 'might rip [him] vein by vein and carve revenge / In bleeding rases' (3.3.22–3), explicitly figuring his retribution as a type of dissection, one that would culminate in the separation of veins.[6] A moment later, he revels in the specific corporeal properties of the very air, or fume, accompanying Julio's blood, declaring, 'Ghost of my poisoned sire, suck this fume; / To sweet revenge, perfume thy circling air / With smoke of blood', and he will boast 'Look how I smoke in blood, reeking the steam / Of foaming vengeance' (3.3.63–5; 3.5.17–18). Such blood that emits fume, smoke and even foam permeates the play. Piero brags that he has 'been nursed in blood, and still [has] sucked / The steam of reeking gore (2.1.19–20); Antonio claims that 'all hell-strained juice / Is poured to [man's] veins, making him drunk / With fuming surquedries' (3.2.70–2); and Antonio even dismisses Seneca's *De providentia* (and, thereby, Stoic philosophy) by declaring, ''tis naught / But foamy bubbling of a fleamy brain, / Naught else but smoke' (2.3.53–5). This recurrent link of the respiratory to the specifically vascular suggests an especially coherent, particularised physiology operant within the play, a physiology attuned to the faintest bits of corporeal matter, just shy of immateriality, which appear at every stage of the revenge narrative, even in Marston's most overt assault on Stoic thought.

Marston's *Antonio's Revenge* appears deeply invested, then, in figurations of the vascular and respiratory systems and, more precisely, the pneumatic theories of its age. Written before William Harvey's discovery of the circulation of blood, Marston's play, I will argue, draws upon a markedly Galenic conceptualisation of pneumatics, a theory both medical and more broadly philosophical, which envisages air joining with and conditioning all blood distributed throughout the body. The veins and arteries in Marston's play carry not only blood but also fume, smoke and foam, in part, because Galenic physiology demanded it: such fusion of blood and *pneuma* remained crucial to the essential workings of the well-ordered body.[7] Yet the detailed anatomical functions in Marston's play operate beyond mere academic interest or symbolic ornament, recalling attention instead to a fundamental ontological ground that will condition the terms upon which the characters govern their actions throughout the play. For in order to show the limits of Stoic resignation – indeed, to debunk *apatheia* and reveal it as inherently incompatible with nature – Marston represents the body's subtlest operations as instinctively countering the trauma wrought by tragedy through its pneumatic systems. Moreover, by affiliating revenge with a pneumatic process of instinctive self-healing, Marston undercuts Stoicism's broader cosmological notion of *pneuma* as a 'containing cause', a pervasive force that imbues the universe with rationality and provides for the Stoic sage tranquillity amid suffering.[8] By appropriating Galen's theory of corporeal pneumatics and sharing the physician-philosopher's anti-Stoic sentiment, Marston creates an ontological framework for his play that will help situate Antonio's final vengeance as acting in accordance with how his world, at its most rudimentary levels, operates. Drawing on Galenic medical theory and anti-Stoic philosophy, Marston surprisingly figures retribution, that is, as physiologically beneficial, a visceral response to trauma that addresses the body's intrinsic need for constitutional equilibrium. In doing so, Marston's play introduces a therapeutic register to revenge attentive, unlike the rigours of Stoicism, to the body's inherent impulse – extending even to its most attenuated material components – toward attaining palliation for the debilitating effects of physical and emotional trauma.[9]

Galenic Pneumatics and Early Modern Medical Theory

Although Andreas Vesalius' *De humani corporis fabrica* (1543) would eventually help displace Galenic authority – an epistemic shift more fully realised only with William Harvey's discovery of the circulation of blood in 1628 – Galenism still served as the principal source of medical theory during Marston's career as a playwright. As the foundation for medical study during the medieval period, Galen's texts had long received attention throughout European centres of learning. Medieval scribes, indebted to Arabic translators, preserved the Galenic *oeuvre,* and where 'monastic libraries [. . .] contained Latin versions of Galen' as early as the ninth century, Niccolo da Reggio's fourteenth-century translations directly from the Greek helped ensure that 'by the end of the Middle Ages, most of Galen's major works had been translated'.[10] The sixteenth century, moreover, witnessed 'phenomenal interest in Galen [as] evinced by the multitude of editions published in Basle, Lyons, Paris and Venice' that followed the Aldine *editio princeps* of 1525, published in Greek.[11] In addition to further promulgating and refining the Galenic corpus as then known, humanists also recovered previously lost works, most notably *De placitis Hippocratis et Platonis*, or *On the Doctrines of Hippocrates and Plato*, a work renowned as well for its anti-Stoic sentiment.[12] Throughout most of the period, individual editions of Galen enjoyed high publication rates, declining only later in the sixteenth century, perhaps due to the arrival of the more comprehensive *Omnia opera*.[13] Amid those published by Continental presses, 'the first printed edition of Galen in English appear[ed] as part of a compilation titled *The Questyonary of Cyrurgyens*, in 1542', a work 'popular enough to be reprinted several times before the end of the sixteenth century'[14] and accompanied by numerous other editions and commentaries as well.[15] Even Vesalius' *Fabrica*, published coterminously with this resurgence of Galenic texts, paradoxically perpetuated Galenism. For while Vesalius significantly challenged and revised features of Galenic medicine well before century's end, his work simultaneously reveals a 'complicated mixture of dependence, reworking, and critique',[16] of his predecessor such that 'it is therefore a mistake to think [. . .] that [*Fabrica*] marks the overthrow of Galenism and a complete break with the past'.[17] Galen's work, qualified and refined by Vesalius' contributions, nonetheless remained 'the dominant authority in medicine throughout the sixteenth century' and even beyond.[18]

Amid its encyclopaedic accounts of human physiology, late sixteenth-century Galenism posited a thoroughly-integrated respiratory, cardiac and vascular system where rarefied air, or *pneuma*, moved with blood, via the veins and arteries, and infused the body with vital energy. Different from the modern notion of oxygenated blood, ancient and early modern pneumatics described vascular and respiratory operations as utilising shared conduits to transmit fundamentally distinct substances. As early as Empedocles, for example, pre-Galenic medical theory suggested that 'blood and breath move in the same vessels of the body' and imagined veins and arteries as 'alternately filled with blood and breath'.[19] As the body took in air and generated blood, each would be distributed through the veins and arteries in analogous but essentially distinct processes. Retaining the notion of veins and arteries as conduits for both blood and *pneuma*, however, Galen argued that such substances flow – often simultaneously – through the same passages. As F. David Hoeniger observes, Galenic physiology took seriously pneumatic flow, theorising that:

> *pneuma* derives from the air that is breathed through the trachea into the lungs. There, by making the air more 'subtle', the lungs' [. . .] peculiar flesh begins the process of transformation. This refined air then passes through pores from the lungs into the pulmonary vein [. . .] from whence it is with its blood attracted to the left ventricle of the heart. There it is joined with more blood, and the transformation into vital *pneuma* is completed. The resulting thin blood, charged with vital spirit, is driven from the heart into the arteries, which carry it to all parts of the body.[20]

Galenic physiology depicted the vascular system, then, as useful not only for transporting blood throughout the body but also, just as importantly, for generating, refining and distributing *pneuma* as well. Indeed, if anything, Galenism emphasised this distribution of *pneuma* over the transmission of blood, a concept evinced by the fact that 'the Greek word "artery" [. . .] means "carrier of air", and the term even was commonly applied to the windpipe'.[21] As *pneuma* infused vital spirit throughout the body, it ensured physical health, and the body's capacity to process pneumatic flow consequently remained central to ancient and early modern understandings of the healthy vascular system.

According to Galenic physiology, *pneuma*, in concert with the blood, helps generate a second substance known as 'psychic *pneuma*' in the brain, a type of even more highly-refined corporeal matter – existing just on the border between materiality and immateriality – that serves as interface, as it were, between the rest of the body and the soul.[22] Galen examines the psychic *pneuma* across treatises, drawn to its status as the 'first instrument' of the soul and intrigued by its specific corporeal properties. Differentiating between types of *pneuma* in *De placitis*, Galen explains how the vital *pneuma* gives rise to the psychic:

> [T]he *pneuma* in the arteries [. . .] is called vital, and that in the brain is called psychic, not in the sense that it is the substance, but rather the first instrument of the soul that resides in the brain, whatever [the soul's] substance may be. Just as vital *pneuma* is generated in the arteries and the heart, getting the material for its generation from inhalation and from the vaporization of the humors, so the psychic *pneuma* is generated by a further refinement of the vital. For it was necessary that this *pneuma*, more than anything else, be changed in precisely the right way.[23]

By depicting the psychic *pneuma* as generated by 'the refinement of the vital' which must 'be changed in precisely the right way', Galen posits a continuum between types of *pneuma*, working backwards through increasingly attenuated material states toward, finally, this 'first instrument of the soul'. As he does so, Galen not only signals the notable dependence of the soul upon the proper functioning of the body's broader operations, but also marks *pneuma* as the finest, most-rarefied instance of materiality as it drifts towards the (apparently) immaterial.[24] Indeed, as he contemplates the '*pneuma* in the ventricles of the brain', Galen speculates that, 'if the soul is incorporeal, the *pneuma* is, so to speak, its first home; or if the soul is corporeal, this very thing is the soul'. Officially remaining agnostic on the question of the soul's substance, Galen depicts the soul's immateriality as the most reasonable supposition and concludes:

> It is better, then, to assume that the soul dwells in the actual body of the brain, whatever its substance may be – for the inquiry has not yet reached this question – and that the soul's first instrument [. . .] is this pneuma [. . .] Thus it is reasonable [. . .] that the *pneuma* is, as I said, the first instrument of the soul [. . .] [T]he psychic *pneuma* is neither the essence of the soul nor its dwelling, but its first instrument [. . .][25]

Although speaking more as physiologist than metaphysician here, Galen remains intrigued by the close connection between this *pneuma* and the still-inaccessible soul. In *De usu respirationis*, Galen observes anew, for instance, that 'this *pneuma* is either the very substance of the soul or its primary organ'[26] and, while once more affirming the latter, speculates that if the psychic *pneuma* 'is the *first* organ [of the soul]', 'then the brain necessarily contains within itself the substance of the soul, and this must be either the natural heat, or the pneuma, or the form of the composition taken as a whole, or some incorporeal power beyond it'.[27] Though momentary inquiries borne of his interest in the inscrutable, deeper recesses of the brain, such passages signal the extent to which Galen's theory of *pneuma* posits a corporeal materiality so finely-attenuated as to seem almost immaterial, the last waypoint, so to speak, between the body's perceptible and the soul's imperceptible functions.

Within Galenic physiology, this generation and maintenance of various *pneuma* – so crucial to the constitutional equilibrium of both body and mind – depends upon the close regulation of internal heat via respiration and even the pulsation of veins, a theory that integrates respiratory and vascular functions into one interdependent system. As the principal locus of 'the body's innate heat', the Galenic heart requires the moderation of surrounding temperature.[28] Through both breathing and vascular pulsation, the body supplies the fresh air used by the heart, veins and arteries and discharges by the same mechanism the resultant sullied residue. Declaring that '*pneuma* must of necessity be nourished', Galen asks in *De usu respirationis*, 'from what other source, therefore, will it get nourishment, unless from that which is drawn in while breathing in?'[29] This nourishment is essential for *pneuma* in its various gradations. For while the psychic *pneuma* 'has no need of the substance of the outer air', observes Galen, it does require 'attraction of [the air's] qualities [. . .] and especially of heat' and 'the preservation of heat is impossible without breathing'.[30] 'It remains, then,' Galen concludes, 'that we breathe for regulation of heat. This, then, is the principal use of breathing, and the second is to nourish the psychic pneuma.'[31] What's more, for Galen even the veins help maintain temperature conducive to pneumatic health by absorbing air and releasing internal heat through pulsation.[32] In *De usu pulsuum*, Galen argues, in fact, that 'the use of the pulse and of breathing is the same – preservation of heat, and restoration of the psychic pneuma' and, later, likewise asserts that, 'to both breathing and the pulse the concoction of the psychic *pneuma* is common'.[33] The Galenic respiratory and vascular systems function, then, to stabilise internal temperatures and maintain the health of one's *pneuma*, the very substance that ensures health for body and mind.

In order to regulate heat and sustain psychic *pneuma*, the Galenic body – like those we will see throughout Marston's play – perpetually emanates vapour, smoke and residue drawn from the blood, first, through exhalation by the lungs and, second, through the discharge of waste by veins and arteries, passed through the skin to the surrounding air. The Galenic body, in essence, perpetually smokes. In *De usu respirationis*, Galen argues breathing 'purges the smoky vapor, as it were, of the blood. For soot and smoke and murk and every such waste product of the burning material naturally quench fire just as much as water does'.[34] Galen reiterates this claim a moment later, noting that the very motion of breathing 'is necessary for emptying out the smokiness, as one might say, from the combustion of the blood', and he concludes his treatise by describing exhalation as the 'evacuation of smoky vapor'.[35] Concurrent with such respiratory functions, the Galenic vascular system also purges smoke from the blood, as the body pulls in air and exhales vapour through the very skin itself.[36] As Galenic arteries pulsate, then, they also breathe. As Galen explains in *De usu pulsuum*, 'The expansion of arteries, like breathing in, draws in airy stuff; contraction, like breathing out, discharges smoky residue'.[37] According to Galen, in this way the arteries 'eliminate through the mouths that end in the skin all the waste matter that is vaporous and smoky, and take up into themselves in exchange no small part of the air that surrounds us'.[38] Thus depicting 'the whole body' as 'breath[ing] in and out', Galenic pneumatics posits a cyclical process as the body absorbs ambient air and discharges smoke in an effort to regulate one's internal heat.

By putting forward such a fluid, cyclical physiological system deeply dependent on its environment, the Galenism still prominent in Marston's age proposed an intimate connection between the subtlest operations of the body and the surrounding world and signalled, in the process, the potential for external factors to influence one's physiological and even psychological well-being. Indeed, in early modern England 'the inner affective experience was understood as an aspect of the physics of temperature and hydraulic flow within the body', and such operations depended in large measure on environment. Since conditions ranging from 'ambient air' to the processes of digestion could so thoroughly influence one's interior affective states, collapsing boundaries between 'the inner world of the passions and the surrounding air', *pneuma*, the key mechanism underlying such an 'interconnected system of physical and spiritual health', remains crucial for understanding the effects of trauma and circumstance on both body and mind.[39] For within Galenism even 'mental disease is due to the deleterious effect produced on the brain and its *pneuma* by unbalanced combinations of the basic qualities of heat, cold, dryness, and moisture', suggesting that 'mental disease is essentially physiologic', a condition shaped, in part, by one's surrounding conditions.[40] The body's most fundamental functions, even the ones residing in the deepest recesses of the interior, remain inextricably linked in a literal, physical manner, then, to the events of the outside world and, what's more, affect (through the very same mechanisms) an individual's psychological health.

On Pneuma *and Galenic Anti-Stoicism*

Although Galenic medicine's heavy reliance on *pneuma* as explanatory construct – as well as its appreciation for the interaction of *pneuma* with material reality beyond the body's boundaries – would seem to suggest an inherent affinity with Stoic philosophy, Galenic and Stoic thought differ significantly on the role of *pneuma* outside the domain of the corporeal.[41] The Stoic's theory of *pneuma*, in particular, stresses the substance's cosmological, rather than merely physiological, role.

As R. J. Hankinson notes, Stoicism figures *pneuma* as a pervasive force that holds all levels of the universe together:

> The Stoics held that the world was permeated by a dynamic substance responsible at the lowest level for the cohesion of material objects; at the next level up for the organization of a functioning metabolizing and self-reproducing organism; then for animal perception and voluntary power; and, finally, in humans, for cognition and understanding [. . .] This stuff, light and volatile yet endowed with the ability to generate and maintain structure, they called *pneuma*, and described it variously as a mixture of fire and air, or air endowed with fiery properties, or a dynamic combination of the hot and the cold.[42]

This *pneuma* – unlike the Galenic version, which may be influenced by outside forces but still remains largely centred on the body – operates as a 'containing cause', a prime substance that makes the universe cohere.[43] A 'central feature of Stoic physics', this version of *pneuma* operates as both substance and agent, 'an all-pervading medium which intelligently directs the cosmic cycle'.[44] Rather than principally explaining corporeal operations, Stoic pneumatics, then, functions more as a vehicle for providing a totalising taxonomy, designed to structure Stoic cosmology, physics, ethics and related fields – as well as to signal the Stoic belief in a wholly interdependent, rational cosmos. To some extent, the Stoics' liberal appropriation of *pneuma* derived from the simple fact that, conceptually, it proved 'notoriously the most volatile of all substances in Greek physical theory',[45] but this rather free use of pneumatic theories troubled Galen, however, who specifically targeted the Stoics for censure. Explaining how 'Galen indeed takes them to task', R. J. Hankinson observes that the physician-philosopher pointedly asked the obvious questions invited by Stoic eclecticism, namely, 'Why posit something to prevent solid things from falling apart? And in any case, how could something as volatile as *pneuma* do the trick?'[46]

Beyond proposing a theory of pneumatics that rivals that of the Stoics, Galen – in a manner not unlike what we will find in Marston as well – also marshals his physiological theories as part of a scathing critique of Stoicism more broadly. The principal purpose of *De placitis* is to reconcile Hippocratic medicine and Platonic philosophy, but, to do this, Galen must first counter the rival psychological paradigm posed by Chrysippus, the 'main theorist' of the Stoics.[47] While Galen's main argument against Stoicism focuses on its location of the rational soul in the heart instead of the brain, much of his critique takes issue with the philosophy's inability to explain affective disturbances within the psyche. The Stoics, Galen explains, use the language of disease to describe disorders of the soul, a move the physician finds untenable given the premises of their own philosophy. As Galen observes while refuting Chrysippus:

> Clearly [he] wishes to preserve here a certain analogy between soul and body in their affections, infirmities, diseases, health, robustness, strength, weakness, and, in a word, everything that has the same name in both [. . .] Therefore, whatever universal definition is given to disease in the body, the soul's disease must be defined in the same way. From this it is clear that Chrysippus' purpose is to explain and preserve the entire analogy [. . .][48]

Following Plato's definition in the *Sophist*, however, Galen understands disease as 'the destruction of what is by nature congenial as a result of some dissension',[49] and he faults the Stoics, therefore, for failing to explain how a monistic substance can experience such discord within itself. If the soul and its functions remain unitary, Galen reasons, how can dissension between parts occur? Galen, by contrast, follows both Plato and Aristotle in perceiving the soul's functions as distributed throughout the body and, what's more, understands each, as we have seen, as interfacing closely with the faintest material aspects of the body as well. Though he shares the Stoics' predilection for perceiving an analogy between the diseased or healthy body and the diseased or healthy soul, then, Galen finds Stoic philosophy unequal to the task of diagnosing disorders of the psyche's affective functions. The Stoics, Galen concludes, fail to answer what parts of the soul remain in dissension when the affective functions of the psyche become disturbed, and, as part of his rebuttal, he roots his own explanation in the interaction between the faintest instantiations of corporeality and the imperceptible soul itself, offering in his view a more complete, accurate diagnosis of psychological distress.

Taking seriously Stoic comparisons of the soul's health with that of the body, Galen speculates whether pneumatic functions could account for disorders of the psyche, and, in a manner akin to what will appear in Marston's play, opens a line of critique, rooted in physiology, against Stoic ethical theory and therapeutic models. Galen tasks Chrysippus for failing to demonstrate what constitutes 'mutual proportion and disproportion of the soul's parts by reference to which the soul is said to be healthy or diseased'.[50] Addressing Chrysippus directly, Galen then makes a fascinating move, suggesting that by the notion of 'the soul's parts', the Stoic may, in fact, have meant *pneuma*, since:

> the soul's parts, as you yourself explain fully elsewhere, are the auditory pneuma, the optic (pneuma), and in addition the vocal and generative (pneumas), and over all of them the governing (pneuma) in which, you said, reason is constituted; and you say that it is primarily with reference to this part of the soul that ugliness and beauty are found in it. Now this pneuma has two parts, elements, or states, that are intermingled throughout, the cold and the hot, or, if you wish to use different appellations and give them the names of their substances, air and fire; and it also takes some moisture from the bodies in which it dwells.[51]

Although Galen ultimately turns to other lines of attack, here he interrogates more closely Chrysippus' imprecision towards the soul's component parts by invoking the Stoic's own pneumatic theories, suggesting that, even in this, the very physiological assumptions informing Stoic thought undercut Stoic therapeutics. If the Chrysippean soul lacks distinction between any identifiable parts (the closest, most viable option being found in the *pneuma* itself), the Stoic reading of affective disorder as akin to bodily disease deconstructs, Galen argues, and, along with it, the rationale for the Stoic diagnosis of, and therapy for, such disorders of the affections.

But why broach the matter of *pneuma* only to pursue at length a different avenue of rebuttal against Stoicism? And might Galenism admit here a more comprehensive refutation of Stoic ethics and therapy grounded explicitly in pneumatic theory itself? By drawing attention to the 'certain simple elements' whose 'mutual proportion' produces health or disease,[52] Galen not only lays out the terms one would need in order to plausibly defend Stoic doctrine. He also establishes the predicates for anyone wishing to criticise it as well. For rather than arguing, as Galen does in *De placitis*, that the Stoics ultimately fail to identify the parts of the soul, one could instead simply note the Stoic figuration of the soul as comprised by *pneuma* and assert their therapeutic methods still fail to ensure the 'mutual proportion' of these 'simple elements' nonetheless. Notably, if Galen signals yet suppresses this angle of attack in *De placitis*, he revisits such ideas in his treatise *The Faculties of the Soul Follow the Mixtures of the Body*. He observes that the Stoics:

> hold that the psyche, like nature (*phusis*), is a kind of breath (*pneuma*) but that [*pneuma*] of nature is more humid and colder, whereas that of the psyche is drier and hotter. That is why this *pneuma*, too, is a kind of matter (*hulê*) appropriate

to the psyche and the form (*eidos*) of the matter is such-and-such a mixture (*krasis*), consisting in a proportion of the airy and fiery substance (*ousia*) [. . .] It has, then, become clear to you now that in the view of the Stoics the substance of the psyche comes to be (*gignetai*) according to a particular mixture (*krasis*) of air and fire.⁵³

Describing at length the Stoic psyche as a type of breath or *pneuma* of a particular sort, Galen emphasises the nature of the equilibrium it requires; the Stoic soul, which Galen identifies in *De placitis* as 'composed of certain simple elements', is here more precisely rendered, enabling a different line of critique of Stoic therapy, grounded in pneumatic theory itself. The Galenic corpus, that is, provides the very predicates for inquiring how Stoic *apatheia* could adequately address trauma which extends to the body and soul's most essential pneumatic elements. Might someone – both attuned to the theory of *pneuma* and inclined against Stoic philosophy – not build upon a pervasive cultural tradition of Galenic thought to launch, then, in a slightly different register, a similar criticism? Is it not likely that Stoic therapeutics could be countered on more specifically physiological grounds, especially when the chief authority of medical theory imbued his own writings with such pronounced anti-Stoic sentiment?

Whatever appeal Stoic ethical teachings held during the late sixteenth and early seventeenth centuries, most early modern authors perceived *apatheia* – the principal Stoic doctrine for countering troubled affective states – as unrealistic, even detrimental, since the concept demanded an extirpation of emotions which remained deeply grounded in physiology.⁵⁴ For many writers, 'the Stoic sage [was] an impossible fiction, a philosophical chimera',⁵⁵ one who, by upholding the doctrine of *apatheia* upheld an unattainable, unhealthy value, 'impossible in practice as well as inhumane and un-Christian as an ideal'.⁵⁶ What's more, many simply rejected the Stoic theory of pneumatics, no small matter given the fact that the theory undergirded the concept of *apatheia* itself. For the Stoic sage attains such imperturbablity partly by subscribing to a monist view 'that the active matter or *pneuma* filling or investing passive matter is substantially one and the same as the reason that governs the human subject', a doctrine that helps the sage recognise 'the universe is a seamless whole' and thus move the thinker 'toward perfect rationality, virtue, and invulnerability to the indifferent vicissitudes of the world'.[57] For early modern thinkers, though, 'the status of [. . .] the pneumatic is not altogether clear in itself or in its relation to the world' and often prompted authors to consider anew the constitution and circulation of *pneuma* itself.[58] Thus, amid the many reasons the Stoic doctrine of *apatheia* was found lacking, one could add the failure of its underlying pneumatics to obtain. How, though, might such coincident strands of intellectual history, prominent in the era's writings, be found at work on the early modern stage?

The Pneumatic World of Marston's Antonio's Revenge

Marston establishes pneumatic functions as central not only to his depiction of individual grief but also the very ontological framework of the entire world his play will depict when, through the Prologue, he invites his audience to trace the tragic setting before them back to its underlying causes. The play opens with a lengthy description of the season, explaining its aptness for tragedy, but while Marston 'paints a harsh and barren winter landscape'[59] designed to set the melancholic tone, he also immediately becomes oddly and tellingly specific:

> The rawish dank of clumsy winter ramps
> The fluent summer's vein; and drizzling sleet
> Chilleth the wan bleak cheek of the numbed earth,
> Whilst snarling gusts nibble the juiceless leaves
> From the naked shudd'ring branch, and pills the skin
> From off the soft and delicate aspects. (ll. 1–6)

An attempt to convey a wintery setting suitable for 'a sullen tragic scene' (l. 7), Marston's Prologue also rather cleverly constructs a detailed, coherent image of the nature of physical trauma, one that will permeate the play. Indeed, in this, even the laboured language itself 'is thickened to throat-stomping clumps', a stylistic effort that seems 'deliberately clumsy', an attempt to reproduce the 'somatic dysfunction', particularly the stifled breath, that will characterise those populating the ensuing drama.[60] Aside from such matters of style, however, Marston's Prologue more precisely begins with both the notable conflation of arboreal and corporeal imagery, and, in what makes the conflation intelligible, a keen awareness of pneumatic flow. Thus, this chill scene of earth's 'wan bleak cheek', 'naked' branches, and pilled 'skin' emerges from the forceable rising – the 'ramp[ing]' – of 'rawish dank' within 'fluent summer's *vein*'. The change of season into winter becomes characterised, that is, by an aggressive, deleterious pneumatic process. At once redolent of corporeal operations – as it affects vein, cheek, skin and even soft and delicate aspects – the underlying pneumatic process figured here also signals a larger milieu subject to the flow of unseen but very real forces, forces that influence, among other matters, moisture, temperature and health.

At the same time that the Prologue sets the prevailing conditions for understanding the ontological assumptions undergirding the play's broader depiction of the world, Marston also seeks to establish rapport with the audience by invoking a shared set of assumptions, rooted in the era's Galenism, about the physiology of grief and, what's more, signals that in order to fully appreciate the tragic action about to unfold one must be attuned to this physiology. Marston invites his audience to hear his play, asking them to self-segregate based on their differing physical and emotional states. Notably, he frames this request in Galenic terms as he distinguishes between suffering and lighthearted playgoers, noting the distinctive pneumatic functions operant within their respective bodies. Marston, the Prologue indicates, most prefers an audience familiar with the stifling effects of misery. 'If any spirit breathes within this round / Uncapable of weighty passion', the Prologue intones, then such a person should withdraw:

> But if a breast
> Nailed to the earth with grief, if any heart
> Pierced through with anguish, pant within this ring,
> If there be any blood whose heat is choked
> And stiflèd with true sense of misery,
> If ought of these strains fill this consort up,
> Th' arrive most welcome. (ll. 13–14, 21–7)

Marston's invitation to the grieving and pained to 'fill this consort up' moves beyond a general sense of pathos to a rather particular notion of how the body responds to trauma, placing, in fact, the greatest emphasis on corporeal pneumatics. By setting the 'spirits' who breathe freely, unencumbered by 'weighty passion', against those mourners so 'pierced through with anguish' that they 'pant within this ring', Marston draws attention to how the trauma of grief suffocates the body, a process that will, in turn, lead to the imbalance of internal heat. For when Marston extends welcome to 'any blood whose heat is choked, / And stifled with true sense of misery', he not only identifies his preferred playgoers in a term itself evocative of the scene's underlying physiology but also shows the very real, traumatic effects grief has on the body's operations, as it stifles and chokes the internal heat, the very mechanism Galen posited as crucial for maintaining a well-balanced mind. Through the Prologue, Marston configures his theatrical world as sharing the Galenic assumptions of the audience about how grief affects the body itself, and if this helps generate a sense of fellow feeling among the consort, it also helps establish the ontological predicates which animate the play's particular physiology and which, attuned to the body's subtlest operations, remain essential for making sense of the play's subsequent narrative of retribution.

Marston begins the play proper by having Piero enter and explain his motive for murdering Andrugio in explicitly Galenic terms of corporeal disorder, and while the villain's claim that he killed his rival to ease his physical distress will immediately be exposed as spurious, his attempt to co-opt the language of both therapy and revenge to justify his actions reveals a world where such an explanation proves plausible. Even in his falsehoods, that is, Piero signals the prevailing assumptions governing the world in which he operates. When he first announces the murder to Strotzo, his accomplice, Piero figures the act as a curious battle of organs, one that resulted in the stifling of heat around Andrugio's heart. 'Andrugio sleeps in peace!', Piero boasts, 'This brain hath choked / The organ of his breast' (1.1.14–15). After declaring himself, 'great in blood, / Unequalled in revenge', Piero continues to pretend his perfidy was an act of vengeance that satisfied his body's physical distress when he recounts how his rival obtained the love of Maria:

> He won the Lady, to my honour's death,
> And from her sweets cropped this Antonio;
> For which I burned in inward swelt'ring hate,
> And festered rankling malice in my breast,
> Till I might belk revenge upon his eyes. (1.1.17–18, 25–9)

Piero describes his villainy here by conjoining the rhetoric of both revenge and therapeutic treatment, figuring his aggression towards Andrugio as a kind of exhalation of breath, something he belches at his rival as a means to relieve the heat disordering his own interior, the 'swelt'ring hate' that inwardly burns, festering about his heart. Although Marston's villain lays claim to the notion of revenge as a form of physical therapy, the playwright makes clear the spurious nature of Piero's declaration. The failure to win a lover over a rival hardly provides warrant for retribution; moreover, Piero's own formulation exposes his claims as suspect. For in order to be true, Piero would have had to burn inwardly for years, his breast festering with debilitating disorder as Antonio grew into adulthood. What's more, his rhetoric belies his superficial claim of seeking relief, for his murder of Andrugio results not in any restoration of health but rather in continued erratic behaviour and, indeed, increasingly frenetic bloodlust. The very fact that Piero feels compelled to describe his hatred and justify his behaviour in these terms, however, remains rather telling. For although Piero's mode of self-diagnosis lacks credibility, his rhetoric signals a world where such a claim makes sense, where physiology and emotional state affect each other, and where relief for trauma can be found in physical action, even, it would seem, in the process of revenge.

Throughout the entire opening sequence where Piero boasts of his villainies, often in Galenic terms, Marston further figures his playworld as markedly pneumatic, but the playwright also immediately takes pains to distinguish his conception of the world from that of the Stoics, for whom pervasive *pneuma* functions as a containing cause, imbuing the world with rationality. As Piero recounts the setting in which he murdered Andrugio and articulates his subsequent exultation, the cascade of descriptions he pours forth, full of images of pneumatic flow and stifled breath, can easily appear as the imprecise, perhaps incoherent, raving of a murderer. Upon entering, Piero tells Strotzo to 'bind Feliche's trunk / Unto the panting side of Mellida' (1.1.1–2), and, once alone, observes how:

'Tis yet dead night; yet all the earth is clutched
In the dull leaden hand of snoring sleep;
No breath disturbs the quiet of the air,
No spirit moves upon the breast of earth
Save howling dogs, nightcrows, and screeching owls,
Save meager ghosts, Piero, and black thoughts. (1.1.3–8)

At first glance, Piero's description of the scene seems rather contradictory. For he figures a world where 'No breath disturbs the [. . .] air' and 'No spirit moves', and yet proceeds to enumerate a sizeable contingent of moving spirits which encompasses virtually every level of existence – from animals to ghosts and villains to thoughts – to which we might also add the 'panting Mellida'. Why does Piero figure his world as utterly still except in the myriad ways it is not? Through Piero's speech, Marston subtly establishes the ontological framework for his play, indicating this world is a highly pneumatic yet decidedly *not* Stoic one. Piero reads his entire environment, other entities, and even his interactions in pneumatic terms, but here is no rational containing cause, an idea Marston, in fact, seems to explicitly parody by depicting 'the earth [as] clutched / In the dull leaden hand of snoring sleep'. Figured as held by that which is insentient and thus not purposeful, the world, as Piero has it, becomes understood nonetheless through recourse to the movement of breath and spirits. Indeed, the Duke will proceed to describe virtually all events and interactions in such terms. He murders Andrugio 'in the hush of night' (1.1.71), hopes circumstance might cover his crime, 'might choke the murder' itself (1.1.74), castigates Strotzo for being 'struck in heat with each slight puff' (1.1.51), mocks his accomplice's 'fumbling throat' (1.1.80), and dismisses him to bed to 'snort in securest sleep' (1.1.105). At every stage of Piero's opening remarks, Marston draws attention to even the faintest movements of breath within the antagonist's environment, setting the playworld as a space where pneumatic flow, as a ubiquitous yet notably non-rational reality, remains paramount.

Into this pneumatic world where Galenic physiology but not Stoic cosmology reigns, Marston introduces Antonio, who, disturbed by nocturnal visions of apparitions, immediately registers his mental distress as manifesting itself in physiological disorder, a state that positions the revenging hero, from the outset, as requiring relief from not only affective but also corporeal trauma. After describing dawn as 'breathing fair light about the firmament' (1.3.4), Antonio commands his joking comrades:

> Blow hence these sapless jests. I tell you bloods
> My spirit's heavy, and the juice of life
> Creeps slowly through my stiffened arteries.
> Last night my sense was steeped in horrid dreams:
> [. . .]
> Two meager ghosts made apparition.
> The one's breast seemed fresh-paunched with bleeding
>   wounds
> Whose bubbling gore sprang in frighted eyes:
> The other ghost assumed my father's shape;
> Both cried, 'Revenge!' At which my trembling joints
> (Icèd quite over with a frozen cold sweat)
> Leaped forth the sheets. Three times I gasped at shades
>   [. . .] (1.3.36–48)

As Marston introduces his protagonist, sets the scene's sense of foreboding, and foreshadows the revelation of the *scelus* that will require vengeance, he surrounds the moment's most graphic images of death with allusions to pneumatic flow. For as the dawn 'breath[es] fair light' throughout the sky, Antonio dismisses his companions' jocularity, telling them to 'blow' away such 'sapless jests', and the most quotidian elements of the world, from illumination in the heavens to meaningless banter among friends, become imagined as if they enter into being from the very flow of air. But even as these reduplicated tropes reinforce a sense of the world of the play as a pneumatic one, one shaped by the flow of faintly perceptible forces, the scene's most profound emotional impact comes from Antonio's terrifying vision. The ghosts or shades – entities themselves commonly described as '*pneuma*' in early modern culture – slow Antonio's blood, stiffen his arteries, freeze his joints with cold sweat, force him to gasp. As if to reinforce the point, Marston has Antonio note yet once more how 'the frightful shades of night yet shake my brain; / My gellied blood's not thawed' (1.3.73–4). At every turn, Marston figures Antonio's affective distress as linked to the disruption of his vascular system and the regulation of his internal temperature, and from the very earliest moments of the play, the author signals that the restoration of one's mental and emotional well-being will require, in some fashion, attention to one's internal physiological operations, even to the body's faintest manifestations of material form.

As Marston stages the first confrontation between Antonio and Piero, he makes clear that revenger and villain – and apparently the court as a whole – share a set of assumptions about how the body operates, for Piero openly relies on Galenic ideas as the most plausible way of explaining away his crimes against his enemies. After Piero reveals his murder of Feliche and denounces Mellida as unchaste, Antonio confronts him:

> Ant. Dog, I will make thee eat thy vomit up,
>   Which thou has belked 'gainst taintless Mellida.
> Pie. Ram't quickly down, that it may not rise up
>   To embraid my thoughts. Behold my stomach's –
>   Strike me quite through with the relentless edge
>   Of raging fury. (1.4.5–10)

A curious scene that may seem simply another instance of Marston's delight in grotesque corporeality, this early conflict depicts villain and revenger as mediating their perception of social interaction in remarkably similar physiological terms. More notably, however, it also signals Piero's facility at subtly rooting his crimes in a shared set of cultural assumptions. Antonio figures Piero's false accusation as a foul excretion discharged with a belch, something emanating from the viscera and accompanied by breath. Though figurative, the formulation provides Piero matter for improvisation. After adopting the metaphor and directing attention to his own stomach, Piero poses as though his erratic behaviour derives in part from physiological distress, something that might rise up from the viscera, not to the mouth but the brain, and unsettle his thoughts. Seeking to gloss his crimes by appealing to a common understanding of bodily disorder, Piero operates in a mode here common to the villains of the play. For when Strotzo fabricates an explanation for Andrugio's sudden passing, he does so by marshalling the language of Galenic physiology:

> The vast delights of his large sudden joys
> Opened his powers so wide, that's native heat
> So prodigally flowed t'exterior parts
> That th' inner citadel was left unmanned,
> And so surprised on sudden by cold death. (1.5.9–13)

Appealing to shared assumptions about physiological operations, Strotzo ascribes Andrugio's death to a rapid imbalance of cardiac temperature caused by pneumatic processes, the prodigal flowing of heat from the heart, the 'inner citadel'. Although spurious like Piero's claims about his own disordered health, Strotzo's lie likewise advances an explanation designed to register as plausible within the context of Piero's court. As Marston makes plain through even the villains' machinations, this is a world where the most rudimentary of bodily functions, the flow of air and heat within the body's viscera, are understood as crucial to constitutional equilibrium and where unexpected events and extreme emotions can disrupt one's internal health, affecting even the highly rarefied corporeal matter which serves as mediator between body and soul.

'*I am taking physic, here's philosophy*': Physiology, Trauma, Therapy

As the survivors respond to the traumatic news delivered by Piero, they immediately comment how such tragedy produces very real physiological effects on them – stifling breath, parching viscera – and through these initial reactions, Marston subtly introduces the idea that Stoic resolve alone will prove inadequate to the task of remedying such imbalance. Indeed, in this, the play's Galenism shapes not only its representation of physiology but also, by extension, its repudiation of Stoicism. Maria first responds to the news of Andrugio's death by declaring, 'O, fatal, disastrous, cursèd, dismal! / Choke breath and life. I breathe, I live too long' (1.5.15–16). When Maria ekes out the phrase 'Choke breath and life', it may be a kind of exclamation of wonder at the method of Andrugio's death, but her fractured syntax also points to her own sense of deteriorating well-being since she then notes she breathes and lives too long, before immediately falling into a swoon. At the same time, as Alberto counsels Antonio to be patient and calm in his own reaction, Antonio replies by pointing to his physical distress. Levelling a critique commonly used against Stoic calls for passivity – yet also doing so in tellingly Galenic terms – Antonio counters:

> Lies thy cold father dead, his glossèd eyes
> New closèd up by thy sad mother's hands?
> Hast thou a love as spotless as the brow
> Of clearest heaven, blurred with false defames?
> Are thy moist entrails crumpled up with grief
> Of parching mischief? Tell me, does thy heart
> With punching anguish spur thy gallèd ribs? (1.5.39–45)

If the earlier vision of apparitions had chilled Antonio's arteries, 'gellied' his blood, this new, sudden grief stokes excessive heat, parches his entrails, and sets his heart to violent rhythms. Of a piece within the context of Galenic physiology, Maria's stifled breath and Antonio's irregular temperature and heartbeat signal the body's inherent need to find relief from sudden trauma, a fact Marston introduces in conjunction with a repudiation of the passive acceptance of tragedy. Indeed, immediately after Maria's swoon and Antonio's rebuttal, Marston has Pandulpho, the Stoic, adopt a broadly philosophical tone as he tries to abstract the concept of pneumatic distress into mere generalities. 'Good are suppressed,' he tells Alberto, 'by base desertless clods, / That stifle gasping virtue' (1.5.68–70). Repudiating the revenger's role, at least for the time, Pandulpho refuses 'to stab in fume of blood', opting instead to call up 'louder music' as he concludes, 'let my breath exact / You strike sad tones unto this dismal act' (1.5.89, 103–4). In the immediate aftermath of receiving traumatic news, the principal characters of Marston's play, that is, figure their distress as physiological and, more specifically, as affecting their pneumatic and vascular systems. The Stoic alone – and only temporarily at that – seeks to treat such physical realities as mere metaphors by which he hopes to prop up a philosophy soon to be revealed as insufficient for addressing the body's very real needs.

Although Marston will take pains to expose the limits of Stoicism for dealing with trauma's effects on the body, the playwright first clearly establishes the philosophy's superiority to the passionate intensity of Piero's unbounded cruelty, itself characterised as an ever-metastasising physiological disorder. When Piero enters alone and triumphs over Andrugio's coffin, he privately reveals his insatiable desire for continued villainy. Not content to have 'choked / the organ of [Andrugio's] breast' (1.1.14–15), Piero now desires that 'Oblivion choke the passage of [his] fame' (2.1.1–3). As Piero continues to wax ecstatic, Marston figures the Duke's moral incontinence as itself a kind of perpetual corruption of his body's own pneumatic processes. Piero declares:

> Pale beetle-browed hate
> But newly bustles up. Sweet wrong, I clap thy thoughts.
> O, let me hug my bosom, rub my breast,
> In hope of what may hap. Andrugio rots,
> Antonio lives; umh; how long? ha, ha, how long? (2.1.8–12)

Despite pretending earlier that his deeds served as a mode of vengeance necessary for correcting his own internal distress, Piero confesses here that his crimes have, in fact, only functioned to stoke his intense hatred which will lead to still more murder, a condition he articulates by imagining his body as flowing with unwholesome forces. For Piero figures his hatred as 'pale' and 'beetle-browed', something that 'bustles up' inside him, leading him to 'hug [his] bosom, rub [his] breast', his still-growing enmity a kind of bodily concoction ever-percolating about his heart. Rather than restoring a sense of equilibrium to body and soul, Piero's actions appear, then, as producing and perpetuating disordered pneumatic flow, a sense of physiological imbalance that he lovingly seeks to cultivate in himself. Indeed, when Piero notes just a moment later that he has 'been nursed in blood, and still [has] sucked / The steam of reeking gore' (2.1.19–20), he imagines his previous crimes as nurturing, as something which feeds his continued bloodlust. When Piero later rationalises his crimes to Pandulpho by declaring, 'pollution must be purged' (2.2.3), he states a principle reaffirmed throughout the play but also one radically undercut, therefore, as applicable to his own moral and physical condition. Unlike the victims' central revenging action, which will seek to rectify the imbalance caused by genuine trauma inflicted from without, Piero's crimes perpetuate his own affective and physiological disorder. If Pandulpho's

Stoicism will fail to remedy the trauma acted upon the body, Piero's villainy, Marston makes clear, actively compounds it.

Pandulpho's Stoicism naturally appears noble in contrast to Piero's villany, and it rightly prompts him to perceive the interplay between bodily and external pneumatics endemic to his world, but his philosophy will eventually fail him, in part, because it depends upon imagining a fanciful invulnerability at odds with the reality of embodied experience. As Pandulpho clashes with Piero over Feliche's body, the Stoic interrupts the conversation, directing attention to the corpse:

> Peace, peace!
> Methinks I hear a humming murmur creep
> From out his gellied wounds. Look on those lips
> [. . .]
> look, look, they seem to stir
> And breathe defiance to black obloquy. (2.2.9–16)

As Pandulpho invokes the folklore that a corpse's wounds will bleed anew in the presence of the murderer, he also vividly emphasises the faint passage of air issuing from Feliche's corpse, as the 'gellied wounds' seem to release a 'humming murmur', the lips 'to stir / And breathe'. Pandulpho's imaginative ruminations here register a sense – acknowledged, as we have seen, by the play's other characters as well – that the external world and the faintest elements of air within the body itself remain, in some fashion, interconnected. But when Piero once more mocks Pandulpho by recalling the injustice of his situation, the Stoic notably retreats into platitudes that envision for himself an imperviousness to the vicissitudes of the harsh, destructive world in which he lives. A fantasy redolent in its way of Hamlet's own desire for a fully-realised freedom from suffering, Pandulpho's daydream here appears from the outset, however, as merely a vain yearning after an impossible illusion. Pandulpho may understand his milieu as highly pneumatic, that is, but he concomitantly fancies himself, contrary to all evidence, as immune to its forces, however penetrating and debilitating they might otherwise seem. A sage's breast, Pandulpho asserts, is 'of such well-tempered proof / It may be rased, not pierced by savage tooth / Of foaming malice [. . .]' (2.2.19–21). Indeed, after the exasperated Piero tries to dismiss the 'doting stoic' (2.2.70), Pandulpho, in an effort to sustain his fantasy of invulnerability, even imagines himself, paradoxically, as a type of *pneuma*, unable to be contained. 'Thou canst not coop me up,' Pandulpho avers, declaring that he will 'skip from earth into the arms of heaven', since 'The portholes / Of sheathèd spirit are ne'er corbed up' (2.2.76, 81, 85–6). 'I tell thee, Duke,' Pandulpho boasts by way of conclusion, 'the blasts / Of the swoll'n-cheeked winds, nor all the breath of kings / Can puff me out of my native seat of birth' (2.2.91–3). *Pneuma* may permeate the body and indeed the cosmos, but for Pandulpho – at least as he figures it here – such forces can never unsettle him, a mythical sense of imperviousness that, as will quickly become clear, remains starkly at odds with the reality of the world in which he actually lives.

In contrast to Pandulpho, Antonio rejects Stoicism, perceiving it not only as a philosophy insufficient for remedying the trauma grief causes to the body but also as itself a kind of by-product of physiological disorder, the delusion of a mind compromised by an underlying pneumatic ailment. Throughout the play, Antonio understands grief as generating physiological distress, but when Alberto seeks to comfort him with prosaic dicta encouraging forbearance, the protagonist wittily plays with the image further, claiming grief itself would have to be ill for it to accord with Stoic platitudes. 'That grief is wanton-sick,' Antonio observes, 'Whose stomach can digest and brook the diet / Of stale ill-relished counsel' (2.3.2–4). Openly repudiating, indeed mocking, the thought of Stoicism as efficacious for countering suffering, Antonio even brandishes a copy of

Seneca's *De providentia* and sardonically reassures his friend, 'I am taking physic, here's philosophy' (2.3.42). Antonio follows this sneer by railing at length against Stoicism, and, as he does so, he extends the familiar critique that the philosophy fails to remedy the actual pain caused by tragedy by persistently reminding his auditors that trauma, far from theoretical, operates on very real bodies. Addressing the absent Stoic, Antonio frames his charge, from first to last, in the language of corporeal heat:

> Thou, wrapped in furs, beaking thy limbs 'fore fires
> Forbid'st the frozen zone to shudder. Ha, ha! 'tis naught
> But foamy bubbling of a fleamy brain,
> Naught else but smoke. O, what dank, marish spirit
> But would be fired with impatience
> at my –
> No more, no more [. . .] (2.3.52–8)

Figuring the Stoic as seated before a fire, wrapped in furs, and telling the freezing they should avoid shuddering, Antonio chides the sage for too easily dismissing another's suffering and, more pointedly, depicts him as advocating a useless therapeutic model, detached from the realities of embodied experience. Antonio then levels his most serious charge at the philosophy, dismissing it as nothing more than 'smoke', the 'foamy bubbling of a fleamy brain', a mere fantasy caused by a body diseased. 'Grief', Antonio tells Mellida just a moment later, is 'invisible / And lurks in secret angles of the heart', and the heart itself 'will burst if void of vent' (2.3.70–1). Stoicism, akin to the delusions wrought by a disordered mind, offers a line of treatment antithetical, as Antonio has it, to that which is actually required for correcting such corporeal imbalance.

Before Antonio proceeds with his revenge, Marston recalls to audience attention Piero's unrestrained depravity and indicates how the villain, along with his accomplice, knowingly co-opts the rhetoric of physiological distress in order to mask an increasing desire to commit more crimes, a move that helps establish Piero as wilfully placing himself beyond hope of any form of restoration. In a scene reminiscent of Lorenzo's duping of Pedrigano in *The Spanish Tragedy*, Marston has Piero and Strotzo plan an execution to be enacted before the court, one Strotzo understands as mere theatrics, Piero as a useful way of dispatching a useless conspirator. As they plot, Piero suggests he praise, as a means of explaining Strotzo's sudden confession, 'Thy honest stomach that could not digest / The crudities of murder; but, surcharged, / Vomited'st them up in Christian piety' (2.5.30–2). That Piero and Strotzo consider this a good plan suggests they see the language as something that will register with their auditors and help render the 'gird[ing]' of Strotzo's 'pipe of breath' symbolically apt. But if Piero's court understands traumatic events and bodily operations as inherently interconnected, Piero himself, when finally alone, reveals he delights in all levels of such disorder: '[S]well plump, bold heart / For now thy tide of vengeance rolleth in,' the Duke intones, boasting how 'confusion and black murder guides / The organs of my spirit' (2.5.43–4, 47–8). Whatever language of physical and moral restoration Piero invokes publicly, the Duke intensely desires to give full reign to his incontinence, a depravity he understands as infusing his freshly-animated heart and as guiding the very 'organs' of his 'spirit'. Piero, Marston reminds us, suffers no genuine trauma but rather cultivates his own corruption, even fervently so.

Where Piero employs the rhetoric of physical healing as a *post hoc* rationalisation to cover his crimes, Antonio, traumatised by the suffering imposed on him from without, immediately suggests his revenge will not only propitiate Andrugio's departed spirit but also serve to relieve his own physiological distress. To be sure, Antonio gives considerable weight to his role in providing peace to his father's ghost. But even in his obsequies, the distraught son notably conceptualises the injustice done to his father – the injustice that initiates and grounds his own quest for retribution – in terms of bodily pneumatics. Alone with his father's hearse, Antonio sets himself to 'purify the air with odorous fume' and announces, 'Thou royal spirit of Andrugio, / Where'er thou hover'st, airy intellect, / I heave up tapers to thee' (3.1.8–20). As Antonio wonders 'in what orb thy mighty spirit soars', he implores his father to 'stoop and beat down this rising fog of shame / That strives to blur thy blood and girt defame' (3.1.27–9). By conceptualising Piero's villainy as if a fume sullying Andrugio's blood, Antonio registers his sense of such crimes as affecting even pneumatic operations and lays the groundwork to then figure revenge itself as something that brings an element of physical relief. Indeed, just a moment later, he articulates this very notion by posing the inverse, imagining the additional bodily suffering he should endure if he were to abrogate his duty to revenge:

> May I be cursèd by my father's ghost
> And blasted with incensèd breath of heaven
> If my heart beat on ought but vengeance.
> May I be numbed with horror and my veins
> Pucker with singeing torture, if my brain
> Digest a thought but of dire vengeance;
> May I be fettered slave to coward chance,
> If blood, heart, brain, plot ought save vengeance! (3.2.34–41)

Imagining his 'father's ghost' and the 'breath of heaven', two types of extra-corporeal *pnuema*, as attuned to his heart which must only 'beat on [. . .] vengeance', Antonio connects his larger role as revenger with the faintest movements of his very body. Even as he contemplates his place amid the cosmos and departed spirits, that is, Antonio conceptualises his retributive duty as salubrious, something that promises to stave off 'singeing torture' from his veins. Vengeance, as Antonio figures it, becomes something his brain must 'digest', an image, following Galen, that therefore anchors retribution in the very first instrument of Antonio's body. Through such tropes that transcend conventional appeals to propitiation or, less nobly, mere bloodlust, Marston situates Antonio's quest for vengeance as intimately connected to the most rudimentary components comprising his body's subtlest operations.

Antonio's first act of vengeance, the gratuitous killing of Julio, Piero's son, sits so uneasily with the play's final valorisation of the revengers that critics have responded with considerable consternation to the inclusion of both, but the troubling dissonance has opened within scholarship myriad useful ways for understanding Marston's unique, if grotesque, dramaturgical strategy in this scene. Julio enters, affrighted by 'bugbears and spirits' (3.2.87), and expresses love for Antonio – indeed, a love even greater than that he holds towards his father (3.3.5). After some hesitation, Antonio kills him anyway, a fate the boy seems to accept, reaffirming his love even with his dying breath. Problematic, even unconscionable, the act defies adequate explanation within the world of the play itself, and a sizable contingent of critics has either read the scene as parodistic or interpreted the play's ending as ironic, a final twist akin to that found in *The Revenger's Tragedy*, meant to provide the audience one final surprise. One particularly provocative method of accounting for Marston's choice here, however, has been to understand this scene as something akin to the theatre of the absurd[61] or, at the least, an exceptionally garish moment designed to highlight various strands of symbolic meaning.[62] Whether parodistic or anticipatory of the absurd, the scene certainly self-consciously foregrounds multiple thematic resonances to which we might add that of bodily pneumatics, a trope the entire passage relentlessly invokes. For, indeed,

Marston employs this grotesque moment, it seems, as a particularly arresting way to emphasise the play's investment in a fully-realised physiological theory and how, more specifically, such a theory shapes the quest for Piero's blood.

Amid all the talk of propitiating departed spirits, Marston figures Antonio's attack on Julio as a kind of dissection meant to extract Piero's blood and, by doing so, frames the revenging action, in part, as the attempt to purge an infection that otherwise would run to unrestrained excesses, debilitating all in its compass. Immediately prior to Julio's entrance, Antonio ruminates on the state of the world and, describing his bleak view of humanity in terms evocative of the Prologue's pneumatic imagery, bemoans how '[M]ature age grows only mature vice, / And ripens only to corrupt and rot / The budding hopes of infant modesty' (3.2.65–7). Prompted by the thought of Piero's villainies yet implicating all people, Antonio more explicitly extends the image, rueing how 'man' has 'all hell-strained juice [. . .] poured to his veins, making him drunk / With fuming surquedies, contempt of heaven, / Untamed arrogance, lust, state, pride, murder' (3.2.70–3). The sense of disorder Piero earlier figured as bustling up within him, a disorder he sought to nurture and loose upon the world, reappears here in Antonio's speech, a disorder, however, that he finds repulsive, one he seeks to counter. Into this context, Marston introduces Julio. Propelled by Andrugio's ghost yet flagging at the impossible predicament in which he finds himself, Antonio imagines his assault on Julio as a type of dissection:

> O that I knew which joint, which side, which limb
> Were father all, and had no mother in't,
> That I might rip it vein by vein and carve revenge
> In bleeding rases! But since 'tis mixed together,
> Have at adventure, pell-mell, no reverse –
> Come hither, boy. This is Andrugio's hearse. (3.3.20–5)

As Antonio stabs Julio, Marston notably *avoids* framing the assault as one that seeks a life-for-a-life; for all the talk of revenge here, there is remarkably little sense that Antonio attempts to exchange a son's life in place of a father's. Instead, Marston has Antonio remain singularly concerned with extirpating any aspect of Piero, the villain whose very existence has infected, and continues to infect, the court. Indeed, Antonio seems intent on looking past the realities of personalities and affective ties – Piero's to Julio, his own to Julio, Julio's to him – to the matter of sheer physicality alone. However distracted, perhaps even deluded, Marston's revenger may be, he remains principally preoccupied with differentiating vein from vein, joint from joint, in the inevitably fraught desire to enact revenge on Piero's 'blood' but not – if only the realities of the world would allow it – Julio himself.[63] If Marston's grotesque aesthetic troubles reception of the literal action onstage, the playwright seems content to marshal such shocking dramaturgy as a means to underscore his interest in the imagery of staunching infection as part of the therapy requisite for countering the very real physiological trauma caused by grief.

As Marston emphasises the purging of even the faintest traces of Piero's blood, the playwright also depicts the inhalation of its accompanying fume as central to the act of revenge, a curious image designed to signal how retribution will help relieve the trauma caused by the play's initial crime. The inhalation of fume that has been relentlessly characterised throughout the play as corrupted may seem an unusual method for conveying a sense of healing. But Marston, having established how the *scelus* disrupts even the subtlest pneumatic operations of the victims' bodies, remains especially concerned with linking the act of vengeance to a physiological relief that extends even to the deepest recesses of the body's interior. At the death of Piero's son, the revenger, who had vowed to 'suck red vengeance / Out of Piero's wounds (3.2.78–9), stresses that he perceives Julio's body as wholly representing Piero alone. '[N]ow there's nothing but Piero left,' Antonio declares, 'He is all Piero, father, all; this blood, / This breast, this heart, Piero all' (3.3.55–7). Addressing Julio's corpse directly, Antonio concludes that it is 'thy father's blood / I thus make incense of' (3.3.61–2). As Antonio 'make[s] incense' of Piero's blood extracted from Julio, he stresses how its pneumatic properties should bring peace to his father: 'Ghost of my poisoned sire,' he intones, 'suck this fume; / To sweet revenge, perfume thy circling air / With smoke of blood' (3.3.63–5). But if 'these fresh-reeking drops' (3.3.66) affect Andrugio, if 'revenge as swift as lightning [. . .] clears [his] heart' (3.3.32–3), Antonio also emphasises the influence retribution has on himself. For when he again draws attention to the blood's fume – 'Look how I smoke in blood, reeking the steam / Of foaming vengeance' – Antonio does so in order to convey his altered state as well: 'Methinks I am all air and feel no weight / Of human dirt clog' (3.5.17–18, 20–1). As imperfect and unsettling as Marston's vehicle for conveying this sense of relief may be, the playwright, by marshalling the pneumatic trope once more, this time as a means of symbolising triumph over disorder, depicts Antonio's revenge, then, as something that counters his position as victim and helps ease the physiological distress grief wreaks on the body.

Marston against the Stoics, or, the Therapy of Revenge

Through Antonio's subsequent disguise as a fool, adopted so he can get close to Piero, Marston subtly reinforces the recurring, interconnecting claims of the play as a whole, namely, that vengeance offers a physiological relief that Stoicism, in its fanciful view of the world, never adequately addresses. Antonio's disguise, that is, functions not only as the practical means of enabling access to Piero. It also provides Marston an opportunity to underscore Antonio's imperative that he find release from the corporeal effects of grief and, at the same time, to assault Stoicism's false comfort – specifically, its notion of *pneuma* as 'containing cause' – by aligning it with pure folly. When the newly-invigorated Antonio adopts the habit of a fool, he wryly notes that, were he a genuine fool, he would 'want sense to feel / The stings of anguish shoot through every vein' (4.1.50–1). Akin to Hamlet's yearning for *ataraxia*, yet here acknowledged as only truly available as the by-product of mental impairment, Antonio envies the fool his immunity to the trauma caused by grief, a trauma this revenger registers as extending even to one's veins. Antonio's disguise thus gestures to a relief that he himself can only find in retribution, but the revenger also cleverly uses the fool's habit to mock the Stoics as well. When he first appears before Piero, Antonio feigns madness by blowing bubbles, a scene that seems, at first glance, rather inconsequential:

> Ant. [Blowing bubbles.] Puff! hold, world! Puff! hold, bubble! Puff! hold, world! Puff! break not behind! Puff! thou art full of wind; puff! keep up thy wind. Puff! 'Tis broke; and now I laugh like a good fool at the breath of mine own lips: he, he, he, he, he. (4.2.28–32)

Easily overlooked as mere playacting, Antonio's antics subtly satirise the Stoicism that would seek to deny him a claim to revenge. For as Antonio blows bubbles, he figures each one as a little 'world', begging each to 'hold' and 'break not'. Adopting the role of the fool and imagining little pneumatic worlds that he wishes would – but ultimately cannot – cohere, the revenger parodies the Stoic philosophy that has posited, against the evidence of his own embodied experience, a containing cause that holds a fragile, tragic world together. Antonio had earlier deemed Stoicism nothing more than the 'foamy bubbling of a fleamy brain', and, here, in the habit of a fool, suggests it amounts to the mere babbling of a madman who 'laugh[s] like a good fool at the breath of [his] own lips'.⁶⁴ Antonio's disguise gains access to Piero, but it also gestures, then, to both the relief he seeks in revenge and the fictions of the Stoics which would otherwise deny that relief.

Marston levels his final, most devastating critique of Stoicism by having Pandulpho openly repudiate the philosophy he has espoused throughout the play, and the rationale justifying this crucial pivot in his thinking principally centres on his realisation that the traumatised body, in a world lacking a 'containing cause', demands a therapeutic response. Marston underscores, that is, that Pandulpho has had pneumatics all wrong: the body *does* require release, the cosmos does *not* cohere in rational harmony. Antonio, mourning the recent death of Mellida, identifies her as his 'vital blood', his trauma as 'stifling' (4.4.10, 21), yet when he shares his sorrows with Pandulpho, the struggling Stoic replies at first with familiar, stale *sententiae* that provide no real relief for his pains. Confronted once more with the corpse of his own family member, however, Pandulpho becomes unable to maintain his pose any longer. Discarding his affectation and its accompanying platitudes, the grieving father recants:

> Man will break out, despite philosophy.
> Why, all this while I ha' but played a part,
> Like to some boy that acts a tragedy,
> Speaks burly words and raves out passion;
> But when he thinks upon his infant weakness,
> He droops his eye. I spake more than a god,
> Yet am less than a man.
> I am the miserablest soul that breathes. (4.5.46–53)

The explicit renunciation of Stoicism by the play's most vocal Stoic, Pandulpho's lines here carry significant weight. Notably, Marston has the distressed father reject Stoic thought, in particular, for its failure to adequately address the reality of severe trauma. Indeed, through the very structure of the first line – 'Man will break out, despite philosophy' – Marston sets in direct opposition to each other the pressing needs of the grieving individual and the dictates of a received tradition. Stoic *sententiae* may well prescribe forbearance, but a truly traumatised victim will inevitably seek release; 'burly words' may help in posing as 'more than a god', but the person reduced to 'infant weakness' requires more than a merely theoretical therapy.[65] In fact, by depicting himself in doubly pneumatic terms, as 'the miserablest soul that breathes', Pandulpho gestures to the effect sorrow has on even his body's most fundamental aspects, an awareness of the extent of his trauma that, as it happens, coincides with a marked shift in his perception of the cosmos. For when Pandulpho concludes 'all the strings of nature's symphony / Are cracked and jar' (4.5.69–70), he registers a sense of the universe not as ordered by a rational containing cause but rather as broken, discordant. Racked by grief, his image of a rational cosmos shattered, Pandulpho seeks instead a new method for responding to his trauma.

With Pandulpho joining the ranks of the conspirators, Marston frames the impending revenge by recalling how Piero's crimes represent a kind of physiological disorder, and he consequently figures the final retribution as a cleansing that heals not only the revengers themselves but also, in a move that broadens his use of the pneumatic trope, the state as well. Before the conspirators meet, Andrugio's ghost enters and delivers a monologue, anticipating the revenging action in what might otherwise seem rather unusual terms:

> The fist of strenuous Vengeance is clutched,
> And stern Vindicta tow'reth up aloft
> That she may fall with a more weighty peise
> And crush life's sap from out Piero's veins.
> Now 'gins the lep'rous cores of ulcered sins
> Wheel to a head [. . .] (5.1.3–8)

The novelty of Andrugio's imagery here should not be lost. For the vengeful ghost expresses his desire for retribution not in the common tropes of *lex talionis* – an eye for an eye, a tooth for a tooth – but rather in those of vascular distress. Andrugio imagines a personified Vindicta as striking from on high, as falling from a great height and with considerable weight, in order to purge the very blood from the tyrannical Duke's veins by a great force. The disorder Piero has lovingly nurtured in himself and loosed upon others Revenge, Andrugio hopes, will now expel. As if to make the implications of this purgation more clear, Marston immediately follows this curious formulation by recalling how Piero's crimes appear as a disease, as 'lep'rous cores of ulcered sins', now swelling into boils, a corruption that has started to affect an even broader segment of the populace. 'I do find the citizens grown sick / With swallowing the bloody crudities / Of black Piero's acts' (5.1.17–19), Pandulpho asserts a moment later, depicting the Duke's villainies as a sickness starting to distemper the citizenry as well. The disordered populace thus desires, Pandulpho determines, to 'vomit him from off their government' (5.3.20). If such rhetoric signals Pandulpho's fresh awareness of the physiological aspects of the trauma Piero's villainies provoke, it also establishes the need for retribution to purge an ever-increasing corruption infecting the court. Whether the crushing of blood from out of the corrupt Duke's veins or the vomiting of Piero from the state itself, Marston figures the revenging action as a mode of healing, not only of the revengers' bodies but also, then, of the body politic itself.

Depicting Piero throughout the play's denouement as intoxicated by his own depravity, his body itself as infused with corruption, Marston indicates that the revengers, as part of their own quest for healing, must also staunch the contagion perpetually emanating from the tyrannical Duke, a clever move by which the author further anchors the drama's final revenging action into the subtle ontological framework which has governed the play throughout. During the masque which precedes the revenge, Marston presents Piero revelling in what he considers his moment of triumph. Calling for more wine, Piero commands his auditors to drink as he celebrates his secure position:

> Force the plump-lipped god
> Skip light lavoltas in your full-sapped veins!
> 'Tis well, brim-full. Even I have glut of blood.
> Let quaff carouse: I drink this Bordeaux wine
> Unto the health of dead Andrugio,
> Feliche, Strotzo, and Antonio's ghosts. (5.4.21–6)

By having Piero's thoughts turn from the spirits in his veins to the spirits of his victims, Marston subtly figures the Duke as drunk on his own villainies, aligning the intoxicating effects of the wine with those of his previous crimes. Directly linking the cup of wine which is 'brim-full' with Piero's claim that he has 'glut of blood', Marston invites us to consider the play's crimes, that is, as, like wine itself, generating an airiness, a fume, within Piero's blood, creating the effect of 'light lavoltas' dancing within 'full-sapped veins'. This is the corruption the revengers are up against, and this the tyranny they seek to overthrow, their revenge, linked to the play's prevailing ontology, taking on the nature of a therapeutic restorative to this widespread infection. Notably, the conspirators understand their act of retribution as the shutting down of a source of corruption that originates, in markedly physiological terms, from deep within Piero himself. For as the revengers kill the Duke who has so traumatised them and infected the court, they repeatedly depict the villain as diseased, invoking 'his black blood', his 'black liver', and even noting the pulsation of his veins (5.5.37, 41). After the revengers cut out Piero's tongue, for instance, Antonio boasts, 'I have't, Pandulpho;

the veins panting bleed, / Trickling fresh gore about my fist', a moment that prompts Andrugio's ghost to delight in seeing Antonio 'triumph in his black blood' (5.5.34–5, 37). As the principal source of corruption, Piero must be stopped, and Marston consequently figures his death as a kind of stifling, a suffocation, as even the Duke's veins pant before eventually going still. Lest the emphasis be missed, Marston has Antonio declare, 'Thus the hand of heaven chokes / The throat of murder. This is for my father's blood!' (5.5.72, 76–7). Whatever the extent this scene contains tropes common to the denouement of revenge tragedy, Marston markedly infuses each with a sense that the revengers are stifling the principal origin of their own distress, a source diseased to its very core.

As the senators praise rather than punish the revengers for killing Piero, Marston mutes the rhetoric of *lex talionis* in the play's final moments, stressing instead the flow of the tyrant's blood as integral to the healing of the victims and, more broadly, the court. Jostling to take credit for killing Piero, the revengers direct attention not to the equalisation of wrongs – not, that is, to the justice of their actions taken on behalf of those murdered – but rather to the simple fact that they spilled the tyrant's blood. 'I pierced the monster's heart / With an undaunted hand,' Antonio boasts, while Pandulpho, not wishing to be outdone, likewise brags, ''Twas I sluiced out his life-blood' (5.6.5–6, 8). These mentions of the piercing of Piero's heart and sluicing of his blood prompt Galeatzo, addressing Antonio, to declare, 'Thou art another Hercules to us / In ridding huge pollution from our state' (5.6.12–13). By alluding to the flushing of the Augean stables, Galeatzo adopts the pneumatic imagery by which the revengers have principally framed their deed, and the entirety of the play's survivors – avengers and court authorities alike – share a sense that the flowing of Piero's blood serves as a crucial means for restoring health. The salubrious effect of ridding the corrupt Duke registers as immediate, but Marston also indicates, however, that those most profoundly victimised by Piero will require still more time to recuperate. Rejecting the possibility of suicide, Pandulpho, for instance, promises to enter religious orders, since they must 'keep this lodge / Of dirt's corruption till dread power calls / Our souls' appearance' (5.6.32–4). Where Pandulpho registers an awareness of their continued corruption, Antonio likewise signals their need for additional healing, asserting he and his conspirators must 'cleanse our hands, / Purge hearts of hatred', and himself promising, while mourning Mellida, to 'weep away my brain / In true affection's tears' (5.6.37–40). Through the reduplication of such tropes at the play's end – the state as flushed of pollution by the sluicing of Piero's blood; the heart and brain as purged and cleansed, even as the soul awaits its final release – Marston reinforces the play's investment in pneumatics as central to all modes of therapeutic response.

By making pneumatics and the vascular system so central to every stage of his play, Marston infuses the bloody imagery of the final revenging action – imagery that might otherwise seem quotidian for a revenge tragedy – with a clearer sense that retribution functions in this particular world as a kind of therapeutic response to trauma, one that reaches even to the body's most attenuated substance which mediates between material flesh and immaterial soul. Amid all the ways Marston's play examines the social, political and metaphysical implications of retribution, *Antonio's Revenge* remains especially attentive to the corporeal effects of grief. Indeed, Marston's curious preoccupations that have seemed something of a muddle when considered independently – his obsession with valorising the revengers, with repudiating Stoicism, and with detailing the interior workings of the body – all cohere remarkably well when considered in light of the age's familiar Galenism. For following Galenic assumptions about pneumatic flow and sharing the philosopher's anti-Stoic disposition, Marston depicts his characters as subject to a complex, sophisticated physiological regime that assumes the body's subtlest operations demand relief in response to intense distress. In particular, the playwright renders grief as not only upsetting the body's internal temperature but also, by extension, affecting even the pneumatics of the vascular system. Drawing attention at every stage to the temperature, fume, smoke and foam within the body's blood and organs, Marston figures trauma, that is, as reaching the most attenuated matter of the body, the *pneuma*, which, as Galenism has it, ultimately interfaces with the very soul itself, a quantity so crucial, in fact, in mediating between material and immaterial that one can reasonably wonder, as Galen himself momentarily does, which side of the dividing line it actually occupies.[66] Representing grief as affecting the deepest recesses of one's body, even to the point of impacting, in a quite literal way, the psychological mechanisms of the victim, Marston invites consideration of what, if anything, could alleviate such suffering. As Marston exposes Stoicism's doctrine of *apatheia* as unable to provide genuine relief, the playwright offers revenge, then, as the most viable alternative, tethering the play's final retributive act into the prevailing ontological ideas which, from first to last, have subtended the world he has created. Within this world where trauma ravages the innermost parts of the body, Marston thus figures retribution as providing what Stoic *apatheia* cannot: namely, a means for quelling any persistent source of ongoing abuse as well as a method for relieving internal distress that plagues, and would otherwise continue to debilitate, the victim. In doing so, Marston renders Antonio's revenge, however fraught it may ultimately prove, as a mode of therapeutic relief more attuned to the most fundamental operations of the world than that offered by the fanciful theories of the Stoics.

Notes

1. See W. Reavley Gair, 'Introduction', in *Antonio's Revenge*, ed. W. Reavley Gair, *The Revels Plays* (Manchester: Manchester University Press, 1999), 12–19.
2. T. S. Eliot, *Essays on Elizabethan Drama* (New York: Harcourt, Brace, and Company, 1932), 165.
3. Phoebe S. Spinrad, 'The Sacralization of Revenge in *Antonio's Revenge*', *Comparative Drama* 39.2 (2005): 171.
4. Joseph Loewenstein, 'Marston's Gorge and the Question of Formalism', *Renaissance Literature and its Formal Engagements*, ed. Mark David Rasmussen (New York: Palgrave, 2002), 97.
5. Samuel Schoenbaum, 'The Precarious Balance of John Marston', *PMLA* 67.7 (1952): 1075, 1072. See also Loewenstein, 'Marston's Gorge', 98–101 and Georgia Brown, 'Disgusting John Marston: Sensationalism and the Limits of a Post-Modern Marston', *Nordic Journal of English Studies* 4.2 (2005): 121–41.
6. All quotes come from John Marston, *Antonio's Revenge*, ed. W. Reavley Gair, *The Revels Plays* (Manchester: Manchester University Press, 1999).
7. On *pneuma* as used to explain 'neurological or psychological function', see P. N. Singer, 'Introduction', *Galen: Selected Works*, trans. P. N. Singer (Oxford: Oxford University Press, 1997), xii. On the pulse as cause – rather than merely symptom – of physiological and psychological disorder, see also Galen, 'The Pulse for Beginners', in *Galen: Selected Works*, 335–44.
8. On Stoic *pneuma* [as] an attempt to give a causal explanation of all events by making them stages in the history of a single, rational, continuously changing substance', see A. A. Long, 'The Stoic Concept of Evil', *The Philosophical Quarterly* 18.73 (1968): 332.
9. On revenge's therapeutic capacity, see Linda Woodbridge, *English Revenge Drama* (Cambridge: Cambridge University Press, 2010), 22–6.

10. Richard J. Durling, 'A Chronological Census of Renaissance Editions and Translations of Galen', *Journal of the Warburg and Courtauld Institutes* 24.3/4 (1961): 232–3, 236.
11. Ibid. 231.
12. *De placitis*, in Galen, *On the Doctrines of Hippocrates and Plato*, ed. and trans. Phillip De Lacy, 3 vols (Berlin: Akademie-Verlag, 1984), 236. All *De placitis* quotes come from vol. 2.
13. Durling, 'A Chronological Census', 242.
14. Mary C. Erler, 'The First English Printing of Galen: The Formation of the Company of Barber-Surgeons', *Huntington Library Quarterly* 48.2 (1985): 159.
15. See Durling, 'A Chronological Census', 275–8, 299.
16. Nancy Siraisi, 'Vesalius and the Reading of Galen's Teleology', *Renaissance Quarterly* 50.1 (1997): 2.
17. Durling, 'A Chronological Census', 245. See also Erler, 'The First English Printing of Galen', 168–9 and Vivian Nutton, *Ancient Medicine* (New York: Routledge, 2004), 376–8.
18. Nancy Siraisi, 'Anatomizing the Past: Physicians and History in Renaissance Culture', *Renaissance Quarterly* 53.1 (2000): 109; see also Durling, 'A Chronological Census', 244.
19. David J. Furley and J. S. Wilkie, *Galen: On Respiration and the Arteries* (Princeton: Princeton University Press, 1984), 3.
20. F. David Hoeniger, *Medicine and Shakespeare in the English Renaissance* (Newark: University of Delaware Press, 1992), 93.
21. Ibid. 93.
22. See also Heinrich von Staden, 'Body, Soul, and Nerves: Epicurus, Herophilus, Erasistratus, the Stoics, and Galen', in *Psyche and Soma: Physicians and Metaphysicians on the Mind–Body Problem from Antiquity to Enlightenment*, ed. John P. Wright and Paul Potter (Oxford: Clarendon Press, 2000), 79–116.
23. *De placitis*, 445–7. See also *De usu pulsuum*, in *Galen: On Respiration and the Arteries*, ed. David J. Furley and J. S. Wilkie, 201 and Hoeniger, *Medicine and Shakespeare*, 94.
24. On the psychic *pneuma*, 'the distinctive bodily matter used uniquely by *psychē* as its tool', see von Staden, 'Body, Soul, and Nerves', 113.
25. *De placitis*, 445–7.

26. *De usu respirationis*, in *Galen: On Respiration and the Arteries*, ed. David J. Furley and J. S. Wilkie, 121.
27. Ibid. 131.
28. Hoeniger, *Medicine and Shakespeare*, 133–4.
29. *De usu respirationis*, 121. See also 119. Galen also allows for the possibility that psychic *pneuma* needs vapour arising from blood as nourishment (*De usu pulsuum*, ed. Furley and Wilkie, 127).
30. *De usu respirationis*, 125, 127.
31. Ibid. 133.
32. On Galen's theory that pulse contributes to 'the restoration of psychic pneuma', see Furley and Wilkie, 'Introduction', in *Galen: On Respiration and the Arteries*, 68.
33. *De usu pulsuum*, 190, 207. See also 227.
34. *De usu respirationis*, 109.
35. Ibid. 109, 133. See also 119 and *De usu pulsuum*, 207.
36. See Furley and Wilkie, 'Introduction', in *Galen: On Respiration and the Arteries*, 5 and Hoeniger, *Medicine and Shakespeare*, 144–5.
37. *De usu pulsuum*, 190.
38. Ibid. 213.
39. William W. E. Slights, *The Heart in the Age of Shakespeare* (Cambridge: Cambridge University Press, 2011), 27.
40. I. E. Drabkin, 'Remarks on Ancient Psychopathology', *Isis* 46.3 (1955): 229.
41. On the differences between Galenic and Stoic *pneuma*, see Ian Johnston, *Galen: On Diseases and Symptoms* (Cambridge: Cambridge University Press, 2006), 11–20.
42. 'Stoicism and Medicine', *The Cambridge Companion to the Stoics*, ed. Brad Inwood (Cambridge: Cambridge University Press, 2003), 298–9.
43. Ibid. 301.
44. Peter Barker, 'Stoic Contributions to Early Modern Science', in *Atoms, Pneuma, and Tranquillity*, ed. Margaret J. Osler (Cambridge: Cambridge University Press, 1991), 138.
45. *Galen*, ed. Furley and Wilkie, 37.
46. Hankinson, 'Stoicism and Medicine', 301.

47. Christopher Gill, 'Galen and the Stoics: Mortal Enemies or Blood Brothers?' *Phronesis: A Journal for Ancient Philosophy* 52.1 (2007): 90.
48. *On the Doctrines of Hippocrates and Plato: Books I–V*, ed. and trans. Phillip de Lacy. 3rd edn (Berlin: Akademie Verlag, 2005), 301.
49. Ibid. 303.
50. Ibid. 303–5.
51. Ibid. 307.
52. Ibid. 309–11.
53. Qtd in Gill, 'Galen and the Stoics', 102.
54. On early modern 'suspicion of Stoic apathy', see Jessica Wolfe, *Humanism, Machinery, and Renaissance Literature* (Cambridge: Cambridge University Press, 2004), 214.
55. Ibid. 215.
56. Joshua Scodel, *Excess and the Mean in Early Modern English Literature* (Princeton: Princeton University Press, 2009), 2.
57. Reid Barbour, *English Epicures and Stoics: Ancient Legacies in Early Stuart Culture* (Amherst: University of Massachusetts Press, 1998), 15–16.
58. Ibid. 16.
59. Schoenbaum, 'The Precarious Balance of John Marston', 1071.
60. Joseph Loewenstein, 'Marston's Gorge and the Question of Formalism', in *Renaissance Literature and Its Formal Engagements*, 93.
61. See Rick Bowers, 'John Marston at the "mart of woe": The "Antonio" Plays', in *The Drama of John Marston: Critical Revisions* (Cambridge: Cambridge University Press, 2000), 18–21.
62. On this scene as conspicuously invoking pagan ritual, biblical sacrifice and Senecan convention, see G. K. Hunter, 'Introduction', in *Antonio's Revenge* (Lincoln, NB: Regents Renaissance Drama, 1965), xvii; Spinrad, 'The Sacralization of Revenge in *Antonio's Revenge*', 173–9; and Brian Shireen, 'Patronage and Perverse Bestowal in *The Spanish Tragedy* and *Antonio's Revenge*', *English Literary Renaissance* 41.2 (2011): 276, respectively.

63. Marston reiterates this idea when Antonio tells Julio: 'Thy father's blood that flows within thy veins / Is it I loathe, is that that revenge must suck' (3.3.33).
64. On the fool's windiness, see Brown, 'Disgusting John Marston', 123.
65. On Pandulpho as now understanding Stoicism 'as a kind of dramatic posturing', see Jonathan Dollimore, *Radical Tragedy: Religion, Ideology and Power in the Drama of Shakespeare and his Contemporaries*, 3rd edn (New York: Palgrave, 2010), 33.
66. Brown argues that even through his 'exploitation of disgust' Marston probes the 'inescapable relationship between the internal and external, between the body and the soul, between materiality and abstraction' ('Disgusting John Marston', 139).

CHAPTER 5

PROHAIRESIS ON THE INSIDE: *THE DUCHESS OF MALFI* AND EPICTETIAN VOLITION

So far, this book has argued that the distinctive atmospheres of early modern revenge tragedies derive, in significant measure, from the subtle shaping influence of classical ideas conventionally overlooked in existing literary criticism. In this final chapter, I'd like to turn to the Stoicism of John Webster's *The Duchess of Malfi* in order to examine the extensive influence and the full performative force of classical ideas previously acknowledged as present within Webster's play but only in a markedly narrow and circumscribed way. Though occupied with other matters, we have witnessed in each preceding chapter hints of the limited philosophical horizons traditionally attributed to revenge tragedy through the various protagonists' flirtation with the idea of Stoic resignation. From Hieronimo's ambiguous declaration of *vindicta mihi* (does he invoke here Seneca or St Paul?) to Titus' temporary pause before giving vent to his own fury to Hamlet's envy of Horatio (who, 'hast been / as one in suffering all, that suffers nothing') to Antonio and Pandulpho's repudiation of Stoic quiescence (''tis naught / But foamy bubbling of a fleamy brain' and 'man will break out despite philosophy'), Stoicism has emerged as something to be considered, at times deeply desired, but always discarded, and, in some instances, outright mocked. Such is the more familiar ground of revenge tragedy's engagement with classical philosophy. But while these flashes of Stoic thought appear amid the tempestuous happenings of other plays, John Webster's *The Duchess of Malfi* has long been understood as especially indebted to this philosophical lineage, second only to George Chapman's *Bussy d'Ambois* in its sympathetic approach toward, even valorisation of, Stoic ideals. Curiously, however, our understanding of the play's investment in this particular strand of classical philosophy has remained unaccountably restricted to the moment of the Duchess' death itself. In her resolute confrontation of imminent, violent death – most notably her defiant declaration 'I am Duchess of Malfi still' – critics have rightly marked one of the early modern stage's paradigmatic moments of Stoic resolve. But what of the rest of the play? Why have we casually noted the sudden emergence of Stoic philosophy here at the end of the Duchess' life but not before – or, since the play famously doesn't end with the death of its heroine, after as well? Why has a philosophy as developed and multivalent as Stoicism not registered as obtaining more broadly, not only as an ethos animating the Duchess' character in her final moments but also as a pervasive ontological framework shaping the rest of the world Webster so assiduously constructs?

The Duchess' final resolve which has resonated so profoundly with audiences, has, at the same time, also seemed largely out of step with the rest of the play's characteristic impulses – indeed, has stood out as so remarkable in the first place precisely on account of how effectively it serves to elevate the Duchess beyond her debased and debasing environment. In this chapter, however, I'd like to suggest that Stoicism provides Webster with much more than simply an incidental mechanism for setting his heroine apart from the play's villains in her dying moments. In much the same way that the other philosophies studied throughout this book have generated fully-realised, conditioning frameworks for various retribution narratives, Stoicism helps inform not only the entire cast of variegated characters populating Webster's play but also, often in rather subtle ways, the very distinct atmosphere for which this brooding Jacobean revenge drama has long been praised. Indeed, although occasionally criticised for its cumbrous *sententiae* and melodramatic moments, *The Duchess of Malfi* has captivated audiences with its foreboding aura of 'dark sensationalism and menace', as a world 'full', in Rupert Brooke's evocative phrase, 'of the feverish and ghastly turmoil of a nest of maggots'.[1] Encroaching on Webster's characters at every turn, this menacing atmosphere impinges on their desires, threatens their ability to know themselves as fully human, capable of determining their own courses of action independent of autocratic supervision. Indeed, this sense of an ever-present threat from coercive forces pits the internal workings of the individual – his or her intangible thoughts, perceptions and resolutions – against the physical dangers of the Amalfi court but also, less materially, against the subtle ideological pressure brought to bear by the tyrannical ruler's manipulative rhetoric. A nightmarish world which promises to dehumanise all within its compass, the court Webster presents remains intrinsically hostile to the social aspirations of its citizens, each desiring to advance his or her own state. The Duchess' final act of defiance, her refusal to assent within the untouchable recesses of her own thoughts, even as her body remains subject to tyrannical coercion, exists, that is, within a larger, more extensively entrenched system where internal desire continually encounters external oppression. This atmospheric condition endemic to the entire Amalfi court invites inquiry, then, into how, if at all, the underlying tenets of Stoic philosophy, promising as they do an immaterial, interior space ultimately secure from the intrusion of others, might reverberate beyond the narrow confines of the Duchess' prison cell itself and, instead, find expression throughout the play as a whole.

Dividing the role of protagonist between remarrying widow and masterless man, Webster's *The Duchess of Malfi* takes as its central concern the expression of human agency within the suffocating milieu of a controlling court, a despotic political regime obsessed with surveilling and dehumanising its own citizenry.² Despite the ostensible power enjoyed by the Duchess as an aristocrat and the seeming freedom afforded Bosola by his masterless status, both protagonists exist within a conscripted, limited world, hostile to individual autonomy. The Duchess, both lauded and faulted by critics for remarrying beneath her caste, has seemed fundamentally circumscribed, even prior to her literal imprisonment.³ Bosola, likewise, has appeared to many as trapped by the inherent inequities of Ferdinand's court. Notably, Webster repeatedly articulates this repressive, closed world through tropes of subjugated or contained animals, constructing his ghastly milieu not by invoking the otherworldly but rather by persistently figuring the play's inhabitants as something subhuman. Bosola, consequently, appears a mere 'creature' (1.2.204), the Duchess a caged bird (4.2.12–13) or 'English mastiff [. . .] fierce with tying' (4.1.13), and Julia a subdued falcon (2.4.28–30) or 'tame elephant' (2.4.32). Even Ferdinand, the character with the most power, imagines himself a wolf, declaring he 'account[s] this world but a dog-kennel' (5.5.67), while the Cardinal, too, perceives himself as dying 'like a leveret / Without any resistance' (5.5.45–6). *The Duchess of Malfi*, in short, teems.⁴ But *why* does its court prove a veritable menagerie, a 'rank pasture' (1.2.222) full of predators and parasites, a space where its inhabitants – masters and servants alike – remain dehumanised within the existing hierarchical structure?⁵ In an era when alignment with the creaturely could just as easily take on positive associations as negative ones, Webster creates a world saturated (with the notable exception of the Duchess' perception of herself) with the assumption that association with the bestial signifies a marked falling away from human dignity.[6] Why, in the end, does Webster specifically turn to the enclosure of animals as a means of creating his nightmarish world and examining thereby the politics of human autonomy?

Webster's persistent and multivalent use of tropes of the bestial as a way of exploring agency and repression emerges, I will argue, in large measure from his indebtedness to Epictetian Stoicism, specifically its doctrine of *prohairesis*, the innate capacity for rational choice that differentiates humanity from the subhuman. For Epictetus, *prohairesis*, or volition, principally manifests itself in one's assent to (or withholding assent from) various impressions, or *phantasiai*, that strike the mind. Those who assent to false impressions constrict their mental horizons, diminish their own humanity; conversely, those who disregard false impressions remain free and fully human, even if otherwise repressed by tyrants. In this way, Epictetian *prohairesis* also promises, therefore, a unique form of liberty by positing the mind as ultimately unassailable: one's freedom or even life may be taken away, Epictetus asserts, but never one's *desire* for such things. Interestingly, as much as assent to false impressions precipitates a loss of full humanity, the retention and cultivation of one's faculty of choice becomes understood as a kind of living in accordance with one's intrinsic nature, a state frequently (and arguably best) elucidated by recourse to the trope of the unrestrained animal, living freely in nature. While the doctrines of Epictetian philosophy may seem a retreat from the political sphere into the untouchable recesses of an imperceptible interiority, Webster's play subtly reveals the threat such a radical notion of liberty might pose to a repressive regime. Amid the menagerie of other debased humans, the

Duchess and Bosola – at different moments and in vastly different ways – resist the dehumanising impressions reinforced by their milieu, the former most fully cultivating the *intrinsic* capacity for choice which was distinct to Epictetian philosophy. Where the Duchess presents an alternative model for managing aristocratic power in the service of a more equitable ethos, Bosola eventually seeks to dispatch tyrannical figureheads by force. As Webster tellingly depicts both modes of resistance as failing to remedy the court's ubiquitous corruption, the playwright gestures to the still more radical prospect that solidarity across the various strata of society might prevail, where secret defiance and violent rebellion had not, in displacing systemic inequity. By aligning Bosola's revenge, as well as the Duchess' remarriage and death, with a strain of Epictetian *prohairesis*, then, Webster tethers the play's multiple acts of resistance into a complex yet coherent ontological ground, and, in doing so, figures the imperceptible stirrings of human volition not as a means of retreat into the untouchable mind but rather as a force – if distributed broadly among the dehumanised and dispossessed – rife with revolutionary potential.

Prohairesis, Phantasiai, *Assent: Epictetian Thought and the Nature of Human Liberty*

By the time Webster wrote *The Duchess of Malfi*, the works of Epictetus had enjoyed considerable popularity throughout Europe, principally on account of the philosopher's *Enchiridion* but also through the more expansive explication of his ideas found in the *Discourses*. The *Enchiridion*, a condensed review of the central tenets of Epictetian thought, received sustained attention from late antiquity through the early modern period and beyond. Simplicius' extensive sixth-century commentary on the text, 'one of the few surviving commentaries on any ancient philosopher other than

Plato or Aristotle', attests in particular to Epictetus' early and pronounced appeal. After Poliziano's 1497 translation of the *Enchiridion* into Latin, vernacular copies abounded.[7] Following James Sanford's landmark English translation of 1567,[8] John Healey published *Epictetus his manuall* in 1610, an edition popular enough to be reprinted in 1616 and again in 1636. Although not translated into English until the eighteenth century, Epictetus' *Discourses* likewise received marked attention throughout the period, thanks in large measure to the *editio princeps* produced by Vettore Trincavelli in 1535 and the substantial Latin translations published by Jacob Schegk in 1554 and Hieronymus Wolf in 1560, an edition which also incorporated the *Enchiridion* as well.[9] Further disseminated through the writings of prominent neo-Stoics such as Lipsius and Guillaume du Vair, Epictetian thought found a wide audience, and the philosopher's influence reached especial prominence in the earliest decades of the seventeenth century.[10]

In both its ancient and early modern iterations, Epictetian philosophy centres on the doctrine that one's *prohairesis*, or volition, remains the only thing an individual ultimately controls, a theory of agency that invites detachment from the material world and the cultivation instead of proper desire within the intangible recesses of one's mind. Positing the material world as beyond one's capacity to control, that is, the philosophy figures the impalpable, interior world of the mind as a space of potentially perfect freedom. For although Epictetus likely 'accepted the standard Stoic position on the physicality of all existing things', his doctrine of *prohairesis* understands volition 'as abstracted from the body'. In this, we may see in Epictetian *prohairesis* a kind of intrinsic defence to the strain of Galenic critique we saw levelled at Stoicism in the last chapter, for there is a sense throughout the philosopher's work of a deep reserve of human will existing just beyond the reach of external, material force.[11] Providing his definition of freedom in the *Discourses*, Epictetus asserts that 'he is free for whom all things happen in accordance with his choice, and whom no one can restrain',[12] but since everyone remains subject to potential physical subjugation, Epictetus conditions his understanding of liberty by stressing that the only quantity truly free from restraint remains one's mental disposition itself. 'In our own power,' explains the philosopher, 'are choice, and all actions dependent on choice; not in our power [are] the body, the parts of the body, property, parents, brothers, children, country, and, in short, all with whom we associate.'[13] Epictetian liberty points, then, not to the absence of oppression but rather to an interior mental resolve that, regardless of material conditions, remains unassailable. The workings of the mind – untouchable and, in essence, immaterial – remain therefore perfectly free, detached from all forces that would otherwise impinge upon them, so long as one maintains a proper disposition towards external things.

According to Epictetus, in order to maintain this proper disposition, one must take care to give assent only to impressions (*phantasiai*) that are true, and by training one's faculty of choice in this way, the individual secures freedom from the false impressions that perpetually threaten mental slavery. For Epictetus, 'impressions' refers to the ideas, notions, or appearances that occur to the rational mind. Since humans, alone among all living things, possess the unique capacity for contemplating the 'propositional content'[14] of thoughts, it becomes incumbent upon the ethical person to interpret them properly, recognising what lies within the purview of one's control and what does not. In the *Discourses*, Epictetus identifies the 'reasoning faculty' as the 'most excellent faculty of all' precisely because it wields the 'power to deal rightly with our impressions', a capacity for choice that prompts the philosopher to declare *prohairesis* a divine gift and source of consolation given to humanity alone.[15] Since the '*prohairetic* faculty [...] is unimpeded, unconstrained, unhindered', nothing can conquer the individual except one's own desires,[16] and problems only arise, therefore, when one assents to false impressions, and becomes encumbered by the burdens such false ideas create. 'The only way to a happy life,' Epictetus concludes, 'is to stand aloof from things that lie outside the sphere of choice' and, instead, 'to devote yourself to one thing only, that which is your own and free from all hindrance', namely, the capacity of choice itself and the ability, more specifically, to reject the false impressions that seek to oppress the mind.[17]

As Epictetus counsels his readers on the importance of rightly addressing the *phantasiai* that strike one's thoughts, the philosopher reveals the subtle, insidious nature of false impressions that, if left unattended, can take root in the mind, enthralling and debilitating the incautious individual. Epictetus praises the person, who, 'withdrawing himself from externals, turns to his own faculty of choice, working at it and perfecting it, so as to bring it fully into harmony with nature', a process of habituation that ultimately renders one 'elevated, free, unrestrained, unhindered, faithful, [and] self-respecting'.[18] Setting such a liberated, ennobled person in contrast with one who desires 'things outside his own power' – a yielding to false impressions that inevitably results in becoming 'subject to others, who can procure or prevent what he desires or wants to avoid'[19] – Epictetus emphasises the need for perpetual circumspection. Indeed, by portraying such progress as essential but, admittedly, laborious, the philosopher signals the intense, almost elemental, pull falsehoods can have on the mind. Cautioning against letting oneself be 'swept away' by any given false impression, Epictetus advises: 'But, in the first place, do not allow yourself to be carried away by its intensity, but say, "Impression, wait for me a little. Let me see what you are, and what you represent. Let me test you."'[20] The insidious power of false impressions to dominate the mind requires from the individual, therefore, continual effort, a 'kind of exercise', that will cause the practitioner to marvel at 'what shoulders, what sinews and what vigour' develop as a result.[21] By detailing at length the persistent, arduous training required to resist false impressions, Epictetian philosophy underscores both the intensity and subtlety of the forces that threaten to sway the unsuspecting mind and reduce an individual's sense of personal value and liberty.

According to Epictetus, the pernicious effects of such false impressions stand in direct opposition to our preconceptions (*prolêpseis*), the innate sense shared by all humanity of what constitutes the good and just, for conflicts only arise, argues the philosopher, when people yield to false *phantasiai* and act out of alignment with this natural orientation towards the ethical. 'Preconceptions,' Epictetus asserts, 'are common to all men, and one preconception does not contradict another.'[22] As compelling as false impressions may be, humanity, as figured in Epictetian thought, begins in a state of harmonious agreement about distinctions between the just and unjust. Crucially, while this 'natural origin of preconceptions goes back to early Stoicism', Epictetus appears 'alone in making them equivalent to an *innate* moral sense',[23] and the philosopher's notion that such *prolêpseis* form a set of shared assumptions, rooted in nature itself, establishes an essential context for understanding his larger concern with the insidiousness of false impressions.[24] Injustice and conflicts arise, Epictetus argues, when humanity, deviating from innate preconceptions, yields to false impressions and errs. 'What, then, is it to be properly educated?' asks the philosopher, 'To learn how to apply natural preconceptions to particular cases, in accordance with nature' and to thus avoid yielding to false impressions.[25] Representing two very different ways of governing one's mind and conceptualising self-worth, Epictetian philosophy posits yielding to false impressions as standing in direct contrast to living in accordance with preconceptions. If a person applies preconceptions properly, he or she resists false impressions; conversely, to yield to false impressions is to deviate from the innate preconceptions that would otherwise naturally direct a person towards what is truly just.

Although most directly concerned with the subtlest, even immaterial, operations of the mind, Epictetian Stoicism carries enormous political implications, since the repudiation of false impressions helps the citizen maintain a proper sense of self-value no matter what external pressures, even death itself, may be threatened within the polity at large. Amid a discussion about the relative stations people hold within society, Epictetus considers the matter of whether certain functions prove too debasing to perform. Rather than weigh the relative merits of certain occupations or societal roles, however, the philosopher turns the question back to one's *prohairesis*, noting that the real issue of concern lies in how one perceives oneself. '[I]t is you who know yourself, and what value you set upon yourself, and at what rate you sell yourself: for different people sell themselves at different prices,'[26] the philosopher observes, dismissing the importance of conventional means of determining social status. There is grave danger, after all, in worrying about relative social positions and perceiving one's value by recourse to one's status within a given hierarchy. 'For as soon as a person even considers such questions, comparing and calculating the values of external things,' explains Epictetus, 'he draws close to those who have lost all sense of their proper character.'[27] At the same time, imagining a dialogue between Helvidius Priscus and Vespasian, who seeks to bar Priscus from the Senate, Epictetus depicts the Stoic as replying, 'It is in your power not to allow me to be a senator; but as long as I am one, I must attend.' Subsequently threatened with death, Priscus, in similar fashion, responds, 'Did I ever tell you that I was immortal? You will do your part, and I mine: It is yours to kill, and mine to die without trembling.'[28] Not unlike Webster's Duchess, the ideal Stoic as described by Epictetus concomitantly understands his true value, whatever different prices others may set upon him, acknowledges his legally-conferred title, fulfilling its corresponding social role, and yet maintains a disposition towards disenfranchisement and even death notably marked by its absence of fear. The resolve Epictetus imagines here – exemplified simultaneously by an emotional detachment from the accoutrements of political power and a marked imperturbability in the face of impending death – emerges directly from the prior training of the *prohairetic* faculty that helps ensure a proper sense of self-value.

As Epictetus invites his audience to recall their proper place as free citizens within a polity, the philosopher grounds such exhortations by positing *prohairesis* as that which distinguishes humanity from animals, asserting in the process that misperceiving one's true intrinsic worth transforms the individual into the bestial, akin, that is, to a being lacking the capacity to even weigh the propositional content of impressions striking the mind. Although humans have 'two elements mingled within us, a body in common with the animals, and reason and intelligence in common with the gods', Epictetus declares, 'many of us incline towards the former kinship, miserable as it is and wholly mortal'.[29] Indeed, he continues:

> Because of this kinship with the mortal, some of us deviate towards it to become like wolves, faithless and treacherous and noxious; others, like lions, wild and savage and untamed; but most of us become like foxes, the most roguish of living creatures. For what else is a slanderous and ill-natured man than a fox, or something yet more wretched and mean? Look, then, and take care that you do not become one of these roguish creatures.[30]

Extending beyond mere metaphor, Epictetus' point is to contrast those who have 'a securely grounded use of their impressions' and who 'will harbour no abject or ignoble thought about themselves' with 'the multitude [which] will think the opposite',[31] as he figures human subservience as dependent upon our own interior interpretations of external conditions. Since, according to Epictetus, 'there is nothing more sovereign than [the] power of choice' and since 'choice itself is free from slavery and subjection', he concludes: 'Consider, then, what you are separated from by reason. You are separated from wild beasts [. . .] Furthermore, you are a citizen of the universe, and a part of it; and no subservient, but a principal part of it.'[32] Within Epictetian thought, then, debasement occurs not from the degradation or oppression inflicted by one person upon another, but more precisely from the improper interpretation of impressions within our own minds. What's more, while this doctrine directs attention to the untouchable and imperceptible reaches of human interiority, Epictetus notably concludes with a provocative statement of the implications such a philosophy might hold for one's position in the broader order, figuring each person as a 'citizen of the universe', and, moreover, a 'principal part' of it.

As a corollary to this admonition that citizens remember their innate sovereignty, reject the falsehood of their supposed subservience, and retain thereby their full humanity, Epictetus concomitantly argues that tyrants, by yielding to false impressions in their own way, in fact dehumanise themselves by abusing others. Imagining a dialogue with a slave, the philosopher responds to the question whether a master can flog a subject with impunity. '[H]e cannot do so with impunity,' Epictetus determines, 'for the very reason that it is not in his power; for no one can act unjustly with impunity.'[33] When the imagined interlocutor presses him on the matter, asking 'what punishment does a man suffer who puts his own slave in chains, when he so wishes', Epictetus retorts, 'The very act of putting him in chains.'[34] If this seems tautological and thus unsatisfactory, the rebuttal stems directly from the philosopher's underlying assumptions. 'This you yourself must grant,' Epictetus claims, 'if you want to hold to the principle that man is not a wild beast but a civilized animal', for humanity's true nature, he asserts, runs counter to the desire 'to bite and kick and throw people into prison and behead them'.[35] Tyranny thus is a form of 'acting against [one's] own nature', which is 'to do good, to cooperate with others and pray for their good'.[36] However else it may seem, Epictetus avers, the tyrant 'is faring badly whenever he acts unreasonably'.[37] Indeed, in language that will resonate in Webster's play, Epictetus concludes that the abusive ruler is 'the person who is truly harmed', 'the one who suffers the most pitiful and shameful fate', namely, 'that of becoming a wolf or a serpent or a wasp instead of a human being'.[38]

Although Epictetus figures yielding to false impressions as a descent into the subhuman, the philosopher also, at times, notably adduces animals as *exempla* of the innate desire for liberty common to every living thing, a natural desire he contrasts with the impulse towards slavery evinced by those who continually confuse liberty with social preferment. 'Now consider how we apply the concept of freedom with regard to animals,' Epictetus begins his discussion of liberty in the *Discourses* before proceeding to note how various animals resist enslavement.[39] Observing how people keep 'lions as tame creatures in cages', Epictetus wonders 'who will say any such lion is free', and, after suggesting he lives 'more slavishly the more he lives at ease', declares that no 'lion, if he acquired sense and reason, would wish to be one of those lions'.[40] In a similar fashion, 'birds [. . .] when they are captured and reared in cages', the philosopher muses, resist their subjugation, even 'starv[ing] themselves to death rather than endure such a life' since they possess '[s]uch a desire [. . .] for natural freedom, and to be independent and free of restraint'.[41] Indeed, he continues, 'Therefore we shall call free only those creatures that are unwilling to put up with captivity, but, as soon as they are taken, escape by dying.'[42] This natural impulse towards liberty stands in stark contrast to the foolish man who confuses advancement through the ranks of society for genuine freedom. For immediately after adducing the *exempla* of lions, birds and even fish that prefer death to captivity, Epictetus charts the life of perpetual enslavement suffered by those who always seek preferment from the powerful. 'A slave,' Epictetus explains, 'prays to be set free [. . .] because he fancies that up until now [. . .] he has lived under restraint and in misery,' but, once freed, finds himself continually discontented, subject to restraints of simply a different kind. Epictetus imagines this slave, not unlike Webster's Bosola, as entering the army but 'suffer[ing] as much as any convict' and, even when he meets with worldly success, encountering slavery still on account of his remaining beholden to others.[43] His failure, Epictetus asserts, lies in his inability to understand the 'true nature of each reality', as he doesn't realise that by 'grovelling to another, or flattering him contrary to his own opinion', that 'he too is not free'.[44] In this respect, such people who misuse their *prohairesis* and improperly respond to impressions simply become slaves of another sort; they have fallen for an unnatural servitude, becoming akin to the subjugated and contained animal.[45]

The Politics of Prohairesis *in Early Modern England*

The philosophy of Epictetus appealed to a wide range of early modern authors for a variety of reasons,[46] but of particular interest was the philosopher's notion that assent to false impressions could cause profound misery, even a sense of debasement into something subhuman. For those receptive to Epictetian ideas, a proper sense of one's volition promised a degree of solace in a harsh and unforgiving world. Montaigne, for instance, perceives in volition a kind of bulwark against the misfortunes of life, something

Nature provides 'for comfort of our miserable and wretched condition', since, as he observes while citing the philosopher, 'man hath nothing that is properly his owne, but the use of his opinions'.[47] The proper formulation of opinion may provide a source of comfort, but misguided assent to false impressions generates misery, perpetuates a destructive kind of folly. Expounding on Epictetian thought and, specifically, 'the thinges that mannes minde seeth, which [the Stoics] cal fantasies', Roger Edgeworth, for example, cautions against 'appl[ying] the assent of [one's] minde' to folly, which only causes distress.[48] Such assent to false impressions signals not only an induction into folly, however, but also a deep sense of deprivation and even a lessening of one's humanity. Robert Greene, glossing Epictetus' claim that wisdom is 'the touchstone of mortality', notes how 'reason [. . .] distinguisheth a man from a brute beast',[49] while, in a similar vein, Thomas Walkington cites the philosopher as he counsels his readers not to 'satisfie [. . .] bestiall appetite'.[50] Most explicitly, Angelo Poliziano, who translated the *Enchiridion*, observes how Epictetus despaired of the 'person who had degenerated so far below human nature that he could be ranked with the beasts'.[51] A source of potential comfort, human volition for early modern thinkers could become, then, the mechanism for profound misery and a degradation that rendered one bestial, given to base and reactive impulses, that is, but not to the full and proper perception of one's intrinsic worth as a reasoning being.

The emphasis among early modern authors on regulating one's desire sometimes served to promote quiescent acceptance of one's lot in life, a critical application of the philosophy most saliently demonstrated in the era's popularisation of the apothegm 'sustain and abstain', sometimes expressed as 'bear and forbear', a phrase absent from Epictetus' own works but an accretion used to articulate the philosopher's doctrine of volition throughout the early modern period.

Calling 'susteyne and absteyne' a dictum 'worthie to be written [. . .] wheresoever a man casteth his eye', Erasmus asserts that by these two words Epictetus advises people 'strongly to beare adversitie' and 'to absteyne from all unlefull pleasures and pastimes'.[52] The advice appears with some regularity, and such emphasis on Epictetian forbearance as a form of endurance or continence could lend itself, in some quarters, to arguments for maintaining the political status quo. Indeed, a few authors marshal this apocryphal phrase to advise against specific actions or dispositions, including revenge or the harbouring of class-inflected resentment. Matthieu Coignet, for instance, advises that one should follow 'the precept of *Epictetus,* in yeelding vnto the greater sort' and 'keeping vnder the desire of reuenge',[53] a sentiment echoed by Pierre de La Primaudaye who notes 'It is a great vertue (saith Epictetus) not to hurt him of whom thou art misused.'[54] Jean Guillemard, more broadly, draws on the philosopher to counsel contentment with one's station, observing that if one's role is to play 'a begger, or a lame man, a King or a rogue, thou must act it as naturally as thou canst, and onely feare to faile'.[55] Invoked to promote endurance and self-mastery, Epictetus' central notion of a fundamentally unassailable will – even when pressed into service by some authors to advocate a particular kind of political or social quiescence – thus found wide dissemination among early modern thinkers, carrying with it to a broad audience the predicates for its more levelling, more socially radical, implications as well.

While Epictetian doctrines sometimes served as a means for reinforcing the status quo, even admonitions drawn from the philosopher counselling forbearance could gesture – at times rather subtly – to the need for a check on excessive power and wealth, and, indeed, in both the countering of aristocratic privilege and the valorisation of each citizen's intrinsic worth, Epictetian thought carried marked revolutionary potential.[56] For as much as early modern invocations of Epictetus caution against discontent with poverty, they also critique the perils of decadence. When Thomas Lodge notes how '*Epictetus* counsailed' that 'it is better in health to bee layd on a meane matteris, then to be sicklie on a magnificent and ritch bed', he presents an adage that at once advises contentment but also remains suggestive of a levelling *ethos* in its acknowledgement of the limits of wealth, a resonance other writers bring out more explicitly.[57] Jacques Hurault, for instance, glosses 'the goodly precept of *Epictetus*, which commaundeth to beare and forbeare' as cautioning against becoming 'corrupted by prosperitie'. For as Pierre de La Primaudaye, citing the philosopher, likewise notes, wealth has the potential to 'stir us up to superfluity [. . .] [and] it is a very hard matter for a rich man to be temperate'.[58] A corollary to such critique of aristocratic wealth and privilege is, as Reid Barbour has noted, Epictetus' elevation of 'the power of the atomized will'. Epictetus, Barbour reminds us, 'is dangerous because he is so critical of the imperial colonization of the will', and Epictetian thought remains a constant 'threat to imperial control', as 'the perfect "libertine" is freer and more powerful than the emperor'.[59] For all the ways that Epictetian forbearance could be marshalled to foster a sense of contentment within a given political arrangement, Epictetian philosophy, in a rather more republican vein, could also serve to moderate aristocratic power and challenge entrenched political privilege.

Popular across a diverse range of writing, Epictetus also received considerable attention in the early modern theatre, and Webster would find among his contemporaries allusions to the philosopher that would complement his own subtle appropriation of Epictetian thought. For some, Epictetus provided fodder for passing references that, if not integral to the play's sensibilities, signal a confidence in audience familiarity with the thinker nonetheless. Even John Marston, for whom, as we have already seen, Stoicism is at the very least a deeply-flawed philosophy, refers in *The Fawn* (1606) to his 'bosom friend Epictetus'[60] and has Gonzago advise Tiberio to 'both forbeare and beare, / *Anexou è ampexou*, (that's Greeke to you now)'.[61] Beaumont and Fletcher's *The Captain* (c. 1609) – a play, incidentally, that shared three of its principal actors with *The Duchess of Malfi* – stages Angelo avowing he has read 'Epictetus twice over against the / Desire of these outward things',[62] and both James Shirley and Thomas Heywood casually invoke the philosopher by name as well.[63] George Chapman, whom Webster considered a friend and occasionally borrowed from,[64] draws heavily on Epictetus to craft Clermont d'Ambois, constructing at least 'five long passages' of *The Revenge of Bussy d'Ambois* by 'translat[ing] or adapt[ing] from specific *dicta* in the *Discourses*'.[65] Indeed, Chapman, it has been shown, went so far as to consult Wolfius' translation of the *Discourses* and *Enchiridion*, Simplicius' *Commentaries*, and Stobaeus' *Epicteti sententiae*.[66] If Chapman was unique in interpolating such long passages directly from the *Discourses*, Renaissance dramatists certainly found in Epictetus a figure who evidently resonated with their broader audiences. When Webster turned to Stoicism to develop the character of his play's heroic Duchess, he adapted the work of a classical philosopher not only widely known throughout Europe for his comprehensive theory of innate volition but also one immediately recognisable within the world of the early modern English theatre.

Aristocratic Privilege, False Phantasiai, *and the Place of the Citizen in* The Duchess of Malfi

From the outset, Webster signals his investment in the principal concerns which occupy the core of Epictetian thought as he frames his play with an *ethos* that markedly valorises individual autonomy and merit, unfettered by the constraints of false impressions, over the ideological manipulations of a corrupt aristocracy. As Webster opens the play with Antonio's homily on good governance, the dramatist directly establishes the ontological framework which will shape the rest of the play by foregrounding how political regimes, when corrupt, can sit at profound odds with an otherwise intrinsic sense of liberty and personal value common across a broad citizenry. Indeed, Webster immediately indicates how the ensuing play will be especially concerned with the ways a corrupt milieu can reinforce – particularly through the subtle, insidious power of manipulative rhetoric – false impressions about one's personal worth within civic contracts. Interestingly, Webster depicts both aristocracy and citizen alike as susceptible to the distorting effects that language can have on one's perceptions. Praising the French court to Delio, Antonio reflects on the maintenance of a well-ordered state. 'A prince's court,' Antonio explains,

> Is like a common fountain, whence should flow
> Pure silver drops in general. But if 't chance
> Some cursed example poison 't near the head,
> *Death and diseases through the whole land spread.*
>   (1.1.11–15)[67]

In many respects a commonplace of the era, Antonio's depiction of the court nonetheless gestures beyond general ruminations on statecraft to more specifically recall how false impressions can infect a polity at all levels. For Antonio indicates the kind of poisonous, 'cursed example' he has in mind immediately prior to this commentary when he praises the 'judicious king' of France for, first and foremost, banishing 'flatt'ring sycophants' from his court. The term 'sycophant' suggested in early modern culture not only servile parasites but also 'tale-bearers', people who distort perception through their misleading speech.[68] Indeed, this preoccupation with the shaping power of misleading fiction leads to

Antonio's concluding observations on 'Blessed government' where clarifying, rather than distorting, rhetoric prevails and where the citizenry, in a more republican vein, may 'freely / Inform [the prince] the corruption of the times'. If Antonio bemoans the manipulative power of tale-bearers found in the diseased court, he likewise values the rhetoric found in the healthy state, rhetoric that facilitates right perception. On the cusp of introducing the degrading world of Ferdinand's court, then, Webster signals how one's proper sense of value can be threatened by the pervasive, insidious influence of distorting rhetoric, figuring the agency of the otherwise free citizenry as always vulnerable to not only outright force but also the constricting power of language and even prominent *exempla*.

At the end of Antonio's homily, Webster introduces Bosola, the play's disenfranchised malcontent, who, from the outset, evinces all the hallmarks of the Epictetian slave, dehumanised by his attachment to external things as he labours for preferment within a debased and debasing milieu. Upon his entrance, Bosola instantly registers a sense of himself as something less than human, locating the cause of his utter abjection in the neglectfulness of those in power. Informing his would-be patron, 'I do haunt you still' (1.1.29), the servant, in his very first lines, indicates his status as a mere shadow of his powerful rulers, perhaps even of his former self, and as emptied, it would seem, even of intrinsic value. Indeed, when Bosola complains that he has 'done [. . .] better service than to be slighted thus' (1.1.29–30), he equally describes the Cardinal's disregard of the remuneration due for his service as well as his own physically-wasted condition, a double resonance he explicitly evokes just a moment later: 'slighted thus? I will thrive some way. Blackbirds fatten best in hard weather: why not I, in these dog-days?' (1.1.37–9). In this first of many identifications of the subjugated citizen with the animal world, Webster presents the servant as assenting to false impressions about his intrinsic value and own capacity for autonomy, an internal disposition towards abjection that the dehumanising court of Malfi actively seeks to reinforce. In fact, in language notably redolent of Epictetian thought, Webster infuses Bosola's assessment of the Cardinal and, by extension, the court with an unambiguous sense that buying into a corrupt system invariably dehumanises all involved:

> He and his brother are like plum trees that grow crooked over standing pools: they are rich and o'erladen with fruit, but none but crows, pies, and caterpillars feed on them. Could I be one of their flattering panders, I would hang on their ears like a horse-leech till I were full, and then drop off [. . .] Who would rely upon these miserable dependencies in expectation to be advanced tomorrow? What creature ever fed worse than hoping Tantalus? [. . .] There are rewards for hawks and dogs, and when they have done us service; but for a soldier [. . .] (1.1.49–60)

Where Epictetus argues one relinquishes true liberty and even full humanity by yielding to 'abject or ignoble thought[s]' and by seeking social preferment, 'groveling to another, or flattering him contrary to his own opinion',[69] Bosola here perceives the court as full of 'crows, pies, and caterpillars', mere 'flattering panders', who seek 'miserable dependencies'. As if the sense of infestation were not pronounced enough already, Bosola yearns to 'hang [. . .] like a horse-leech till [. . .] full, and then drop off', a brutally debased image that figures the servant so low that he *aspires* to the role of mere parasite. Faulting the corrupt aristocracy for his wasted condition, Bosola may, at this early moment, misperceive his own role in creating his sense of degradation, but he rightly diagnoses from the outset, however, the very real structural inequities of the court that facilitate and capitalise upon such subjugation of the citizenry.

Throughout the first scene, Webster underscores the dehumanisation of both servants and rulers alike within the court by foregrounding the aristocracy's obsessive efforts to proscribe any hint of autonomous action among its citizenry. For if the world of Ferdinand's court appears brutal, the people animalistic, Webster quickly makes clear such a state emerges not only from individual citizens assenting to debased images of themselves but also from those in power actively cultivating such impressions at every turn. After Bosola's tirade against the parasitic court, for instance, Antonio claims, ''Tis great pity / He should be thus neglected' since 'This foul melancholy / Will poison all his goodness'. Fearing a kind of 'inward rust unto the soul', Antonio concludes that this 'close rearing' will 'Like moths in cloth, hurt for want of wearing' (1.1.74–82). Antonio perceives in Ferdinand's neglect an attempt to delimit Bosola's agency, and Webster yields the diagnosis additional warrant just a moment later when he further emphasises the court's despotic desire to surveil even the faintest expression of personal volition. For after his courtiers momentarily jest among themselves, Ferdinand issues a sharp rebuke: 'Why do you laugh? Methinks you that are courtiers / Should be my touchwood: take fire when I give fire – / That is, laugh when I laugh, were the subject never so witty' (1.2.42–4). A momentary flash of autonomous action, a hint of intangible will made manifest at court, and Ferdinand instantly attempts to circumscribe what, in truth, he ultimately cannot control, seeking, as Frank Whigham aptly observes, to transform the courtiers into 'his creatures, without will or spontaneity'.[70] In the wake of this display, Antonio and Delio further note the dehumanising mode of governance that prevails in Malfi, perceiving in the Cardinal 'nothing but the engendering of toads' (1.2.76) and observing how, to Ferdinand, the law 'is like a foul black cobweb to a spider: / He makes it his dwelling and a prison /

To entangle those shall feed him' (1.2.96–8). In the predatory world ruled by Ferdinand and the Cardinal, the privileged few aggressively control, as fully as they can, both behaviour and mind, seeking to perpetuate the conditions that help render the citizens of Malfi subhuman.

Webster portrays Ferdinand and the Cardinal as wielding the combined power of dehumanising rhetoric and the promise of patronage in order to purposely reinforce Bosola's false impressions about his own personal value, an effort indicative of the aristocracy's desire to maintain a type of subhuman, disposable underclass that helps secure their own continued dominion. Indeed, throughout the first scene, Webster follows Bosola's multiple expressions of his abject status, moments where the servant exhibits a sense of self-awareness, however limited, of his fall from full humanity, with the active cultivation of such thinking by those in power. 'I was lured to you' (1.2.148), Bosola tells the Cardinal, employing the language of angling to depict himself a hooked creature, and he later observes to Ferdinand, 'It seems you would create me / One of your familiars' (1.2.175–6). By holding out the promise of advancement, Ferdinand explicitly encourages this debased thinking. For the Duke readily reaffirms Bosola's perception, admitting 'such a kind of thriving thing / I would wish thee; and ere long thou mayst arrive / At a higher place by 't'. (1.2.178–80). Significantly, the more the aristocracy figures Bosola as bestial, the more he adopts such language himself. When Ferdinand likens him to 'a politic dormouse', Bosola interjects, concluding the sentence for him: 'As I have seen some / Feed in a lord's dish' (1.2.199–200). Readily assenting to the dehumanised role prearranged for him, Bosola indeed seems incapable of imagining anything else. In fact, on the verge of finally receiving some preferment, he inquires 'What's my place? / The provisorship o'th' horse?' – a position that could indeed suggest a degree of status at last – and concludes that they should 'say then, my corruption / Grew out of horse dung: I am your creature' (1.2.202–4). Perceiving his appointment not as an honour but as a placement of himself among the merely animal, Bosola describes his condition as concomitantly corrupted and bestial, a status derived from his own assent to a false sense of himself but one, at the same time, systematically perpetuated by Ferdinand's deft use of political favour and imaginative rhetoric.

Extending the Sphere of Volition: The Duchess and the Egalitarian Potential of Prohairesis

Against this backdrop of a corrupt court that actively dehumanises its citizenry, Webster presents the Duchess as remarkable for acting in accordance with her preconceptions, or *prolêpseis*, regarding both her personal value and liberty – for resisting, that is, all encroachments on her own expression of free choice. In a scene that brings the play's contrasting views of human will and dignity into stark relief, Ferdinand and the Cardinal counsel their sister against remarriage, and as they confront their inability to exert control over the Duchess' deepest reserves of volition, the Aragonian brothers redouble their efforts to shape her self-perception by figuring her as bestial, as lacking the genuine autonomy of choice reserved for humanity alone. The moment, often considered paradigmatic of the play's animating *agon*, places centre-stage multiple Epictetian assumptions about volition, tyranny and most pointedly the determinative role of assent in shaping one's condition. For the Duchess, however politically and physically constrained she may be, evinces a remarkable sense of interior liberty, steadfastly withholding assent to her brothers' false and dehumanising narratives. Ferdinand and the Cardinal, at the same time, exhibit the tyrant's impulse towards restricting liberty, something that, as the play will later bear out, ultimately marks their own subhuman natures. Throughout the scene, the brothers persistently frame the Duchess as bestial, even going out of their way to recast her unimpeachable volition as a debased feature of herself. When the Cardinal informs the Duchess, '[Y]our own discretion / Must now be your director,' for instance, Ferdinand rapidly interjects that those who 'will wed twice' have 'livers [. . .] more spotted / Than Laban's sheep', reminding his sister that she 'live[s] in a rank pasture here i'th' court' (1.2.208–9, 214–15, 222). And when the Cardinal sneers at the Duchess' capacity to choose – 'You may flatter yourself, / And take your own choice' (1.2.232–3) – the Duke once more aligns her volition with the subhuman, describing her as 'like the irregular crab, / Which, though 't goes backward, thinks that it goes right / Because it goes its own way' (1.2.235–7). What's more, after Ferdinand crudely asserts that 'women like that part, which like the lamprey, / Hath ne'er a bone in 't', the Duke quickly amends the initial innuendo to instead emphasise rhetoric's capacity to shape perception and curtail volition. 'Nay, / I mean the tongue,' Ferdinand protests, for, after all, 'What cannot a neat knave with a smooth tale / *Make* a woman believe?' (1.2.253–7). Ferdinand's overt avowal of rhetoric's power simply expresses more explicitly the mode of coercion operant throughout the scene, as the brothers, encountering a will they cannot, in truth, govern, attempt to secure their sister's assent to false impressions about her intrinsic value.

The Duchess resists her brothers' attempts at distorting her self-perception, but she also, more remarkably, immediately expands the space for autonomous action to include others regardless of rank, a beneficent, levelling application of power that gestures to the revolutionary potential of *prohairesis*, of an unassailable internal liberty, if broadly realised across a receptive citizenry. Upon the conclusion of her brothers' conversation, the Duchess scoffs, 'shall this move me?' (1.2.256) and sets to work to enact her own designs. Although she will later claim, upon her exposure to

Ferdinand, that she did not marry secretly 'to create / Any new world or custom' (3.2.109–10), privately she declares here, 'Let old wives report / I winked and chose a husband' (1.2.263–4). Imagining her free choice as something recounted among a broader network of people, the Duchess perceives her impending marriage to Antonio as exemplifying for others a volition unconstrained. The Duchess' inclination to understand her marriage as a kind of broadening of the range of free action can be observed as well in the way in which she frames the idea to Antonio himself. For when Antonio voices concern over the Duke and the Cardinal, the Duchess' response gestures to an expanded sense of the sphere of *prohairesis*, a sense that the range of uninhibited volition might be able to extend beyond the confines of the individual body itself. 'Do not think of them,' she advises, for 'All discord without this circumference / Is only to be pitied and not feared' (1.2.377–9). A piece of advice redolent of Epictetus' own counsel to ignore the fearful phantasms external to oneself, the Duchess, renowned for her Stoic resolve evinced elsewhere in the play, notably expands the principle to incorporate *two* minds, extending the 'circumference' of untouchable volition across multiple bodies. Indeed, a similar ethic may be seen at work when the Duchess privately reproves Antonio for underestimating his true value – for 'darkening of [his] worth' when, in fact, he is 'a complete man', a descriptor, incidentally, that echoes an Epictetian passage out of Chapman – and then, later and more publicly, when advising him to be 'the example to the rest o'th' court' by refusing to remove his hat before the king (1.2.343, 346; 2.1.130).[71] Beginning with Antonio and Cariola, as well as the imagined community of 'old wives' and, then, courtiers, the Duchess perceives the unrestrained will not as inevitably isolated, but rather as capable of existing in concert with other similar instantiations of it, perceives, that is, multiple points of unrestrained wills, broadly distributed, as fashioning a kind of network or community in their own right.

This theoretically unassailable – and markedly more egalitarian – world of fully-realised volition, a world which extends Stoic ontological assumptions about the immaterial will into a broader political sphere, requires co-operation, of course, depends upon another's acceptance of the proffered solidarity. As we have seen in the chapter on *The Spanish Tragedy*, the language of households carries profound political implications, and the Duchess' proposal, for all its potential romance, is couched in the rhetoric of social advancement, an improving of one's estate that requires Antonio awakening his own agency as well, as they seek, collectively, to expand their range of autonomous action. 'Sir,' the Duchess declares:

> This goodly roof of yours is too low built;
> I cannot stand upright in 't, nor discourse,
> Without I raise it higher. Raise yourself;
> Or, if you please, my hand to help you.
> [*Gives her hand. Antonio rises.*] So. (1.2.326–30)

By explicitly envisioning her union with her steward as an instance of estate management, or the improving of one's household, the Duchess seeks to level social distinctions, a fact Webster reinforces through the formal stylistics of the line.[72] Thus, the caesura 'I cannot stand upright [. . .] Without I raise it higher. Raise yourself' juxtaposes the Duchess' aristocratic largesse with an emphasis on the middling steward's own agency, an implicit sense of *co-operation* physically enacted a moment later with the joining of hands. The Duchess, as the stage directions indicate, may prove the mechanism that 'raises him' but he – unlike, as we will see, Bosola – participates in this venture and accepts, along with her hand in marriage, a renewed way of perceiving his own value.

Through the discovery of the secret marriage, Webster further contrasts the Duchess' impulse towards social levelling with Ferdinand's desire to contain and dehumanise the citizenry, but he also begins to signal her conceptualisation of liberty, grounded it would seem in a different way of perceiving the natural world itself, as carrying, in fact, an ontological warrant lacking in Ferdinand's repressive politics. Indeed, in the Duchess we can see a mode of conceptualising the creaturely that actively resists the pejorative connotations which dominate the world of Ferdinand's court. This mode of understanding affinity with the animal world as carrying marked positive valences resonates, as Julia Lupton and others have persuasively shown, across the period more broadly,[73] but Webster inflects the entirety of the Duchess' defiant behaviour with a particular emphasis on the role of innate volition in shaping one's actual condition, a move that, significantly, also helps account for the different dispositions toward the creaturely evident throughout the play. When the Duchess informs Ferdinand of her marriage, for instance, the ensuing dialogue suggests distinctly divergent ways of understanding the issue of native volition, a fundamental disagreement that quickly finds expression in allusions to the animal world. After announcing the marriage, the Duchess describes her brother as powerless to restrain Antonio: 'Alas, your shears do come untimely now / To clip the bird's wings that's already flown' (3.2.83–4). Indicative, as she will soon explain, of a disposition towards reading the animal world as enjoying a natural state of liberty, the Duchess' retort draws from Ferdinand a torrent of invective designed to reduce the spouses to mere creatures – as he understands them – containable and subject to his tyrannical whims. 'The howling of a wolf / Is music to thee, screech-owl. Prithee, peace!' (3.2.87–8), Ferdinand declares as he attempts to silence his sister, before recalling Antonio and erupting:

> I would have thee build
> Such a room for him as our anchorites
> To holier use inhabit. Let not the sun
> Shine on him till he's dead. Let dogs and monkeys
> Only converse with him, and such dumb things
> To whom nature denies use to sound his name.
> Do not keep a paraquito, lest she learn it [. . .] (3.2.100–6)

As the dark enclosure envisioned by Ferdinand transforms from 'such a room' inhabited by 'anchorites' into a type of cage – full of 'dogs and monkeys' and 'such dumb things' – his rhetoric blurs the distinction between human and subhuman, imagining Antonio as occupying the same confined space as subjugated animals. Confronted with a human volition revealed as beyond his capacity to fully control, Ferdinand attempts to align the liberated citizen, that is, with creatures unable to identify and express a sense of autonomous, individuated self. The Duchess replies to Ferdinand's abuse with simple logic, asking 'Why might I not marry?' and, again, 'Why should only I, / Of all the other princes in the world, / Be cased up like a holy relic?' (3.2.107, 135–6). In doing so, she challenges the very predicates undergirding her brother's fantasies of containment, posing as well a starkly different vision of personal volition from that found in the dark, enclosed spaces inhabited, as her brother would have it, by a dull subhumanity.

Contrasting Phantasiai with Preconceptions: Refashioning the Creaturely as Exempla

As the Duchess gradually loses her freedom to act autonomously in anything that resembles a more public fashion, she herself articulates her subjugation as akin to the containment of the captured animal, yet, significantly, persists in emphasising that the natural world holds no inherent precedent, no ontological predicate, for her brothers' restrictions. Indeed, resisting to the end their attempts to distort perception of her own intrinsic value, the Duchess repeatedly marshals tropes of the animal world, in a manner strikingly similar to what we have also seen in Epictetus' *Discourses*, as *exempla* for illustrating the pleasures of living in accordance with one's own preconceptions. Her volition inhibited from manifesting itself in any meaningful way beyond the confines of her own body, that is, the Duchess adopts the court's prevailing imagery of the contained animal in order to reveal such repression as fundamentally *un*natural. Forced to take leave of the banished Antonio, for instance, the Duchess observes:

> The birds that live i'th' field
> On the wild benefit of nature live
> Happier than we; for they may choose their mates,
> And carol their sweet pleasure to the spring. (3.5.17–20)

Perceiving in the animal world the freedom to act according to one's own will, the Duchess implicitly marks herself as subjugated and contained, and, what's more, artificially so, unable to enjoy 'the wild benefit of nature'. The strictures enforced by her brothers, the Duchess suggests, appear as contrary to 'nature', imposed from an external and false authority onto an entity that otherwise would live in liberty. Webster further emphasises the capture of the Duchess' family as both dehumanising and contrary to a naturally-free existence by having Bosola act as one that 'frights the silly birds / Out of the corn' and 'allure[s] them / To the nets' (3.5.100–2). Later still, the Duchess will carry the metaphor even further when, responding to Bosola's claims that the brothers are being in fact merciful, she sardonically observes, 'With such pity men preserve alive / Pheasants and quails, when they are not fat enough / To be eaten' (3.5.109–11). Immediately preceding her singular fable of the salmon and the dogfish, the Duchess casts her brothers' tyranny, then, as running contrary to the unrestrained volition exhibited in nature, a nature that consequently functions as a model of – and vehicle for communicating – her own understanding of intrinsic value and autonomy.

Amid these redoubled tropes of contained or liberated animals, the Duchess defends Antonio, recounts her own plight, and, crucially, invites Bosola to reconsider his perception of his own personal worth by telling the rather curious fable of the salmon and dogfish, an effort designed at heart to sever the tie in Bosola's mind between external circumstance and one's intrinsic value. Bosola exhorts the Duchess to forget Antonio, but, by employing the very mechanism of reading humanity through the animal world that the servant has so thoroughly practised himself, the Duchess invites him to re-evaluate his understanding of existing hierarchies and his place within them. Complex, curious and appearing at a critical juncture of the play, the Duchess' fable warrants quoting in full:

> I prithee, who is greatest can you tell?
> Sad tales befit my woe; I'll tell you one.
> A salmon, as she swam unto the sea,
> Met with a dogfish, who encounters her
> With this rough language: 'Why are thou so bold
> To mix thyself with our high state of floods,
> Being no eminent courtier, but one
> That for the calmest and fresh time o'th' year
> Dost live in shallow rivers, rank'st thyself
> With silly smelts and shrimps? And darest thou
> Pass by our dog-ship, without reverence?'
> 'O,' quoth the salmon, 'sister, be at peace:
> Thank Jupiter we both have passed the net!
> Our value never can be truly known
> Till in the fisher's basket we be shown;
> I'th' market then my price may be the higher,

> Even when I am nearest to the cook and fire.'
> So, to great men, the moral may be stretched:
> 'Men oft are valued high, when they're most wretched.'
>   (3.5.121–39)

Notably, the Duchess presents the fable not only as a defence of Antonio against Ferdinand but also as illustrative of her own interaction with Bosola. For the variability of the fable's referents align the salmon, alternately, with either Antonio or the Duchess and the dogfish with either Ferdinand or, more surprisingly, Bosola. Despite setting out to prove Antonio's worth, the Duchess begins by claiming 'sad tales befit *my* woe; I'll tell you one', affiliating the ensuring narrative with *her* own condition. Likewise, the fable's moral focusing on ensnarement – of waiting 'in the fisher's basket [to] be shown' – remains most evocative of the Duchess' current situation as the one presently ensnared and 'nearest to the cook and fire'. Thus, while the salmon may signify Antonio (as one of low rank who remains free nonetheless), the salmon's imagined demise seems apposite to the Duchess' particular predicament, and the story that 'befits [her] woe' concludes with a statement of resignation regarding her fate: 'But come; whither you please. I am armed 'gainst misery' (3.5.140). If, therefore, the Duchess invites us to read the salmon as Antonio or herself, she likewise suggests the dogfish, despite its alignment with high rank, may signify Bosola. Immediately preceding the fable, for instance, Bosola launches into a strident attack on Antonio and urges the Duchess to 'forget this base, low fellow [. . .] one of no birth' (3.5.315–17). The dogfish, in similar fashion, upbraids the salmon 'with [. . .] rough language', disdaining her as one that 'rank'st thyself / With silly smelts and shrimps'. While the fable of the salmon and dogfish, then, focuses largely on depicting Ferdinand's reaction to Antonio's low birth, the tale itself registers, only slightly less overtly, the interaction between the Duchess and Bosola as well. Since the parameters of fabulist language prove malleable indeed – the Duchess, after all, notes that 'the moral may be *stretched*' – she uses the fable to defend Antonio, bemoan her own plight, and, through it all, invite Bosola to be wary of his misplaced confidence, predicated on false impressions of value and expressed through his unwarranted, rough language.

By using the human-as-animal trope to resist the dehumanising effects of the court – by inverting, that is, the very rhetorical devices employed as methods of political repression – the Duchess seeks to have Bosola perceive his intrinsic worth, and, in doing so, tries to invoke a sense of natural solidarity, a type of inherent kinship, with another repressed citizen. Just as the Duchess offered to raise Antonio by helping him to perceive himself 'a complete man', she here invites Bosola to see himself anew. The Duchess marshals the fable as potentially subversive, a means of generating solidarity between captive and captor, both possessing an intrinsic worth and an ultimately inviolable volition that corrupt agents more politically powerful than themselves would otherwise deny. By opening her fable with the dual questions 'who is greatest, can you tell', the Duchess simultaneously draws attention to the ascription of value to a human life and the capacity of Bosola to accurately perceive it. She invites Bosola, that is, to rethink eminence, and she invites the audience to rethink Bosola, to attend more closely to his process of ethical perception, to wait and see whether he will, in fact, be able to 'tell'. On one level, then, the fable operates in defence of Antonio, who mingles 'with our high state of floods' despite 'being no eminent courtier' who 'darest' to transgress class boundaries 'without reverence'. But it also functions to challenge Bosola's perception of humanity as akin to the subhuman by turning to the animal fable, by reading, that is, the human through the animal in order to affirm the value of the former. Appealing to a 'value' that 'never can be truly known' until a later time, the Duchess concludes that 'Men oft are valued high when th' are most wretched', a move, evocative of Epictetus' ruminations on the 'different prices' people set upon others,[74] that opens a theoretical alternative to the determination of value by reference to externals alone. The fable, as the Duchess wields it, focuses its energies on prompting Bosola to reconceptualise social relations, particularly the definition of eminence, the valuation of the human, and the servant's own relation to power; prompts him, in short, to abandon the false impressions enthralling his mind and reinforced by Ferdinand and, instead, to return to the preconceptions of human value manifested before him in the Duchess' Stoic resolve.

If the deafening silence that follows this fable underscores the gulf between the Duchess and Bosola, between their various capacities for appreciating themselves as possessing an inviolable and defining human volition, Webster again emphasises such distance as Bosola persists in imagining the human as *inevitably* subjugated – a view starkly at odds with the Duchess who retains autonomy even in her final moments. Bosola imagines that Ferdinand's 'restraint' of the Duchess makes her 'like English mastiffs that grow fierce with tying', but the Duchess remains, in fact, quietly resigned. For when Cariola calls for her 'to shake this durance off', the Duchess – in a moment that recalls Epictetus' own declaration that 'birds [. . .] when they are captured and reared in cages' prefer death 'rather than endure such a life' – replies, 'Thou art a fool. / The robin redbreast and the nightingale / Never live long in cages' (4.2.12–14). Both Bosola and the Duchess may perceive subjugation as akin to 'tying' or caging an animal, but the Duchess resolutely points up the unnatural essence of such circumscription, defying it to the end. In fact, resisting attempts to render her subhuman even when literally placed in captivity, the noble prisoner retains her sense of true value, defiantly asserting in her most widely-recognised expression of Stoic resolve,

'I am Duchess of Malfi still' (4.2.137).⁷⁵ Man, as Pandulpho had it, may 'break out despite philosophy', but (this) woman markedly will not. Bosola, by contrast, perceives the human condition as inherently and unalterably subhuman; for Bosola, the metaphors of degrading entrapment signify, even at this late moment, immutable reality. Thus, when the Duchess inquires of Bosola, disguised as a madman, 'who am I', he dubs her 'a box of worm-seed', and claims:

> Our bodies are weaker than those paper prisons boys use to keep flies in; more contemptible, since ours is to preserve earthworms. Didst thou ever see a lark in a cage? Such is the soul in the body; this world is like her little turf of grass, and the heaven o'er our heads, like her looking-glass, only give us a miserable knowledge of the small compass of our prison [...] Thou sleepest worse than if a mouse should be forced to take up her lodging in a cat's ear [...] (4.2.119–34)

Notably, the sequence of images here depicts not only a debased humanity but an enclosed one, and Bosola expresses through each trope an inherently oppressive power relation. While Bosola's rhetoric remains conventional enough in each selected image, the sheer quantity and the condensed reduplication of such tropes signal their centrality to Bosola's mode of self-evaluation. Whereas, to the end, the Duchess rejects the manipulative rhetoric of Ferdinand's court that seeks to foster false impressions of her true value, Bosola has so internalised them that his perception remains almost irrevocably distorted.

Kinds of Nothing and Deep Pits of Darkness: Systemic Inequity and the Limits of Isolated Resistance

Through the Duchess' execution, a moment long recognised as emblematic of Stoic resolve, Webster depicts the heroine as alert to volition as the only thing truly within her own control, a mental disposition that affords her a kind of autonomy, even authority, when facing death, and enables, in turn, her lucid assessment that her brothers have, in fact, dehumanised themselves by abusing their power. As with the rest of the play, the Duchess' death emphasises that political oppression debases only if one assents to the false impressions of one's value, a marked reminder that one's internal choice, not material circumstances, determines one's sense of liberty. Subjected to torment and threatened with death, the Duchess responds to her captors' machinations with a simple acknowledgement of her own mortality and a coincident *ataraxia* startling for such a dark setting. 'I know death hath ten thousand several doors / For men to take their exits,' the Duchess declares and, deeming death a 'gift', tells her captors with the bearing of one still in authority herself, 'Dispose my breath how please you' (4.2.211–12, 217, 220). Responding to the threat of death with a simple rhetorical question – 'Did I ever tell you I was immortal?' – the Stoic, as Epictetus has it, adopts such serene resignation, observing, 'You will do your part, and I mine: It is yours to kill, and mine to die without trembling.'[76] Paradigmatic of Stoic tranquillity, this noble autonomy finds compelling expression in Webster's drama, and the playwright explicitly sets it in contrast with the tyrants' bestial natures, natures they have brought on themselves by their unjust actions. The abusive ruler, Epictetus reminds us after all, 'suffers the most pitiful and shameful fate [. . .] of becoming a wolf or serpent or a wasp instead of a human being',[77] an idea so crucial to the play's denouement Webster takes pains to recall it at the very moment of the Duchess' death. 'In my last will I have not much to give,' the Duchess tells Cariola, since 'many hungry guests have fed upon me', and she again registers the predatory nature of the court just a moment later in her final lines: 'Go tell my brothers, when I am laid out, / They then may feed in quiet. *They strangle her*' (4.2.193–4, 228–9). In this moment of redoubled physical circumscription – imprisonment coupled with strangulation – the Duchess exhibits a commanding presence, even issuing a final edict of her own, and, what's more, indicating with profound clear-sightedness an awareness that, by abusing their temporal power, her brothers have in truth sacrificed the distinctive feature of their own humanity.

At the moment of her death, the Duchess' assessment may seem fanciful, but through Ferdinand's disintegration into *lycanthropia* and the Cardinal's seizure of Antonio's land Webster makes manifest the fact that tyranny dehumanises the very rulers who otherwise would seem most privileged and secure within an inequitable society. Indeed, though neglected in existing criticism, just as the playwright's interest in Stoicism has surprisingly informed the entire action preceding the Duchess' death, so too does it outlive in this way the eponymous heroine herself, as the ontological framework so carefully wrought around the issue of the political import of the immaterial will shapes the demise of all the remaining characters as well. Where Epictetus had asserted that yielding to false impressions prompts some 'to become like wolves, faithless and treacherous and noxious' and others to 'become like foxes, the most roguish of living creatures', Webster exposes his tyrannical rulers as likewise bestial despite their exalted social positions. For although Ferdinand dismisses the murder of the Duchess' children by declaring 'the death / Of young wolves is never to be pitied' (4.2.249), the animalistic imagery famously obtains to himself as his own psychological condition almost literalises the play's understanding of what causes descent from one's fully-realised humanity. After imagining that 'The wolf shall find her grave, and scrape it up, / Not to devour the corpse, but to discover / The horrid murder,' Ferdinand exits, promising 'I'll go hunt the badger by owl-light: 'Tis a deed of darkness' (4.2.298–300, 323–4). During the Duke's absence and before his imminent return, Webster likewise signals the brutal nature of the Cardinal, depicting 'Antonio's land' as 'ravished from his throat / By the Cardinal's entreaty' (5.1.41–3). Framed as an act of predation, the theft recalls the Duchess' grim prediction that, upon her death, her brothers could feed in quiet, and Webster quickly underscores the brothers' rapaciousness even further by having Ferdinand return to the stage exhibiting signs of 'lycanthropia', joining those who 'imagine / Themselves to be transformed into wolves' (5.2.6, 9–10). Where the Duchess' *prohairesis* elevated her very humanity, the tyrannical Ferdinand becomes something subhuman, his untouchable interior 'a wolf's skin', his condition 'hairy [. . .] on the inside' (5.2.17–18). If the Cardinal becomes more openly predatory, prompting Bosola to observe that 'this fellow doth breed basilisk in 's eyes' and acts as a deceptive 'old fox' (5.2.135, 140), Ferdinand's bestial nature manifests itself in the overt disintegration of personality, as both men suffer more openly the debilitating effects wrought by their own abuses of power.[78]

After the Duchess' death, Bosola, unlike the tyrannical brothers, evinces a burgeoning awareness that he has assented to myriad false impressions about his own value, yet even as he attempts to remedy his subjugation, still retains a misguided attachment to externals, failing to conceive a mode of resistance beyond the physical deposition of tyrants. Inspired in part by a clarified understanding of his intrinsic worth, Bosola's opposition to tyranny, that is, takes shape as an action with less lasting effect than the widespread solidarity envisioned by the Duchess in her own form of political resistance. As Bosola realises his debased condition, he depicts himself as no longer held in thrall by the repressive aristocratic system of patronage and, resolving to rebel against tyranny, opts for solidarity with the outcast Antonio. Asking himself, 'What would I do, were this to do again,' Bosola concludes, 'I would not change my peace of conscience /

For all the wealth of Europe' (4.2.228–30), his utter debasement prompting him to turn from external metrics of value to prefer instead the serenity available within the recesses of his own mind. Depicting his reformation as deriving from his emancipation from anxiety, Bosola begins to perceive more clearly, if still imperfectly, alternative responses to the 'cruel tyrant' (4.2.352–3, 361). Consequently, when Bosola observes that 'these most cruel biters [. . .] have got / Some of [Antonio's] blood already', he nonetheless joins forces with Antonio even though these 'cruel biters' still hold power (5.2.325–6). 'It may be,' Bosola imagines, 'I'll join with thee in a most just revenge. / The weakest arm is strong enough that strikes / With the sword of justice' (5.2.326–9). Bosola, increasingly alert that his subjugation need not be an inevitable one, perceives his world more clearly, even as he, in his vision of a purely physical assault on the brothers, fails to appreciate how Ferdinand and the Cardinal operate as mere figureheads of a corrupt system.

Bosola's growing awareness of the court's pervasive influence over perception, its capacity to reinforce false impressions about one's intrinsic worth as a means of propping up a corrupt regime, becomes more acute after his revenge miscarries, his accidental murder of Antonio further propelling him to break from such a destructive aristocracy, noble in its external forms only. Mistaking Antonio for Ferdinand and stabbing the very man he sought to join, Bosola berates himself in a rather curious fashion. For as he confronts his tragic error and recalls the Cardinal whom he next plans to kill, the revenger exclaims, 'O direful misprision! / I will not imitate things glorious, / No more than base; I'll be mine own example' (5.4.79–81). The promise to be one's own example may seem dissonant at the very moment when the would-be revenger, having decided to pursue his own course of action, errs so profoundly as to murder the man he desired to assist. Yet in the accidental killing of Antonio, Bosola confronts the full force of his dejected condition and continues to awaken to just how thoroughly his misperceptions have governed his life. Indeed, although his tragic mistaking of Antonio for Ferdinand serves as the occasion for this outburst, Bosola tellingly identifies his 'misprision' not by noting his miscarried revenge but rather by citing his very assent to false modes of conceptualising human value that has brought him to this tragic point in the first place. Instead of a single, clear epiphany, Bosola gradually awakens, here at the end of the play, to the pervasiveness of the brothers' influence over the minds of those at court, and when he vows to 'be mine own example', begins – in a manner not unlike the Duchess – to make his own assay away from false impressions and the rhetoric marshalled by a corrupt court designed to reinforce its own power.

In his revenge, Bosola gestures towards a type of political levelling, a materialisation of his new awareness not only of his own personal worth as greater than previously supposed but also of the aristocratic system as itself hollow, a construct with no intrinsic value, predicated simply on the exploitation of the underclass. Though imperfectly working out the assumptions regarding human liberty and volition as embodied by the Duchess, Bosola sheds in his final actions the false impressions reinforced by the court regarding his supposedly inherent inferiority and starts to perceive more clearly the very artificiality of the system of patronage upon which he had depended for so long. In his limited, halting way, Bosola at last begins to imagine an alternative to such a repressive structure. 'Now it seems thy greatness was only outward,' Bosola declares as he finally stabs the Cardinal, marvelling at how the villain's superior image deflates before his eyes: 'thou fall'st faster of thyself than calamity / Can drive thee!' (5.5.40–2). No longer enthralled by such a thoroughly-ingrained sense of personal debasement, Bosola becomes free to perceive in the tyrannical aristocrats their own bestial natures, natures previously gilded over with the accoutrements of rank. Webster emphasises this reversal of fortunes at the moment of death for each of the brothers, contrasting Bosola's increasingly lucid assessment of himself and the court with the brothers' exposure as subhuman themselves. For where the Cardinal laments that he 'shall [. . .] die like a leveret / Without any resistance', Ferdinand, having been mortally wounded in his scuffle with Bosola, declares he 'account[s] this world but a dog-kennel' (5.5.43–4, 65). Striking the aristocratic figures who actively reinforced his own sense of degradation, Bosola inverts the power structure momentarily and proudly describes this instance of usurped authority as an object lesson of sorts, as revelatory of the true essence of courtly politics:

> I do glory
> That thou, which stood'st like a huge pyramid
> Begun upon a large and ample base,
> Shalt end in a little point, a kind of nothing. (5.5.73–7)

His sense of worth no longer conditioned by the actions of a predatory aristocracy, Bosola delights not only in the awareness that this once-imposing ruler now dissipates into nothing but also in his epiphany that such a seemingly impressive figure had to rely, in life, 'upon a large and ample base'. The privileged aristocrat, like the apex of the pyramid, only exists because of the indispensable bottom, and Bosola signals just prior to his own death that where the mighty prove 'a little point, a kind of nothing', the base, or lowborn, remain both more numerous and in themselves sufficient.

By depicting Bosola as inspired, in part, by his revitalised sense of personal value and his realisation of the regime's claim to true authority as spurious, Webster animates the play's final acts of retribution with the same philosophical predicates that informed the Duchess' own mode of resistance – a resistance that characterised her life as well as her final Stoic approach toward death – and anchors the servant's vengeance, however limited or compromised it may be, into a deeper ontological ground that has underwritten the entire play. As Frank Whigham has astutely noted, at the play's end, 'Bosola seeks his ontological grounding anew in a succession of chosen actions that he sees as neither derived from another (as his service was) nor evasively contemplative'.[79] Indeed, where Whigham argues that 'personal vengeance will at least make [Bosola] his own deed's creature',[80] Ralph Berry observes how 'the animal references die away in the closing scenes as Bosola's "good nature" asserts itself'.[81] In this, Bosola's shift in perception and, surprisingly, even his resultant revenge exhibit a philosophical disposition akin to that of the Duchess, awakening as he does to an alternative way of understanding personal value and liberty, a way exemplified most bracingly in the heroine's death but also embodied more subtly throughout. But in playing Juliet to the Duchess' Romeo, Bosola awakens too late, his chance at communion tragically past, leaving the servant to improvise a new course of action – much as the Duchess herself found 'nor path nor friendly clue' to be her guide – in his desperately isolated world. If Stoicism proper repudiates the act of revenge, early modern invocations of Epictetian philosophy, as we have seen, often signalled the revolutionary potential implicit in such an absolute theory of the immaterial and unconquerable will. Throughout the end of the play, Webster takes pains to figure Bosola's retribution – whatever its limitations as an act of political resistance and however adaptive as an expression of Epictetian ideals about agency – as emerging from a developing sense of his own personal value and capacity for autonomous action, as well as from his repudiation of the aristocracy as a genuine arbiter of value in the first place. As Bosola vows to be his 'own example', perceives in the tyrannical aristocrats a greatness that in truth was only 'outward', and sheds the habit of thinking of himself in subhuman terms, Webster's revenger reveals a revitalised way of thinking about his own agency, as he translates a rather radical notion of individual liberty into a forcible attempt at political levelling.

Although theatrically satisfying, Bosola's retribution ultimately falls short, however, not simply as an expression of Stoic resolve but also as a mode of effective political resistance, for by killing Ferdinand and the Cardinal, the revenger merely displaces the figureheads of the corrupt regime he loathes, and he fails, thereby, to fully counter the pervasive methods of ideological control that helped perpetuate the court's systemic inequity in the first place. Even as he rightly notes the imperative to cast off false impressions, that is, Bosola, his chances of a broadly-distributed solidarity with others now past, only manages to kill his oppressors, not the ideas which sustained their power. In the moments before his death, the revenger notes that in life he had acted 'Much 'gainst mine own good nature, yet i'th' end / Neglected' (5.5.84–5). As he reaffirms a sense of his actual, intrinsic value and confesses his own role in yielding to false impressions, Bosola also implicates here the court's system of patronage as a significant contributor to his corruption. In doing so, he underscores for the audience once more the court's capacity to inculcate by means of misleading fictions a sense of degradation within the underclass. During his final lines, the revenger significantly casts genuine nobility as a function of *thought* rather than of cultural position, admonishing, 'Let worthy minds ne'er stagger in distrust / To suffer death or shame for what is just' (5.5.98–103). Yet while Bosola exhibits in this moment a depth of political awareness regarding the need to resist tyranny – even in one's very thoughts – he fails to undo the underlying assumptions regarding hereditary privilege that helped foster his debasement in the first place. For the projected action of the play ultimately perpetuates the existing power structure, as 'the noble Delio' promotes the 'pretty gentleman, [Antonio's] son and heir' in order to 'establish this young, hopeful gentleman / In 's mother's right' (5.5.104, 110–11). On the play's final note, hereditary privilege persists, its validating narrative reinforced by distinguishing between noble and ignoble humanity, between the 'wretched eminent things' now openly represented by Ferdinand and the Cardinal and the 'great men' ready to take up their prescriptive function as 'lords of truth', a function putatively ascribed to them by 'Nature' itself (5.5.111, 116–17).

Webster thus depicts both the Duchess' secret resistance to her brothers and Bosola's violent rebellion against tyranny as ultimately failing, as, respectively, avoiding or displacing mere figureheads of a corrupt system but not, in the end, undoing the ideological substructure of the system itself. Through both tragic narratives, Webster presents two failed counter-discourses – revolt from above and revolt from below – to the aristocratic system of patronage. In doing so, however, he invites consideration of what *might* succeed in displacing an entrenched political system, rather than merely its temporary leaders, and the compelling cases of both the Duchess and Bosola suggest that where each failed individually, both, if operating together, could perhaps sustain a viable alternative. What would happen, Webster's play seems to ask, if the radical notion of individual volition and autonomy embodied by the Duchess and gradually accepted by Bosola were to become more widespread, across an ever-expanding group of citizens? Webster depicts Ferdinand's and the Cardinal's dominion as relying in large measure on the power of rhetoric to enthral and dehumanise a citizenry not always alert to its own intrinsic value, and the play stages the greatest threat to their power as taking place in the untouchable recesses of the individual citizen's mind. The Duchess' sense that her will – immaterial and unassailable – always remains her own proves disruptive to the oppressive regime she inhabits, but her scandalous ideology broaches an even greater transgressive possibility when she invites Bosola to appreciate his position as akin to her own. The prospect of solidarity across class lines, among the repressed and disenfranchised citizens of all kinds, remains the unrealised promise suggested throughout *The Duchess of Malfi*, and through the play's various moments in which the unassailability of human volition comes to the fore, Webster gestures towards alternative political possibilities – in many respects, ones only faintly adumbrated – that such a radical notion of personal liberty can hold.

While critics have long noted the central role of Stoic resolve in shaping Webster's depiction of the Duchess' death, the influence of the philosophy on the play as a whole has been curiously neglected, and it seems odd indeed to simply accept Stoicism as paramount to the play's most compelling moment yet largely absent from the rest of the dramatic action. By attending to Webster's indebtedness to Epictetian thought in particular, however, we can see how the dramatist animates his entire play with a coherent set of ontological predicates regarding human volition and how such an intangible quantity, always capable of remaining beyond the scope of repressive forces, can indeed carry profound and widespread political ramifications. Taking the trope of the contained animal as his principal vehicle for portraying the difference between those who assent to false impressions about their own value and those who properly understand themselves as free, whatever constraints they otherwise encounter, Webster constructs his play as something of a study of individual autonomy within the confines of a corrupt regime. Where Bosola, enslaved by his desire for patronage, understands his abject condition as akin to the subjugated animal, the court's tyrannical rulers, who seek to reinforce such abjection for their own advantage, likewise debase themselves and become exposed by play's end as, in truth, bestial. Amid this dark world rife with degradations to human dignity, Webster presents the Duchess as keenly alert to her own will as something that remains exclusively within her control, ultimately inviolable. Inclined to perceive animals as *exempla* of the liberty that exists in nature, the liberty promised by adherence to one's latent preconceptions of intrinsic value, the Duchess invites Bosola through her fable to reconsider his own self-worth, and, although the servant rejects this proffered solidarity, he gradually becomes, in the wake of her death, increasingly aware of his own worth, a realisation, tragically, that comes too late. What else is tragedy, asks Epictetus, but the depiction of 'the sufferings of men who have devoted their admiration to external things', and if the misguided adherence to externals sets the prevailing conditions for Webster's nightmarish milieu, the dramatist offers glimpses of an alternative way of approaching the world. For by anchoring the play's multiple acts of resistance into a shared set of ontological assumptions about the nature of the human will, Webster reveals how the faintest, virtually immaterial, stirrings of untouchable volition can resist the reach of tyrannical power, yielding a radical notion of liberty that carries the potential – if distributed across many – to disrupt even the most repressive of political regimes.

Notes

1. *John Webster and the Elizabethan Drama* (New York: Russell & Russell, 1916), 158.
2. Bosola appears at the head of the play's *dramatis personae* and serves as principal focus after the Duchess' death for the play's entire fifth act.
3. Charles Forker observes that 'the Duchess is a virtual prisoner in her own realm long before she is physically incarcerated' (*Skull beneath the Skin: The Achievement of John Webster* [Carbondale: Southern Illinois University Press, 1986], 301).
4. As Ralph Berry notes, 'animal images continuously underscore the action' and 'well over sixty different *sorts* of animals are

alluded to in *The Duchess of Malfi*' (*The Art of John Webster* [Oxford: Clarendon Press, 1972], 111).

5. On the play's persistent imagery of 'preying forms of life', see Nigel Alexander, 'Intelligence in *The Duchess of Malfi*', in *John Webster*, ed. Brian Morris (London: Ernest Benn Limited, 1970), 104–5.
6. For the positive valences of the creaturely in the era, see Julia Reinhard Lupton, 'Creature Caliban', *Shakespeare Quarterly* 51.1 (2000): 1–4 and Erica Fudge, *Perceiving Animals: Humans and Beasts in Early Modern English Culture* (Urbana: University of Illinois Press, 2002), 153–66. Since Webster insistently associates the bestial with debasement, except with notable departures in the Duchess' own speech, I have largely retained these terms and connotations.
7. See A. A. Long, *Epictetus: A Stoic and Socratic Guide to Life* (Oxford: Clarendon Press, 2002), 261.
8. Sanford's translation was published by Henry Bynneman, the same printer who, incidentally, produced William Painter's *The Palace of Pleasure*, Webster's source for *The Duchess of Malfi*, in the same year.
9. See W. A. Oldfather, 'Bibliography', in *Epictetus. The Discourses as Reported by Arrian Books I–II*, trans. W. A. Oldfather (Cambridge, MA: Harvard University Press, 1979), xxxii–xxxiv.
10. Long, *Epictetus*, 263.
11. Ibid. 28.
12. Unless otherwise noted, all citations from Epictetus come from *The Discourses of Epictetus*, ed. Christopher Gill, trans. Robin Hard (London: J. M. Dent, 1995), 1.12.9; p. 33.
13. 1.22.10–11; p. 51. On the 'unprecedented emphasis' Epictetus places on this distinction, see Rodrigo Sebastián Braicovich, 'Freedom and Determinism in Epictetus' *Discourses*', *The Classical Quarterly* 60.01 (2010): 203.
14. Christopher Gill, 'Introduction', in *The Discourses of Epictetus*, xx.
15. 1.1.4, 7; p. 5.
16. Qtd in Long, *Epictetus*, 209.
17. 4.4.39; p. 252.

18. 1.4.18; p. 13.
19. 1.4.19; p. 13.
20. 2.18.23–4; p. 121. See also 3.12.14–15; p. 175.
21. 2.18.26; p.121.
22. 1.22.1; p. 50.
23. Long, *Epictetus*, 83.
24. See also Matt Jackson-McCabe, 'The Stoic Theory of Implanted Preconceptions', *Phronesis* 49.4 (2004): 324–7 and 346–7.
25. 1.22.9; p. 51. See also 4.1.42; p. 230.
26. 1.2.11; p. 8.
27. 1.2.14; p. 9.
28. 1.2.19–21; p. 9.
29. 1.3.3; p. 11.
30. 1.3.7–8; p. 11.
31. 1.3.4; p. 11.
32. 2.10.1–3; p. 95.
33. 4.1.119; p. 239.
34. 4.1.120; p. 239.
35. 4.1.120; p. 239.
36. 4.1.121–2; p. 239.
37. 4.1.122; p. 239.
38. 4.1.119–27; p. 240. See also, 2.9.5, 7; p. 93.
39. 4.1.24; p. 228.
40. 4.1.25; p. 228.
41. 4.1.26–7; p. 228–9.
42. 4.1.29; p. 239.
43. 4.1.39; p. 230
44. 4.1.41, 55; pp. 230–1.
45. See 4.1.55; p. 232.
46. See Long, *Epictetus*, 259–66 and Gillian Wright, 'Women Reading Epictetus', *Women's Writing* 14.2 (2007): 322–7.
47. 'The Apologie of Raymond Sebond', in *The Essayes or Morall, Politike and Millitarie Discourses of Lo: Michaell de Montaigne*, trans. John Florio (London, 1603), 282.
48. *Sermons very fruitfull, godly, and learned* (London, 1557), Pir-v.
49. *Euphues* (London, 1587), F1r.

50. *The optick glasse of humours* (London, 1607), B4r-B4v, D8r.
51. 'A Letter to Bartolomeo Scala in Defence of the Stoic Philosopher Epictetus', in *Cambridge Translations of Renaissance Philosophical Texts: Moral and Political Philosophy*, ed. Jill Kraye (Cambridge: Cambridge University Press, 1997), 195.
52. *Proverbs or Adages, Gathered out of the Chiliades and Englished (1569)* (Gainesville: Scholars' Facsimiles and Reprints, 1956), 41r-42r.
53. *Politique discourses upon trueth and lying* (London, 1586), 49.
54. *The French academie* (London, 1618), 157.
55. *A combat betwixt man and death: or A discourse against the immoderate apprehension and feare of death* (London, 1621), 397.
56. On the counsel of 'bear and forbear' as supporting the active, rather than passive, life, see Peter Bement, 'The Stoicism of Chapman's Clermont d'Ambois', *Studies in English Literature, 1500–1900* 12.2 (1972): 349–50.
57. *Euphues shadow* (London, 1592), C3r.
58. *The French academie* (London, 1618), 144.
59. *English Epicures*, 160, 165–6.
60. 'To my equall reader', in *Parasitaster, or The Favvne* (London, 1606), A2r.
61. Fv. Marston also invokes Epictetus in *The scourge of villanie. Three bookes of satyres* (London, 1598), n.p.
62. *The Works of Francis Beaumont and John Fletcher in Ten Volumes*, ed. A. R. Waller, vol. 5 (Cambridge: Cambridge University Press, 1907), 4.4.1–19.
63. James Shirley, *Changes: OR, Love in a maze. A comedie* (London, 1632), 4.2 and Thomas Heywood, *Londini emporia, or Londons mercatura* [1633], in *Thomas Heywood's Pageants: A Critical Edition*, ed. David M. Bergeron, The Renaissance Imagination, vol. 16 (New York: Garland Publishing, 1986), ll. 366–71, p. 63.
64. See Forker, *Skull beneath the Skin*, 110 and John Russell Brown, *The Duchess of Malfi: John Webster* (Manchester: Manchester University Press, 1997), 52, n. 158; 137, n. 102–3.

65. Frederick S. Boas, 'Introduction', in Bussy d'Ambois: And The Revenge of Bussy d'Ambois by George Chapman (Boston, MA: D. C. Heath & Company, 1905), xxxvi. See also xxxv–xxxvi.
66. Gunilla Florby, The Painful Passage to Virtue: A Study of George Chapman's The Tragedy of Bussy d'Ambois and The Revenge of Bussy d'Ambois (Lund: CWK Gleerup, 1982), 196.
67. All citations from the play come from John Webster, The Duchess of Malfi, ed. Leah S. Marcus (London: A. & C. Black, 2009).
68. George Downame's warning to avoid 'the tale-bearer and the sycophant' (Lectures on the XV. Psalme [London, 1604], 125–6) and Robert Horne's advice that magistrates should punish 'the malitious Tale-bearer, and Sycophant' (The Christian Gouernour [London, 1614], M4v) may be considered representative.
69. Discourses, 1.3.4; p. 114.1.55; p. 231.
70. Seizures of the Will in Early Modern English Drama (Cambridge: Cambridge University Press, 1996), 195.
71. On George Chapman's 'complete man' as indebted to 'the Latin Stoics' and his play as drawing on Epictetus in particular, see N. S. Brooke, 'Introduction', in Bussy d'Ambois: George Chapman (Manchester: Manchester University Press, 1999), xxii. On Antonio as fulfilling Chapman's ideal, see Ellen R. Belton, 'The Function of Antonio in The Duchess of Malfi', Texas Studies in Literature and Language 18.3 (1976): 474.
72. See also Forker, Skull beneath the Skin, 362.
73. See n. 6.
74. Discourses, 1.2.11; p. 8.
75. As noted above, Epictetus himself argues that a correct sense of one's value can include dispassionate recognition of one's actual social position. See Discourses, 1.2.19; p. 9.
76. Ibid. 1.2.19–21; p. 9.
77. Ibid. 4.1.127; p. 240.
78. On Ferdinand's disease as staging a 'double-crosssing' between 'inner and outer worlds, psychic and somatic experience', see

Lynn Enterline, '"Hairy on the In-side": *The Duchess of Malfi* and the Body of Lycanthropy', *Yale Journal of Criticism* 7 (1994): 103–14.
79. *Seizures of the Will*, 221.
80. Ibid. 221.
81. Berry, *The Art of John Webster*, 113.

EPILOGUE: A KIND OF SENSIBLE JUSTICE

In the final act of *The Duchess of Malfi*, the corrupt Cardinal, soon to be struck down by the revenging sword of Bosola, enters and in a moment of quiet reflection, discloses:

> I am puzzled in a question about hell.
> He says in hell there's one material fire,
> And yet it shall not burn all men alike.
> Lay him by. [*Puts down the book.*]
>   How tedious is a guilty conscience!
> When I look into the fishponds in my garden,
> Methinks I see a thing armed with a rake
> That seems to strike at me. (5.5.1–7)[1]

In my chapter on Webster's play, I elucidated the ways in which the dramatist anchors a critique of class structure into the deeper ontological ground found in Epictetian notions of volition; the Cardinal's private confession here is indeed telling in the way it conflates a guilty conscience with fear of retribution delivered from the hand of one wielding an implement of the underclass. But the Cardinal's initial rumination, juxtaposed with this fear of an impending act of vengeance, also reveals something of the peculiar concerns of revenge drama. For as the Cardinal muses about the state of his soul, he envisions an afterlife where judgement cuts across the material and immaterial divide. With the immaterial soul parted from the material body, the Cardinal imagines a spiritual reckoning that at once takes shape in the form of a 'material fire' yet also affects individual souls in different ways. How will the material fire of hell affect his immaterial soul, the Cardinal muses, and how will it do so while affecting the souls of others in varying gradations? The justice of God has prompted in the Cardinal reflection, however fleeting it may be, on the traversal between material and immaterial realms.

Whatever the murderous Cardinal's moral failings, he has the virtue of having considered religious matters more extensively, even in this brief moment, than I have in this book. As outlined in my introduction this has been by design: criticism on revenge tragedy has almost invariably centred on matters of law, politics, or religion, often with the coincident emphasis on trying to ascertain the disposition of the dramatist, audience, or (more broadly) culture towards revenge. Since official or orthodox statements condemn private retribution yet revenge plays remain perennially popular, the matter has proven particularly vexed, and much critical ink has consequently been spilled over the degree of approval or disapproval revenge tragedies elicit for their acts of vengeance. I have held religious discourses on revenge in abeyance in order to move beyond the much-rehearsed debates of the previous century and to instead clear new ground for examining classical philosophies crucial to, but long ignored, within these texts. In closing, however, I'd like to briefly return to such discourses; not to revisit the well-worn concerns of previous criticism but rather to reveal how the concerns this book has taken up find expression in the myriad ways early modern writers discuss revenge itself. For throughout the discourses of the era, writers across a diverse array of backgrounds figure retribution as uniquely concerned at every stage with the interaction between the immaterial and material, the imperceptible and perceptible. Early modern authors, that is, constantly signal the ways in which revenge recalls one's mind to the fundamental ontological realities that undergird embodied experience. Amid the prohibitions against personal revenge and the promises of God's final vengeance, we have missed the ways retribution has served as a means for focusing early modern minds on the dividing line between immaterial and material worlds, on how that line gets crossed, and on how ontological assumptions about the imperceptible directly affect, thereby, in one form or another, embodied action.

The terms 'vengeance' and 'revenge', as Ronald Broude reminds us, were regularly used by early modern authors to signify divine judgement,[2] and the era's homiletic and didactic texts, frequently figuring such vengeance as hovering just beyond the purview of the perceptive faculties, persistently labour to make the unseen seen, the imminent present, the insensible felt. 'God's vengeance which is yet unseen, must come before our eyes, & be considered by faith,' observes John Calvin in Arthur Golding's translation of his sermons on *Deuteronomy* in 1583.[3] Although invisible, such divine vengeance hangs immediately overhead, just beyond one's ken, a fact repeatedly revisited throughout the era's literature. As George Joye informs his readers, 'the imminent hevye wrathe and vengeaunce of God hangeth redy to fall downe from heuen' upon the unrighteous,[4] a sentiment echoed by Thomas Becon, who, inveighing against 'certen ritch and gredy cormorauntes', wonders how 'these deuouring caterpyllers' could ever 'escape the vengeaunce of God, that hangeth ouer theyr heads'.[5] Nearby yet imperceptible, vengeance must be made manifest, then, first by Scripture, second by pious authors. In this vein, Everard Digby, reflecting on the divine judgement of Nebuchadnezzar, counsels that although God does not 'alwaies sende such manifest &

speedy reuenge', his readers should avoid disdaining providence simply 'because vengeance yet lieth hid'.[6] If vengeance may, at present, seem hidden or altogether absent, the devout writers of the era frequently seek through their hortatory prose to make manifest an imminent revenge, envisioned as just on the cusp of material instantiation.

Early modern authors also call to attention the boundary between immaterial and material realms – and, more pointedly, the traversal of that boundary – by continually representing vengeance itself as the sensible manifestation of an invisible God. Where Thomas Becon writes about God's 'vengeance, that is to saye, corporall plages' and the 'manifest tokens of Gods [. . .] vengeaunce',[7] Robert Bolton contemplates 'some remarkable vengeance [. . .] or sensible smart [. . .] from Gods visiting hand'.[8] Vengeance delivered makes visible the otherwise invisible hand of God. Recounting in a sermon a catalogue of tyrants struck down by providence, James Brooks follows every rehearsal of heinous crime, for example, with repeated iterations of the phrase 'did not he fele the hand of Gods vengeance'.[9] The materialised vengeance of invisible divinity could, of course, take multiple forms. Thomas Bilson reminds his readers of the 'corporall fire in hell', asserting that 'the vengeance [. . .] executed on the wicked is sensible and true fire from God'[10] while William Fulke perceives divine providence as oftentimes turning 'the sword of the enemies through their owne bowels' for persecuting the righteous.[11] What's more, even the ostensible absence of vengeance could signify the presence of divine power. William Bradshaw assures his readers that though they may lack 'visible and sensible vengeance' for wrongs, the prayers of the righteous will nonetheless prevail,[12] and Joseph Hall recalls how God 'doth not inflict sensible judgements upon all his enemies, lest the wicked should thinke there were no punishment abiding for them elsewhere'.[13]

Through its enactment – and, remarkably, even in its deferral – divine vengeance directs attention to the material manifestation of otherwise imperceptible providence.

For early modern thinkers, divine vengeance – hovering unseen just overhead, then materially instantiating the invisible hand of God – also worked through its very material blows to affect the inmost spirit of its target. In the same passage where Everard Digby cautions against apathy towards providence when 'vengeance yet lieth hid', for example, he reminds his readers that God's 'sword is sharpe, & passeth swiftly, betwixt the soule and the spirit'.[14] Expostulating on the vengeance of God, Richard Taverner asserts that '[n]o doubte God jugeth rightly [. . .] neyther only after the outward workes but after the harte and outwarde workes too'.[15] That God's vengeance cuts to the heart and even passes 'betwixt the soule and the spirit' reveals yet again the tendency to perceive in revenge a marked capacity for traversing material and immaterial realms; it also provides a fit counterbalance to the imperceptible origins of (unapproved) desires for retribution nestled within the deepest recesses of the human heart itself. Alternately described as emerging from 'invisible tumults'[16] and internal smouldering embers 'which being stir'd never so little, breakes forth againe, inflaming the soule',[17] the human desire for retribution itself traces back to the faintest, most imperceptible movements of the individual's being. The ire that provokes revenge, John Davies explains in *Microcosmos*, is 'a vehement *motion* of the *Hart*', a stirring that reverberates until 'joint by joint, the Soule it rudely rends'.[18] Where unsanctioned revenge emerges from, and threatens to rend, the inmost parts of an individual, even to the very soul, providential retribution, deriving from imperceptible, immaterial divinity and instantiated as a material quantity, remains capable of parsing the most immaterial aspects of the human subject.

As even this briefest of surveys attests, early modern discourses on vengeance persistently encourage the kind of thinking backward to the era's ontological assumptions regarding the imperceptible's relation to the observable world that this book has examined, in a different register, within the revenge tragedies of the popular stage. In the preceding chapters, I have sought to reveal revenge drama's distinctive capacity for exploring – with considerably more latitude than possible in didactic texts centred on religious, legal, or political theory – the complexities inherent in tracing embodied action to its various ontological roots. Retribution quite logically lends itself to consideration of the social and metaphysical implications of violent acts, and it likewise provides a visceral, immediately compelling dynamic for dramatists seeking to garner attention within the competitive world of the commercial theatre. But if our critical tradition, thanks in large measure to the twentieth-century creation of revenge tragedy as a definable genre, has foregrounded matters of law, politics and religion, while also stressing the sensationalism, within these plays, theatrical retribution, as we have seen, can also engage a diverse array of classical philosophies with considerable nuance and subtlety. To be sure, these plays do stage the sensational and histrionic. Thomas Lodge's *Wits Miserie* (1596) famously mocks the ghost calling for revenge as shrieking 'like an oister wife', while the Induction to the *A Warning for Faire Women* (1599) ridicules the 'filthie whining ghost' that enters 'screaming like a pigge halfe stickt, /And cries Vindicta, revenge, revenge'.[19] But amid, and even through, such discordant features we can also find the remarkable appropriation of rather complex philosophical doctrines, ones largely lost to modern perception yet common among the authors and audiences of the sixteenth and seventeenth centuries. Along with cries evocative of 'oister' wives and half-stuck pigs, we might hear as well – if we attend closely enough – the reasoned, deliberative voices, that is, of antiquity's greatest philosophers.

Epilogue [301]

Notes

1. John Webster, *The Duchess of Malfi*, ed. Leah S. Marcus (London: A. & C. Black, 2009).
2. Ronald Broude, 'Revenge and Revenge Tragedy in Renaissance England', *Renaissance Quarterly* 28.1 (1975): 39–42, 52–4.
3. *The sermons of M. Iohn Caluin vpon the fifth booke of Moses called Deuteronomie*, trans. Arthur Golding (London: 1583), 1171.
4. *The defence of the mariage of preistes* (Antwerp, 1541), Div(v).
5. *The new pollecye of warre* (London, 1542), G.iiir-G.iiiv.
6. *Euerard Digbie his dissuasiue from taking away the lyuings and goods of the Church* (London, 1590), 143–4.
7. *An inuectyue agenst the moost wicked [and] detestable vyce of swearing* (London, 1543), Bviiir, Eiir.
8. *Some generall directions for a comfortable walking with God deliuered in the lecture at Kettering in Northhamptonshire* (London, 1626), 40.
9. *A sermon very notable, fruictefull, and godlie made at Paules crosse* (London, 1553), Liiir-Livr.
10. *The suruey of Christs sufferings for mans redemption and of his descent to Hades or Hel for our deliuerance* (London, 1604), 53.
11. *Praelections vpon the sacred and holy Reuelation of S. Iohn* (London, 1573), 39.
12. *A plaine and pithy exposition of the second Epistle to the Thessalonians* (London, 1620), 70.
13. *Contemplations vpon the principall passages of the holy storie. By J.H.* (London, 1612), 211–12.
14. *Euerard Digbie*, 144.
15. *The Epistles and Gospelles with a brief postil vpon the same from after Easter tyll Aduent* (London, 1540), B.ii.r.
16. Gervase Markham, *The most famous and renowned historie, of that woorthie and illustrous knight Meruine, sonne to that rare and excellent mirror of princely prowesse, Oger the Dane* (London, 1612), 85.

17. Mateo Alemán, *The rogue: or The life of Guzman de Alfarache* (London, 1623), 180.
18. (London, 1603), 187.
19. *The Complete Works of Thomas Lodge 1580–1623? Now First Collected*, ed. Edmund Gosse (Glasgow, 1883), 56; Anonymous, *A Vvarning for Faire Vvomen* (London, 1599), A2v.

INDEX

Aaron (*Titus Andronicus*), 105, 110–11, 120–3
Adelman, Janet, 135
Aesop, 42, 46
Alarbus (*Titus Andronicus*), 95, 104–6, 109–10, 130n
Andrugio (*Antonio's Revenge*), 212–14, 217–20, 224–5, 227, 229, 232–5
Antonio (*The Duchess of Malfi*), 262–3, 265, 269–76, 280–3, 286, 293n
apatheia, 29–30, 193–5, 208–9, 237, 241n
Apuleius, 43
Ardolino, Frank, 43
Aristotle, 25–7, 48–9, 91–5, 98–100, 119–20, 144, 186n, 205, 249; *see also* commutative justice; distributive justice; ethical mean; hylomorphism; justice-in-exchange; *Nicomachean Ethics*; ready-wit; rectificatory justice; vegetative soul
Artaud, Antonin, 17–19

ataraxia, 176–7, 181, 183, 192, 230, 279
The Atheist's Tragedy, 12
atomism
  and atheism, 27, 136, 138–9, 143–4, 149, 155, 159, 182–3, 184n
  and Epicureanism, 27, 138–9, 149, 155, 159, 183
  in late seventeenth-century, 143, 148, 183, 184n, 185n
  and memory, 27–8, 137–8, 155, 159–60, 183
  and nothingness/the void, 138–9, 148
  and perception, 27–8, 137–8, 140–2, 159–61, 163, 183
  and theism, 27, 136, 138, 143–4, 146–55, 159, 182–3, 184n, 185n, 187n, 190n
  and time, 27–8, 137, 141–2, 183
atoms
  dust/motes as image for, 31–2, 139, 145–7, 150–2, 160–1

atoms (cont.)
  imperceptibility of, 3, 31, 138–41, 145, 150–5
  indestructibility of, 27, 136–40, 143, 148, 151–5, 187n, 189n
  as reconstitutable, 27, 137, 139, 142–3, 145, 150–1, 153–5, 177–8, 187n
Augustine, 151

Bacon, Francis, 1–2, 36, 144, 148–9, 186n, 187n
Balthazar (*The Spanish Tragedy*), 50, 62–6, 68, 70, 72, 75, 79–80
Banquo (*Macbeth*), 163
Barber, C. L., 50
Barbour, Reid, 260
Bassianus (*Titus Andronicus*), 102–3, 106, 110
Bazulto (*The Spanish Tragedy*), 75–6
Beaumont, Francis, 44, 261
Bel-Imperia (*The Spanish Tragedy*), 68–72
Berry, Ralph, 285, 289n
Bloom, Harold, 39n
Boas, F. S., 1, 13
Bodenham, John, 43
Bosola (*The Duchess of Malfi*), 30, 246, 248, 257, 263–7, 270, 273–8, 281–9, 295
Bowers, Fredson, 1, 7–9, 11, 13–14
Boyle, Robert, 144
Bradley, A. C., 15
Brathwaite, Richard, 99–100

breath/breathing, 207–8, 210–15, 217–19, 221–2, 224–5, 230–2
Brooke, Rupert, 10–11, 245
Broude, Ronald, 297
Brown, Georgia, 242n
Browne, Thomas, 149
Bruno, Giodorno, 144
Bynneman, Henry, 290n

Calvin, John, 297
Cardinal (*The Duchess of Malfi*), 246, 263–9, 280–4, 286–7, 295–6
Case, John, 127n
Cefalu, Paul, 189n
Celia (*As You Like It*), 145, 156
Chapman, George, 43, 244, 261, 269, 292n, 293n
Chiron (*Titus Andronicus*), 105, 110, 120–2
Chrysippus, 205–7
Claudio (*Measure for Measure*), 146
Claudius (*Hamlet*), 39n, 138, 165, 169–70, 180–1
Coleridge, Samuel Taylor, 15
commutative justice, 98, 119
Crane, Mary Thomas, 188n, 189n
creatures/creaturely, 246–7, 254–6, 264–7, 271–2, 280, 285, 290n
Crooke, Helkiah, 55
Cunliffe, John W., 9–10

Davies, Sir John, 57–8, 63, 146–8, 160, 299
Dekker, Thomas, 43
  (as 'Decker'), 44–5, 47

Delio (*The Duchess of Malfi*), 262, 265, 286
Demetrius (*Titus Andronicus*), 105, 110, 120–2
Democritus, 138, 144, 145, 147, 149
Descartes, René, 53–4
Digby, Kenelm, 144
The Discourses (Epictetus), 248–50, 256, 261, 273, 290n, 293n
distributive justice, 95–6, 98, 102, 118, 128n
Dollimore, Jonathan, 242n
Don Andrea (*The Spanish Tragedy*), 9, 59–62, 68–70, 75, 80–1, 87n
Donne, John (and atomism), 145, 151–5, 169, 176–7, 179, 187n, 188n, 189n
Drayton, Michael, 43
Drummond, William, 150
Du Bartas, Guillaume de Saluste, seigneur, 147–8, 186n
dualism, 48, 53–4
Duchess of Malfi (character), 30, 244–8, 254, 261, 267–81, 283–5, 287–9, 290n
Duke of Castile (*The Spanish Tragedy*), 68, 79–80
Duke Vincentio (*Measure for Measure*), 146, 156

Eliot, T. S., 193
Elyot, Thomas, 45
Elysium, 44, 46
Empedocles, 198
Enchiridion, 248–9, 258, 261

Epictetus, 247–61, 264, 269, 273, 277, 279–80, 289, 290n, 293n; see also *The Discourses*; *Enchiridion*; *phantasiai*; *prohairesis*; *prolêpseis*
Epicurus, 138, 149; see also atomism: and Epicureanism
Erasmus, 259
Erne, Lukas, 83n
ethical mean, 3, 26–7, 31–2, 91–2, 94–102, 104, 109, 112–15, 118, 123–5, 130n, 133
as set against extremes, 26–7, 91–2, 95, 99–100, 111–17, 123–4, 133

Feliche (*Antonio's Revenge*), 213, 216, 221, 234
Ferdinand (*The Duchess of Malfi*), 246, 263, 265–9, 271–2, 275, 277–8, 280–4, 286–7, 293n
Ferguson, Margaret W., 135
Fletcher, John, 261
Forker, Charles, 289n
Fudge, Erica, 290n

Galeatzo (*Antonio's Revenge*), 235
Galen, 3, 29, 55, 195–208, 210–13, 215–19, 226, 236–41, 249
Gassendi, Pierre, 144
Gertrude (*Hamlet*), 168–71
ghost (*Hamlet*), (im)materiality of, 159–64
ghosts, as convention of revenge tragedy, 7–12, 20–1

Gibbons, Brian, 11
gratitude, 92, 97–8, 101, 105–9, 123–4, 130n
Gravedigger (*Hamlet*), 176–7
Greene, Robert, 41, 258
Greville, Robert, 144

Hamilton, A. C., 120
Hankinson, R. J., 204
Harriot, Thomas, 143–4
Harris, Jonathan Gil, 94, 143
Harrison, Charles Trawick, 184n
Harvey, Gabriel, 98
Harvey, William, 195–6
Hazlitt, William, 15
Healey, John, 249
Herbert, Edward, 144
hesitation, as convention of revenge tragedy, 7–8, 15
Heywood, Thomas, 261
Hieronimo (*The Spanish Tragedy*), 9, 23, 26, 48–51, 62–4, 66–7, 73–80, 111, 125, 132–3, 192, 243
Hill, Eugene, 43
Hill, Nicholas, 144–5
Hippocrates, 197, 205
Hirsch, David A. Hedrich, 143, 187n, 189n
Hoeniger, F. David, 198
Hopkins, Lisa, 86n, 87n, 188n
Horatio (*Hamlet*), 160–3, 176–7, 180, 182, 188, 192, 243
Horatio (*The Spanish Tragedy*), 9, 48–52, 62–6, 68–75, 79–80
household management *see* oeconomia

Hunter, G. K., 43, 241n
Hurault, Jacques, 98, 260
hylomorphism, 157–8

immateriality, 2–3, 5, 18, 20–2, 24, 29, 31–2, 36, 55, 82, 91, 125–6, 133–4, 156, 160–2, 166, 195, 199–200, 236–7, 245, 250, 253, 270, 280, 285, 287, 289, 296–9
immoderation, 26–7, 90, 92, 100, 111, 113, 124
impressions, 30, 247–8, 250–8, 261–2, 264–6, 268, 276–83, 286, 288; *see also phantasiai*
ingratitude, 107, 109, 122–3
Isabella (*The Spanish Tragedy*), 51, 74, 77–9

Jonson, Ben, 43–4, 47, 145
Julia (*The Duchess of Malfi*), 246
Julio (*Antonio's Revenge*), 194, 226–9, 242n
justice-in-exchange, 97–8, 107, 118–20, 128n

Kahn, Coppélia, 131n
Kargon, Robert Hugh, 185n
Kendall, Gillian Murray, 117
Kerrigan, John, 36, 119, 129n
Kyd, Thomas, 8–11, 13–14, 23–7, 37, 48–56, 58–60, 62–77, 79, 81–6, 88, 94, 125–6, 192–3
  classical learning of, 41–7, 82–3, 83n, 89, 133
  Cornelia (*Cornélie*), 43, 44

The Householder's Philosophy, 25, 48, 51–3, 58, 65
  as 'industrious', 44–7

La Primaudaye, Pierre de, 55–6, 259–60
Lambin, Denis, 148, 154–5, 166, 177–8
Lander, Jesse M., 93
Lavinia (*Titus Andronicus*), 105–6, 108, 110, 112, 114, 116, 118, 120–2, 131n
Leinwand, Theodore B., 50
Leucippus, 138, 149, 184n
Lines, David A., 92
Lipsius, Justus, 249
Lodge, Thomas, 260, 300
Long, A. A., 238n
Long, Zackariah, 83n
Lorenzo (*The Spanish Tragedy*), 50, 63–6, 68, 72–6, 80, 224
Lucius (*Titus Andronicus*), 105, 111, 121–4
Lucretius, 138–42, 145, 148, 154, 160–1, 163, 177–8
Lupton, Julia Reinhard, 271, 290n
lycanthropy, 280–1

McAlindon, Thomas, 189n
Macbeth, 6, 9
McMillin, Scott, 77
madness, as convention of revenge tragedy, 7–8, 12–13, 19–20
The Malcontent (Marston), 10
Marcellus (*Hamlet*), 162

Marcus (*Titus Andronicus*), 101–4, 107, 111, 114–18, 120–1, 123, 130n
Marcus, Leah, 189n
Maria (*Antonio's Revenge*), 212, 218–19
Markham, Gervase, 99
Marlowe, Christopher, 43–4
Marston, John, 11, 23–4, 29–30, 38, 191–6, 202, 205–6, 209–21, 223–4, 226–9, 231–8, 241–2, 260, 292
  anti-Stoicism of, 192–6, 205–6, 213–19, 229–32, 236–7
  and Epictetus, 260–1
  preoccupation with bodily functions of, 192–6, 202, 205–6, 210–11, 216–17, 219, 226–9, 233, 236–7, 242n
Marvell, Andrew, 56–7
materialism, 28, 48, 54, 134, 136, 138–9, 143, 146, 148–9, 155, 158–65, 169, 173, 175, 179–80, 183
matter, 20, 27–9, 135–42, 144, 147–9, 154–5, 157–8, 160, 163–7, 171–3, 175–80, 182–3, 186n, 188n, 194–5, 199, 202, 207–9, 218, 237, 239n, 253, 255, 260, 296
Mellida (*Antonio's Revenge*), 213–14, 216, 223, 231, 236
Mercer, Peter, 38n
Mercutio, 145, 156
Meres, Francis, 43
metadrama, as convention of revenge tragedy, 8, 12, 19–20, 37n

middling sort, 25, 48–51,
    58–60, 62, 64, 66–9, 71–2,
    76, 81–2, 270
moderation, 26–7, 90–3, 95,
    109, 111–12, 114–16,
    120, 122–4, 130n,
    133, 201
Montaigne, Michel de, 145,
    155, 166, 177, 257–8
mortalism, 54–5, 142
Morton, A. G., 67
The Mousetrap (*Hamlet*),
    169–70, 180
Mutius (*Titus Andronicus*), 106

Nashe, Thomas, 41–7, 83
Nicomachean Ethics, 93–8,
    101–5, 107, 110, 119,
    123, 127n
Norford, Don Parry, 135
nothing (in *Hamlet*), 156,
    161–3, 166, 174, 188n

oeconomia, 25, 48–53, 55–9,
    62–3, 65–8, 70, 76–7, 79,
    82–3, 133
ontology, 3–5, 18–24, 26–8,
    30–7, 47–9, 52–3, 58–9,
    82–3, 88, 90–2, 95, 97–9,
    125–6, 132–4, 158–63,
    195–6, 270–3, 288–9,
    295, 297, 300

Painter, William, 290n
Pandulpho (*Antonio's Revenge*),
    192, 219–22, 231–6, 242n,
    243, 278
Parker, Patricia, 135, 184n
Passannante, Gerard, 143
Paster, Gail Kern, 129n

Pedrigano (*The Spanish
    Tragedy*), 68, 73, 224
Perry, Curtis, 43
phantasiai, 30, 247, 250–2, 258;
    see also impressions
Phebe (*As You Like It*), 145, 156
Piero (*Antonio's Revenge*), 195,
    212–14, 216–36
Plato, 55, 197, 205, 249
pneuma, 3, 29, 31–2, 194–209,
    213–16, 221–2, 225–6,
    230, 237, 238n, 239n, 240n
Poliziano, Angelo, 249, 258
Polonius (*Hamlet*), 171–2
preconceptions (*prolêpseis*),
    252–3, 267, 272–3,
    277, 289
Priam, 101
Priscus, Helvidius, 253
prohairesis, 30, 247–51, 253–4,
    257, 268–9, 281; *see also*
    volition
prolêpseis, 252, 267; *see also*
    preconceptions
proportionality, 27, 92, 95,
    97–9, 104, 107, 109–10,
    112, 114, 116–24, 128n
Proserpine (*The Spanish
    Tragedy*), 61–2, 69, 76,
    81, 86n
providence, 34–5, 149–51,
    179–80, 183, 190n, 298–9
psyche, 30, 60, 75–6, 205–8,
    239
Puttenham, George, 144–5,
    160, 185n

ready-wit, 110
rectificatory justice, 95–6,
    104–5, 118, 128n, 130n

respiration, 194–5, 197–8, 200–2; *see also* breath/breathing
revenge, as 'wild justice', 1–2
The Revenge of Bussy D'Ambois, 12, 244, 261; *see also* Chapman, George
revenge tragedy, as genre, 1–21, 37n, 39n, 47, 88–9, 119, 191–3, 296–7, 300
The Revenger's Tragedy, 11–12, 22, 226
Rhadamanth(us), 61, 118

Sanford, James, 249, 290n
Saturninus (*Titus Andronicus*), 92, 102–3, 106–9, 111, 124
scelus, 8, 19, 23, 72–3, 121, 215, 228
Schegk, Jacob, 249
Schelling, Felix E., 10
Schlegel, Augustus, 15
Schmitt, Charles B., 92
Seneca, 16, 42–3, 46, 77, 132, 192, 195, 223, 241n, 243
Sennert, Daniel, 144
sensationalism, 2, 6–7, 13–14, 16–18, 25–6, 32, 36, 82, 89, 91, 191, 245, 300
Shakespeare, William, 2–3, 12–14, 23–4, 26–7, 39n, 43–4, 88–93, 99, 101–2, 104, 108, 110–11, 114, 116–17, 122, 124–6, 132–4, 143–5, 148, 150, 156–61, 163, 170, 183, 191–3
Shirley, James, 261
Siemon, James, 50–1

Simplicius, 248, 261
smoke (associated with blood/*pneuma*), 29, 31–2, 194–5, 202, 223, 229, 237
Solon, 101
Spenser, Edmund, 44, 46, 145
Stewart, Potter (Justice), 6
Stobaeus, 261
Stoicism, 3, 29, 32, 192–7, 203–9, 213–15, 218–19, 221–3, 229–32, 236–7, 243–5, 247, 249, 252–4, 258, 260–1, 269–70, 277–80, 284–6, 288, 293n
and *pneuma*, 196, 203–9, 213–15, 219, 222, 230, 238n, 240n
rejected, 29, 192–7, 205–7, 219, 221–3, 229–32, 236–7, 242n
see also Epictetus
Strotzo (*Antonio's Revenge*), 212–14, 217, 224, 234
Suarez, Franciscus, 54
Sullivan, Garrett, A., 189n
Sylvester, Josuah, 100, 147, 160

Tacitus, 43
Tamora (*Titus Andronicus*), 105, 108–10, 120–3, 130n, 131n
Tasso, Torquato, 25, 42, 48, 51–3, 58, 65–6, 94
temper/temperance, 90–1, 100, 112–16, 222, 260
temperature (of blood, body), 201, 203, 210, 216–17, 219, 237
Theater of Cruelty, 17–19
Thorndike, A. H., 7–13

Titus Andronicus (character),
    27, 89, 92, 101–9, 111–12,
    114–26, 129n, 130n,
    133, 243
The Tragedy of Hoffman
    (Chettle), 12
Trincavelli, Vettore, 249

Urmson, J. O., 130n

vegetative soul, 3–4, 25–6,
    31–3, 48–9, 53–9, 62, 74–6,
    81–3, 85n, 125
veins, 193–5, 197–8, 201–2,
    209–10, 225–8, 230,
    232–5, 242n
Vesalius, Andreas, 196–7
vindicta mihi, 21, 243
Virgil, 43, 46
Vives, Juan Luis, 150–1

volition, 3, 30–2, 247–9, 257–8,
    261, 265, 267–74, 276–8,
    283, 287–9, 295; *see also
    prohairesis*

Warley, Christopher, 162
Webster, John, 10, 23–4, 30–1,
    243–8, 254, 256–7, 260–7,
    270–1, 273, 277–81, 284–5,
    287–9, 290n, 295
Whigham, Frank, 69, 265, 285
Wilkinson, John, 127n
Wolf, Hieronymus, 249, 261
Woodbridge, Linda, 128n,
    238n
Wrightson, Keith, 49–50

Yorick (*Hamlet*), 175, 177

Zamir, Tzachi, 88

EU representative:
Easy Access System Europe
Mustamäe tee 50, 10621 Tallinn, Estonia
Gpsr.requests@easproject.com